Tales of Frontier Texas

Tales of
Frontier Texas

1830-1860

Edited by

JOHN Q. ANDERSON

SOUTHERN METHODIST UNIVERSITY PRESS : DALLAS

© 1966 : SOUTHERN METHODIST UNIVERSITY PRESS : DALLAS

LIBRARY OF CONGRESS CATALOG CARD NUMBER 66-19620

PRINTED IN THE UNITED STATES OF AMERICA

BY THE

SOUTHERN METHODIST UNIVERSITY PRINTING DEPARTMENT

AT DALLAS, TEXAS

Preface

THE POPULARITY of backwoods and frontier material between 1830 and 1860 is illustrated by the fact that two-thirds of the sketches presented herein were published in newspapers; the remainder appeared in magazines in the United States, England, and Scotland. Few, if any, of these sketches have previously been reprinted in the twentieth century.

The sixty-five sketches included in this volume were selected from hundreds of items dealing with Texas. Many are from the widely circulated New York weekly, the *Spirit of the Times,* edited by William T. Porter, who encouraged subscribers to contribute backwoods material and also reprinted sketches from American newspapers and from English and American magazines. Newspapers represented here, either directly or indirectly through the *Spirit,* include *New York Sunday Times,* St. Louis *Reporter,* New Orleans *Picayune* and *Delta, Richmond* (Va.) *Examiner, Richmond* (La.) *Compiler,* and Houston *Telegraph.* American magazines include *Arthur's Home Gazette, Littell's Living Age, Journal of Commerce, United Service Magazine, Harper's, Democratic Review,* and *Noah's Weekly Messenger;* English magazines, *Chambers' Edinburgh Journal, Blackwood's Magazine,* and the *Spectator.* In addition to the sketches that were published in newspapers and magazines, much backwoods material appeared in travel books and collections of humor, most of which were originally issued as inexpensive paperbacks.

Sketches reprinted here are presented with little alteration other than occasional modernization of spelling and removal of excess punctuation.

For financial assistance in completing this project, I am grateful to the officials in charge of the Fund for Organized Research, Texas A & M University.

JOHN Q. ANDERSON

College Station, Texas
May 19, 1966

Contents

Tales of Frontier Texas

Introduction

TEXAS WAS A MAVERICK from the beginning. As a Spanish province, it was too far away from the heart of Mexico to be one of the herd. As a Republic, it was neither Spanish nor Mexican enough to become another Latin nation; it was too small and weak to stand alone as an Anglo-American nation; yet it was too American to become a satellite of England or France. As a state, it was too proud of its blood-bought freedom and its brief taste of nationhood to accept mere statehood and so entered the American Union with concessions granted no other member. Consequently, Texas has always been alongside the Union as much as in it. Geographically, it is Deep South, Southwest, and West. Culturally, it is not entirely Anglo-American. This maverick strain, weakened only externally over the years, has been the chief impetus behind the ever growing Texas myth, now so firmly established that there is little chance its power will diminish.

The Texas myth itself is also a maverick without parallel in history. It has no ancient gods or demigods but has satisfied the need for them in its own heroes, whose feats have sometimes been superhuman. Its tales of the marvelous and fantastic, stemming from a diverse terrain and a violent nature, compare favorably with such stories in older mythologies. Central to the Texas myth has always been a profound belief in the significance of place in the life of man. Defensive in the beginning, this "nationalism" has brought about a unity that has withstood generations of criticism by outsiders, because it results from pride like that which moti-

3

vated the Greeks to refer to all other peoples as barbarians and the
Romans to pity all who were not citizens of Rome. But the saving
grace in the Texas myth is that element which permits Texans themselves to disbelieve in it. Long ago Bigfoot Wallace learned that
people at home in Virginia could not accept the truth about Texas
because it seemed too fantastic, and so he gave them what they
were prepared to believe—fantasy. Texans away from home have
been following his lead ever since, for they know that the Texas
myth exists more for outsiders than it does for them. Thus, with a
keen sense of irony—developed in part from the paradoxes of nature
in their homeland—Texans have laughed at themselves while satis-
fying in others the thirst for the maverick life.

Actually, the Texas myth is not so readily explained; it remains
a maverick no matter how much it is analyzed, attacked, or de-
fended. No attempt will be made here, then, to corral this creature.
It did, however, have a beginning, and the selections presented in
this book show that from the start outsiders greatly influenced
the origin and development of significant elements of the myth.
Travelers, foreigners especially, who came determined to find
uniqueness, who looked briefly, and who went away and wrote
about what they saw, stirred the imaginations of their many readers
who wanted this faraway land to be romantic and strange.

As the tales are told—by adventurers, journalists, traveling Euro-
peans, military officers, and others—the maverick strain will be evident. And when it is remembered that these stories appeared in the
eastern press or in widely-read travel books, it becomes clear why
the Texas myth was born a lusty child—a child who soon grew to
manhood and made himself heard far and wide before he was
twenty years old.

I
The Land of the Lone Star

I. The Land of the Lone Star

THE LAY OF THE LAND *in Texas has had much to do with both the destiny and the lore of the state. The terrain was misleading from the beginning. Travelers arriving by the waters of the Gulf of Mexico saw a seemingly endless plain stretching back from the beach; those riding over the Camino Real, the Old Spanish Trail, from Natchitoches, Louisiana, to San Antonio saw a shifting panorama of dense, well-watered forests, rolling hills covered with post oaks, small open prairies, low-frowning mesas, and finally the vast plains of the buffalo range; those coming south out of Arkansas plowed through the tangled wilderness of the Cross Timbers before they reached the prairie. Sooner or later all travelers experienced the vastness of the ocean-like prairies which made the eye ache from the distance that stretched to far horizons. An American journalist who spent some time in Texas in the 1830's remarked, ". . . the stillness of a large prairie is one of the most painful sensations of loneliness a man ever encountered"* (Jonathan F. Kelley, The Humors of Falconbridge [Philadelphia, 1856]). *But, in contrast, across the prairie lay the colorful old Spanish town of San Antonio, or the bustling seaports of Galveston and Indianola, or a sun-baked army post hidden in the badlands of the upper Brazos River.*

The land was both hostile and friendly. In the semitropical coastal plain the plantation system of the Old South was immediately at home, though the lush vegetation harbored the deadly malaria and yellow fever, and hurricanes sometimes stripped the land bare. The higher, healthier river bottoms inland to the north

7

were excellent for small farms, but the fierce Comanches continued to raid them periodically for many years after Texas became a state. From the Sabine River on the east to the mountains around El Paso, there was a type of terrain to please every taste: hardwood-covered bottom land, small prairies ringed with oak, blackland prairies embracing thousands of acres, cedar brakes along the upper reaches of the rivers, vast tablelands of the High Plains, rocky waterless semi-deserts, and purple-shadowed mesas.

The Texans, like the American frontiersmen elsewhere, paid for their land with endurance, money, and blood, removing the physical obstacles of Indians, wild animals, and trees, shaping the land to their needs and in turn being shaped by it—believing all the while that they were creating something new, and indeed they were.

Arrival in Texas

NOAH SMITHWICK

I AGAIN [1827] took up the line of march for Texas, this time on board a coasting schooner owned by parties in New Orleans, chartered by Carlysle & Smith and laden with supplies for the Mexican army. A steam tug towed us out to the mouth of the Mississippi as far as steamers ventured. The weather was lovely as a dream of Venice, and we rounded the Balize and sped away on the wings of the tradewinds over the placid waters. We passed Galveston Island in plain view. There was no sign of human habitation on it, nothing to give promise of the thriving city which now covers it. It was only noted then as having been the rendezvous of Lafitte and his pirates and as such was pointed out to me. The trip was a delightful one and I was in fine spirits, when on the third day we threaded the Paso Caballo and ran into Matagorda Bay, having made the run in a little over forty-eight hours, a remarkable record in those days. We cast anchor in the mouth of the Lavaca River, where we had calculated to find the Mexican troops, but the movements of the

From *The Evolution of a State, or Recollections of Old Texas Days,* compiled and edited by Noah Smithwick's daughter, Nanna Smithwick Donaldson (Austin, 1900), pp. 12-14. In 1827 Smithwick, at the age of nineteen, left Kentucky for Texas with "a few dollars in money, a change of clothes, and a gun." He rode a flatboat to Natchez and then took a steamer to New Orleans, where, because he was broke, he worked briefly in a foundry. A few months later he arrived in Texas, where he spent most of the remainder of his life, working as gunsmith, blacksmith, Indian fighter, and miller. He knew intimately many of the original colonists.

troops, as well as the government, were very uncertain, and there were no troops, no agent, no one authorized to receive the goods. There was not an American there. The colonization law exempted from settlement all land within twenty-five miles of the coast; so the territory was given over to the Karankawa Indians, a fierce tribe, whose hand was against every man. They lived mostly on fish and alligators with a man for fete days when they could catch one. They were the most savage looking human beings I ever saw. Many of the bucks were six feet in height, with bows and arrows in proportion. Their ugly faces were rendered hideous by the alligator grease and dirt with which they were besmeared from head to foot as a defense against mosquitoes. They rowed outside to our vessel in their canoes, but Carlysle warned them to leave their arms on shore, enforcing the argument by the presence of a wicked looking cannon, which was conspicuously pointed in their direction. The mate and I had made special preparations for their reception, having molded several pints of bullets with which to load the cannon, and we were eager for a chance to turn it loose among them, but they gave us no provocation.

It was a dreary place for a lone stranger to land. A few Mexicans came around, but they spoke no English and I understood no Spanish. At length two men, Fulchcr and McHenry, who had squatted on land six or eight miles up the river, sighted the schooner and came down in a dugout. They took me in with them and I spent my first night in Texas in their cabin. My first meal on Texas soil was dried venison sopped in honey. After having spent some months in New Orleans, where everything of the known world was obtainable, it looked like rank starvation to me, but I was adaptive. The sea voyage had sharpened my appetite and I was possessed of a strong set of grinders; so I set to and made a meal, but I was not anxious to trespass on their hospitality, so next morning I set out on foot for Dewitt's colony, ten miles further up the Lavaca.

On the Prairie of Jacinto

CHARLES SEALSFIELD

WHEN A VERY YOUNG MAN, I found myself one fine morning possessed of a Texas land scrip—that is to say, a certificate of the Galveston Bay and Texas Land Company in which it was stated that, in consideration of the sum of one thousand dollars, duly paid and delivered by Mr. Edward Rivers into the hands of the cashier of the aforesaid company, he, the said Edward Rivers, became entitled to ten thousand acres of Texan land to be selected by himself or those he should appoint under the sole condition of not infringing on the property or rights of the holders of previously given certificates.

Ten thousand acres of the finest land in the world, and under a heaven compared to which our Maryland sky, bright as it is, appears dull and foggy! It was a tempting bait—too good a one not to be caught at by many in those times of speculation, and accordingly our free and enlightened citizens bought and sold their millions of Texan acres just as readily as they did their thousands of towns and villages in Ohio, Indiana, Illinois, and Michigan, and their tens of

Reprinted from *Blackwood's Magazine* in William T. Porter's New York sporting weekly, *Spirit of the Times* (hereafter cited as *Spirit*), XIII, 41 (December 9, 1843), 483-85. This part of "Adventures in Texas" and its sequel (*Spirit*, XIII, 44 [December 30, 1843], 518-21) were written by the Austrian novelist Karl Anton Postl (1793-1864), who used the pen name Charles Sealsfield. Born in Moravia, he was destined for the church but ran away from a monastery and came to New Orleans, where he appeared as Charles Sealsfield in 1823. He traveled through Texas and Mexico, lived in Pennsylvania, and

11

thousands of shares in banks and railways. It was a speculative
fever which has since, we may hope, been in some degree cured. At
any rate, the remedies applied have been tolerably severe.

I had not escaped the contagion, and, having got the land on
paper, I thought I should like to see it in dirty acres; so, in company
with a friend who had a similar venture, I embarked at Baltimore
on board the *Catcher* schooner and after a three-week voyage arrived in Galveston Bay [1832]. The grassy shores of this bay, into
which the River Brazos empties itself, rise so little above the surface of the water to which they bear a strong resemblance in color
that it would be difficult to discover them, were it not for three
stunted trees growing on the western extremity of a long lizard-
shaped island that stretches nearly sixty miles across the bay and
conceals the mouth of the river. These trees are the only landmark
for the mariner, and with their exception not a single object—not a
hill, a house, nor so much as a bush—relieves the level sameness of
the island and adjacent continent.

---

in 1826 returned to New Orleans. The next year he went back to
Europe, where he published a book in two parts, *The United States
as They Are* and *The Americans as They Are; Described in a Tour
Through the Valley of the Mississippi* (1828). Again in the United
States, he published his first novel, *Tokeah; or The White Rose*, in
1828. In that year he returned to the Southwest, where he worked
as a journalist until 1832. He then went to Switzerland and spent
the remainder of his life there, though he retained his American
citizenship. His works were published in fifteen volumes in 1845-47
under the name of Charles Sealsfield. His identity as the fugitive
monk Karl Postl was revealed in his will. He created a new type of
fiction, the ethnographical novel, in which he took whole peoples
as his center of concentration. He was widely read.

"Adventures in Texas" appears in three parts in *Frontier Life, or
Scenes and Adventures in the South West* (1857) by Francis Hard-
man, according to J. Frank Dobie (*Guide to Life and Literature of
the Southwest*, p. 48) another of Postl's pseudonyms. *Frontier Life*
contains a fuller version of the episode presented here; in the introduction the narrator is both *Edwin* and *Edward* Morse on the same
page. Porter may have changed the name to Edward Rivers and
otherwise edited the sketch.

After we had, with some difficulty, got on the inner side of the island, a pilot came on board and took charge of the vessel. The first thing he did was to run us on a sandbank, off which we got with no small labor and by the united exertions of sailors and passengers, and at length entered the river. In our impatience to land, I and my friend left the schooner in a cockleshell of a boat, which upset in the surge, and we found ourselves floundering in the water. Luckily it was not very deep, and we escaped with a thorough drenching.

When we had scrambled on shore, we gazed about us for some time before we could persuade ourselves that we were actually upon land. It was, without exception, the strangest sight we had ever seen, and there was scarcely a possibility of distinguishing the boundary between earth and water. The green grass grew down to the edge of the green sea, and there was only the streak of white foam left by the latter upon the former to serve as a line of demarcation. Before us was a plain, a hundred or more miles in extent, covered with long, fine grass, rolling in waves before each puff of the sea breeze, with neither tree, nor house, nor hill to vary the monotony of the surface. Ten or twelve miles toward the north and northwest, we distinguished some dark masses, which we afterward discovered to be groups of trees; but to our eyes they looked exactly like islands in a green sea, and we subsequently learned that they were called islands by the people of the country. It would have been difficult to have given them a more appropriate name or one better describing their appearance.

Proceeding along the shore, we came to a block house situated behind a small tongue of land projecting into the river and decorated with the flag of the Mexican republic, waving in all its glory from the roof. At that period, this was the only building of which Galveston harbor could boast. It served as customhouse and as barracks for the garrison, as the residence of the director of customs and of the civil and military intendant, as headquarters of the officer commanding, and moreover, as hotel and wine-and-spirit

store. Alongside the board, on which was depicted a sort of hiero-
glyphic intended for the Mexican eagle, hung a bottle doing duty as
a sign, and the republican banner threw its protecting shadow over
an announcement of "Brandy, Whiskey, and Accommodation for
Man and Beast."

As we approached the house, we saw the whole garrison assembled before the door. It consisted of a dozen dwarfish, spindle-
shanked Mexican soldiers, none of them so big or half so strong as
American boys of fifteen and whom I would have backed a single
Kentucky woodsman, armed with a riding-whip, to have driven to
the four winds of heaven. These heroes all sported tremendous
beards, whiskers, and mustaches and had a habit of knitting their
brows in the endeavor, as we supposed, to look fierce and formidable. They were crowding around a table of rough planks and
playing a game of cards, in which they were so deeply engrossed
that they took no notice of our approach. Their officer, however,
came out of the house to meet us.

Captain Cotton, formerly editor of the *Mexican Gazette,* now civil
and military commandant at Galveston, customs-director, harbor-
master, and tavern-keeper, and a Yankee to boot, seemed to trouble
himself very little about his various dignities and titles. He produced some capital French and Spanish wine, which, it is to be
presumed, he got duty free, and welcomed us to Texas. We were
presently joined by some of our fellow-passengers, who seemed as
bewildered as we had been at the billiard-table appearance of the
country. Indeed, the place looked so desolate and uninviting that
there was little inducement to remain on *terra firma,* and it was
with a feeling of relief that we once more found ourselves on board
the schooner.

We took three days to sail up the River Brazos to the town of
Brazoria, a distance of thirty miles. On the first day, nothing but
meadowland was visible on either side of us. On the second, the
monotonous grass-covered surface was varied by islands of trees,
and about twenty miles from the mouth of the river, we passed

through a forest of sycamores, and saw several herds of deer and
flocks of wild turkeys. At length we reached Brazoria, which at the
time I speak of, namely, in the year 1832, was an important city—
for Texas, that is to say—consisting of upward of thirty houses, three
of which were of brick, three of planks, and the remainder of logs.
All the inhabitants were Americans, and the streets arranged in
American fashion in straight lines and at right angles. The only
objection to the place was that in the wet season it was all under
water, but the Brazorians overlooked this little inconvenience in
consideration of the inexhaustible fruitfulness of the soil. It was
the beginning of March when we arrived, and yet there was already
an abundance of new potatoes, beans, peas, and artichokes, all of
the finest sort and most delicious flavor.

At Brazoria, my friend and myself had the satisfaction of learning
that our land certificates for which we had each paid a thousand
dollars were worth exactly nothing—just so much waste paper, in
short—unless we chose to conform to a condition to which our
worthy friends, the Galveston Bay and Texas Land Company, had
never made the smallest allusion.

It appeared that in the year 1824 the Mexican Congress had
passed an act for the encouragement of emigration from the United
States to Texas. In consequence of this act, an agreement was
entered into with contractors, or *empresarios* as they call them in
Mexico, who had bound themselves to bring a certain number of
settlers into Texas within a given time and without any expense to
the Mexican government. On the other hand, the Mexican government had engaged to furnish land to these emigrants at the rate of
five square leagues to every hundred families; but to this agreement
one condition was attached, and it was that all settlers should be,
or become, Roman Catholics. Failing this, the validity of their
claims to the land was not recognized, and they were liable to be
turned out any day at the point of the bayonet.

This information threw us into no small perplexity. It was clear
that we had been duped, completely bubbled by the rascally Land

Company, that as heretics the Mexican government would have nothing to say to us, and that unless we chose to become converts to the Romish Church we might whistle for our acres and light our pipes with the certificates. Our Yankee friends at Brazoria, however, laughed at our dilemma and told us that we were only in the same plight as hundreds of our countrymen who had come to Texas in total ignorance of this condition, but who had not the less taken possession of their land and settled there. They themselves were among the number, and, although it was just as likely they would turn Negroes as Roman Catholics, they had no idea of being turned out of their houses and plantations. At any rate, if the Mexicans tried it, they had their rifles with them and should be apt, they reckoned, to burn powder before they allowed themselves to be kicked off such an almighty fine piece of soil. So, after a while, we began to think that as we had paid our money and come so far we might do as others had done before us—occupy our land and wait the course of events. The next day we each bought a horse, or *mustang* as they call them there, which animals were selling at Brazoria for next to nothing, and rode out into the prairie to look for a convenient spot to settle.

These mustangs are small horses, rarely above fourteen hands high, and are descended from the Spanish breed introduced by the original conquerors of the country. During the three centuries that have elapsed since the conquest of Mexico, they have increased and multiplied to an extraordinary extent and are to be found in vast droves in the Texan prairies, although they are now beginning to become somewhat scarcer. They are taken with the *lasso*, concerning which instrument or weapon I will here say a word or two, notwithstanding that it has often been described.

The lasso is usually from twenty to thirty feet long, very flexible, and composed of strips of twisted ox-hide. One end is fastened to the saddle, and the other, which forms a running noose, held in the hand of the hunter who thus equipped rides out into the prairie. When he discovers a troop of wild horses, he maneuvers to get to windward of them and then to approach as near as possible. If he is an experienced hand, the horses seldom or never escape him, and soon as he finds himself within twenty or thirty feet of them, he throws the noose with unerring aim over the neck of the one he has selected for his prey. This done, he turns his own horse sharp round, gives him the spur, and gallops away, dragging his unfortunate captive after him breathless and with his windpipe so compressed by the noose that he is unable to make the smallest resistance. After a few yards, the mustang falls headlong to the ground and lies motionless and almost lifeless, sometimes badly hurt and disabled. From this day forward, the horse which has been thus caught never forgets the lasso; the mere sight of it makes him tremble in every limb, and, however wild he may be, it is sufficient to show it to him or lay it on his neck to render him as tame and docile as a lamb.

The horse taken, next comes the breaking in, which is effected in a no less brutal manner than his capture. The eyes of the unfortunate animal are covered with a bandage, and a tremendous bit, a pound weight or more, clapped into his mouth; the horse breaker puts on a pair of spurs six inches long and with rowels like penknives, and jumping on his back urges him to his very utmost speed. If the horse tries to rear or turns restive, one pull, and not a very hard one either, at the instrument of torture they call a bit is sufficient to tear his mouth to shreds and cause the blood to flow in streams. I have myself seen horses' teeth broken with these barbarous bits. The poor beast whinnies and groans with pain and terror; but there is no help for him, the spurs are at his flanks, and on he goes full gallop till he is ready to sink from fatigue and exhaustion. He then has a quarter of an hour's rest allowed him; but scarcely does he begin to recover breath, which has been ridden or spurred out of his body, when he is again mounted, and has to go through the same violent process as before. If he breaks down during this rude trial, he is either knocked on the head or driven away as useless; but if he holds out, he is marked with a hot iron and left to graze on the prairie. Henceforward, there is no particular difficulty in catching him when wanted. The wildness of the horse is completely punished out of him, but for it is substituted the most confirmed vice and malice that it is possible to conceive. These mustangs are unquestionably the most deceitful and spiteful of all the equine race. They seem to be perpetually looking out for an opportunity of playing their master a trick, and very soon after I got possession of mine, I was nearly paying for him in a way that I had not calculated upon.

We were going to Bolivar and had to cross the River Brazos. I was the last but one to get into the boat and was leading my horse carelessly by the bridle. Just as I was about to step in, a sudden jerk, a cry of "Mind your beast!" made me jump to one side, and lucky it was that I did so. My mustang had suddenly sprung back, reared up, and then thrown himself forward upon me with such force and fury, that, as I got out of his way, his fore feet went completely through the bottom of the boat. I never in my life saw an animal in such a paroxysm of rage. He curled up his lips till his whole range of teeth was visible, his eyes literally shot fire, while the foam flew from his mouth, and he gave a wild screaming neigh that had something quite diabolical in its sound. I was standing perfectly thunderstruck at this scene when one of the party took a lasso and very quietly laid it over the animal's neck. The effect was really magical. With closed mouth, drooping ears, and head low, there stood the mustang as meek and docile as my old jackass. The change was so sudden and comical that we all burst out laughing, although when I came to reflect on the danger I had run it required all my love of horses to prevent me from shooting the brute upon the spot.

Mounted upon this ticklish steed and in company with my friend, I made various excursions to Bolivar, Marion, Columbia, Anahuac— incipient cities consisting of from five to twenty houses. We also visited numerous plantations and clearings, to the owners of some of which we were known, or had messages of introduction. Either with or without such recommendations, we always found a hearty welcome and hospitable reception, and it was rare that we were allowed to pay for our entertainment.

We arrived one day at a clearing, which lay a few miles off the way from Harrisburg to San Felipe de Austin and belonged to a Mr. Neal. He had been three years in the country, occupying himself with the breeding of cattle which is unquestionably the most agreeable as well as profitable occupation that can be followed in Texas. He had between seven and eight hundred head of cattle and from fifty to sixty horses, all mustangs. His plantation, like nearly all the plantations in Texas at that time, was as yet in a very rough state, and his house, although roomy and comfortable enough inside, was built of unhewn tree trunks in true backwoodsman style. It was situated on the border of one of the islands, or groups of trees, and stood between two gigantic sycamores which sheltered it from the sun and wind. In front and as far as could be seen lay the prairie, covered with its waving grass and many-colored flowers, behind the dwelling arose the cluster of forest trees in all their primeval majesty, laced and bound together by an infinity of wild vines, which shot their tendrils and clinging branches hundreds of feet upward to the very top of the trees, embracing and covering the whole island with a green network and converting it into an immence bower of vine leaves.

These islands are one of the most enchanting features of Texan scenery. Of infinite variety and beauty of form and unrivalled in the growth and magnitude of the trees that compose them, they are to be found of all shapes—circular, parallelograms, hexagons, octagons—some again twisting and winding like dark-green snakes over the brighter surface of the prairie. In no park or artificially laid-out grounds would it be possible to find anything equalling these natural shrubberies in beauty and symmetry. In the morning and evening especially, when surrounded by a sort of veil of light-grayish mist and with the horizontal beams of the rising or setting sun gleaming through them, they offer pictures which it is impossible to get weary of admiring.

Mr. Neal was a jovial Kentuckian, and he received us with the greatest hospitality, only asking in return all the news we could give him of the States. It is difficult to imagine without having witnessed it the feverish eagerness and curiosity with which all intelligence from their native country is sought after and listened to by these dwellers in the desert. Men, women, and children crowded round us, and though we had arrived in the afternoon it was near sunrise before we could escape from the inquiries by which we were overwhelmed and retire to the beds . . . prepared for us.

I had not slept very long when I was roused by our worthy host. He was going out to catch twenty or thirty oxen which were wanted for the market at New Orleans.[1] As a kind of chase which takes place after these animals is very interesting and rarely dangerous, we willingly accepted the invitation to accompany him and having dressed and breakfasted in all haste got upon our mustangs and rode off into the prairie.

The party was half a dozen strong, consisting of Mr. Neal, my friend and myself, and three Negroes. What we had to do was to drive the cattle which were grazing on the prairie in herds of from thirty to fifty head to the house, and then those which were selected for the market were to be taken with the lasso and sent off to Brazoria.

After riding four or five miles, we came in sight of a drove, splendid animals, standing very high and of most symmetrical form. The horns of these cattle are of unusual length and in the distance have more the appearance of stag's antlers than bull's horns. We approached the herd first to within a quarter of a mile. They remained quiet. We rode round them and in like manner got in rear of a second and third drove and then began to spread out so as to form a half circle and drive the cattle toward the house.

Hitherto my mustang had behaved exceedingly well, cantering freely along and not attempting to play any tricks. I had scarcely, however, left the remainder of the party a couple of hundred yards, when the devil by which he was possessed began to wake up. The mustangs belonging to the plantation were grazing some three quarters of a mile off; and no sooner did my beast catch sight of them than he commenced practicing every species of jump and leap that it is possible for a horse to execute and many of a nature so extraordinary that I should have thought no brute that ever went on four legs would have been able to accomplish them. He shied, reared, pranced, leaped forward, backward, and sideways—in short, played such infernal pranks that, although a practised rider, I found it no easy matter to keep my seat. I began heartily to regret that I had brought no lasso with me, which would have tamed him at once, and that, contrary to Mr. Neal's advice, I had put on my American bit instead of a Mexican one. Without these auxiliaries, all my horsemanship was useless. The brute galloped like a mad creature some five hundred yards, caring nothing for my efforts to stop him, and then finding himself close to the troop of mustangs he stopped suddenly short, threw his head between his forelegs, and his hind feet into the air with such vicious violence that I was pitched clean out of the saddle. Before I well knew where I was, I had the satisfaction of seeing him put his fore feet on the bridle, pull bit and bridoon² out of his mouth, and then with a neigh of exultation spring into the midst of the herd of mustangs.

I got up out of the long grass in a towering passion. One of the Negroes who was nearest to me came galloping to my assistance and begged me to let the beast run for a while. He said that when Anthony, the huntsman, came he would soon catch him. I was too angry to listen to reason, and I ordered him to get off his horse and let me mount. The black begged and prayed of me not to ride after the brute. Mr. Neal, who was some distance off, shouted to me as loud as he could, for Heaven's sake, to stop—that I did not know what it was to chase a wild horse in a Texan prairie and that I must not fancy myself in the meadows of Louisiana or Florida. I paid no attention to all this—I was in too great a rage at the trick the beast had played me, and jumping on the Negro's horse I galloped away like mad.

My rebellious steed was grazing quietly with his companions, and he allowed me to come within a couple of hundred paces of him; but just as I had prepared the lasso which was fastened to the Negro's saddle bow, he gave a start and galloped off some distance farther, I after him. Again he made a pause and munched a mouthful of grass—then off, again for another half mile. This time I had great hopes of catching him for he let me come within a hundred yards, but just as I was creeping up to him, away he went with one of his shrill neighs. When I galloped fast he went faster, when I rode slowly he slackened his pace. At least ten times did he let me approach him within a couple of hundred yards without being a bit nearer getting hold of him. It was certainly high time to desist from such a mad chase, but I never dreamed of doing so, and indeed the longer it lasted, the more obstinate I got. I rode on after the beast which kept letting me come nearer and nearer and then darted off again with his loud-laughing neigh. It was this infernal neigh that made me so savage—there was something so spiteful and triumphant in it, as though the animal knew he was making a fool of me and exulted in so doing. At last, however, I got so sick of my horse hunt that I determined to make a last trial, and if that failed to turn back. The runaway had stopped near one of the islands of trees and was grazing quite close to its edge. I thought that if I were to creep round to the other side of the island and then steal across it through the trees, I should be able to throw the lasso over his head or, at any rate, to drive him back to the house. This plan I put in execution—rode round the island, then through it, lasso in hand, and as softly as if I had been riding over eggs. To my consternation, however, on arriving at the edge of trees and at the exact spot where only a few minutes before I had seen the mustang grazing, no signs of him were to be perceived. I made the circuit of the island, but in vain—the animal had disappeared. With a hearty curse, I put spurs to my horse, and started off to ride back to the plantation.

Neither the plantation, the cattle, nor my companions, were visible, it is true, but this gave me no uneasiness. I felt sure that I knew the direction in which I had come, that the island I had just left was one which was visible from the house while all around me were such numerous tracks of horses, and that the possibility of my having lost my way never occurred to me; I rode on quite unconcernedly.

After riding for about an hour, however, I began to find the time rather long. I looked at my watch; it was past one o'clock. We had started at nine, and allowing an hour and a half to have been spent in finding the cattle, I had passed nearly three hours in my wild and unsuccessful hunt. I began to think that I must have got farther from the plantation than I had as yet supposed.

It was toward the end of March, the day clear and warm, just like a May day in the Southern States. The sun was now shining brightly out, but the early part of the morning had been somewhat foggy; and as I had only arrived at the plantation the day before and had passed the whole afternoon and evening indoors, I had no opportunity of getting acquainted with the bearings of the house. The reflection began to make me rather uneasy, particularly when I remembered the entreaties of the Negro and the loud exhortations of Mr. Neal addressed to me as I rode away. I said to myself, however, that I could not be more than ten or fifteen miles from the plantation, that I should soon come in sight of the herds of cattle, and that then there would be no difficulty in finding my way. But when I had ridden another hour without seeing the smallest sign either of man or beast, I got seriously uneasy. In my impatience, I abused poor Neal for not sending somebody to find me. His huntsman, I heard, was gone to Anahuac and would not be back for two or three days, but he might have sent a couple of his lazy Negroes. Or, if he had only fired a shot or two as a signal. I stopped and listened in hopes of hearing the crack of a rifle. But the deepest stillness reigned around; scarcely the chirp of a bird was heard—all nature seemed to be taking the siesta. As far as the eye could reach was a waving sea of grass, here and there an island of trees, but

not a trace of a human being. At last I thought I had made a discovery. The nearest clump of trees was undoubtedly the same which
I had admired and pointed out to my companions soon after we
had left the house. It bore a fantastic resemblance to a snake coiled
up and about to dart upon its prey. About six or seven miles from
the plantation we had passed it on our right hand, and if I now
kept it upon my left I could not fail to be going in a proper direction. So said, so done. I trotted on most perseveringly toward the
point of the horizon where I felt certain the house must lie. One
hour passed, then a second, then a third; every now and then I
stopped and listened, but nothing was audible, not a shot nor a
shout. But, although I heard nothing, I saw something which gave
me no great pleasure. In the direction in which we had ridden out,
the grass was very abundant and the flowers scarce; whereas the
part of the prairie in which I now found myself presented the
appearance of a perfect flowergarden with scarcely a square foot
of green to be seen. The most variegated carpet of flowers I ever
beheld lay unrolled before me—red, yellow, violet, blue, every color,
every tint was there—millions of the most magnificent prairie roses,
tube-roses, dahlias, and fifty other kinds of flowers. The finest artificial garden in the world would sink into insignificance when compared with this parterre of nature's own planting. My horse could
scarcely make his way through the wilderness of flowers, and I for
a time remained lost in admiration of this scene of extraordinary
beauty. The prairie in the distance looked as if clothed with rain-
bows that waved to and fro over its surface.

But the difficulties and anxieties of my situation soon banished all
other thoughts, and I rode on with a perfect indifference through a
scene that, under other circumstances, would have captivated my
entire attention. All the stories that I had heard of mishaps in these
endless prairies recurred in vivid coloring to my memory, not mere
backwoodsman's legends, but facts well authenticated by persons
of undoubted veracity, who had warned me before I came to Texas
against venturing without guide or compass into these dangerous

wilds. Even men who had been long in the country were often
known to lose themselves and to wander for days and weeks over
these oceans of grass, where no hill or variety of surfaces offers a
landmark to the traveller. In summer and autumn, such a position
would have one danger the less, that is, there would be no risk of
dying of hunger; for at those seasons the most delicious fruits,
grapes, plums, peaches, and others, are to be found in abundance.
But we were now in early spring, and although I saw numbers of
peach and plum trees, they were only in blossom. Of game also
there was plenty, both fur and feather, but I had no gun, and
nothing appeared more probable than that I should die of hunger,
although surrounded by food and in one of the most fruitful countries in the world. This thought flashed suddenly across me, and for
a moment my heart sunk within me as I first perceived the real
danger of my position.

After a time, however, other ideas came to console me. I had
been already four weeks in the country and had ridden over a large
slice of it in every direction, always through prairies, and I had
never had any difficulty in finding my way. True, but then I had
always had a compass and been in company. It was this sort of
over-confidence and feeling of security that had made me adventure
so rashly and in spite of all warning in pursuit of the mustang. I
had not waited to reflect that a little more than four weeks was
necessary to make one acquainted with the bearings of a district
three times as big as New York State. Still I thought it impossible
that I should have got so far out of the right track as not to be able
to find the house before night fall, which was now, however, rapidly
approaching. Indeed, the first shades of evening, strange as it may
seem, gave this persuasion increased strength. Home-bred and
gently nurtured as I was, my life before coming to Texas had been
by no means one of adventure, and I was so used to sleep with a
roof over my head that when I saw it getting dusk I felt certain that
I could not be far from the house. The idea fixed itself so strongly
in my mind that I involuntarily spurred my mustang and trotted

on, peering out through the now fast-gathering gloom in expectation of seeing a light. Several times I fancied I heard the barking
of the dogs, the cattle lowing, or the merry laugh of the children.

"Hurrah! there is the house at last—I see the lights in the parlor
window."

I urged my horse on, but when I came near the house, it proved
to be an island of trees. What I had taken for candles were fire flies
that now issued in swarms from out of the darkness of the island
and spread themselves over the prairie, darting about in every
direction, their small blue flames literally lighting up the plain and
making it appear as if I were surrounded by a sea of Bengal fire.[3]
It is impossible to conceive anything more bewildering than such a
ride as mine on a warm March night through the interminable,
never varying prairie. Overhead the deep blue firmament with its
hosts of bright stars, at my feet and all round an ocean of magical
light, myriads of fireflies floating upon the soft still air. To me it
was like a scene of enchantment. I could distinguish every blade
of grass, every flower, each leaf on the trees, but all in a strange
unnatural sort of light and in altered colors. Tube roses and asters,
prairie roses and geraniums, dahlias and vine branches, began to
wave and move, to range themselves in ranks and rows. The whole
vegetable world around me seemed to dance as the swarms of living
lights passed over it. . . .

I now felt so weary and exhausted, so hungry and thirsty, and
withal my mind was so anxious and harassed by my dangerous
position and the uncertainty how I should get out of it that I was
really incapable of going any further. I felt quite bewildered and
stood for some time gazing before me and scarcely even troubling
myself to think. At length I mechanically drew my clasp-knife from
my pocket and set to work to dig a hole in the rich black soil of the
prairie. Into this hole I put the knotted end of my lasso and then
pushing it in the earth and stamping it down with my foot as I
had seen others do since I had been in Texas, I passed the noose
over my mustang's neck and left him to graze while I myself lay

down outside the circle which the lasso would allow him to describe. An odd manner, it may seem, of tying up a horse but the most convenient and natural one in a country where one may often find one's self fifty miles from any house and five-and-twenty from a tree or bush.

I found it no easy matter to sleep, for on all sides I heard the howling of wolves and jaguars, an unpleasant serenade at any time, but most of all so in the prairie, unarmed and defenseless as I was. My nerves, too, were all in commotion, and I felt so feverish that I do not know what I should have done had I not fortunately remembered that I had my cigar-case and a roll of tobacco, real Virginia *dulcissimus,* in my pocket—invaluable treasures in my present situation and which on this as on many other occasions did not fail to soothe and calm my agitated thoughts.

Luckily, too, being a tolerably confirmed smoker, I carried a flint and steel with me, for otherwise although surrounded by lights I should have been sadly at a loss for fire. A couple of Havannahs did me an infinite deal of good, and after a while I sank into the slumber of which I stood so much in need.

The day was hardly well broken when I awoke. The refreshing sleep I had enjoyed had given me new energy and courage. I felt hungry enough, to be sure, but light and cheerful, and I hastened to dig up the end of the lasso and saddled my horse. I trusted that, though I had been condemned to wander over the prairie the whole of the preceding day, as a sort of punishment for my rashness, I should now have better luck and having expiated my fault be at length allowed to find my way. With this hope I mounted my mustang and resumed my ride.

I passed several beautiful islands of pecan, plum, and peach trees. It is a peculiarity worthy of remark, that these islands are nearly always of one sort of tree. It is very rare to meet with one where there are two sorts. Like the beasts of the forest that herd together according to their kind so does this wild vegetation preserve itself distinct in its different species. One island will be entirely composed of live oaks, another of plum, and a third of pecan trees; the vine only is common to them all and embraces them all alike with its slender but tenacious branches. I rode through several of these islands. They were perfectly free from bushes and brushwood, and carpeted with the most beautiful verdure it is possible to behold. I gazed at them in astonishment. It seemed incredible that nature, abandoned to herself, should preserve herself so beautifully clean and pure, and I involuntarily looked around me for some trace of the hand of man. But none was there. I saw nothing but herds of deer that gazed wonderfully at me with their large clear eyes and when I approached too near galloped off in alarm. What would I not have given for an ounce of lead, a charge of powder, and a Kentucky rifle? Nevertheless, the mere sight of the beasts gladdened me and raised my spirits. They were a sort of society. Something of the same feeling seemed to be imparted to my horse which bounded under me and neighed merrily as he cantered along in the fresh spring morning.

I was now skirting the side of an island of trees of greater extent than most of those I had hitherto seen. On reaching the end of it, I suddenly came in sight of an object presenting so extraordinary an appearance as far to surpass any of the natural wonders I had as yet beheld, either in Texas or the United States.

At the distance of about two miles rose a colossal mass, in shape somewhat like a monumental mound of tumulus and apparently of the brightest silver. As I came in view of it, the sun was just covered by a passing cloud, from the lower edge of which the bright rays shot down obliquely upon this extraordinary phenomenon, lighting it up in the most brilliant manner. At one moment it looked like a huge silver cone, then took the appearance of an illuminated castle with pinnacles and towers, or the dome of some great cathedral, then of a gigantic elephant covered with trappings but always of solid silver and indescribably magnificent. Had all the treasures of the earth been offered me to say what it was, I should have been unable to answer. Bewildered by my interminable wanderings in the prairie and weakened by fatigue and hunger, a superstitious feeling for a moment came over me, and I half asked myself whether I had not reached some enchanted region into which the evil spirit of the prairie was luring me to destruction by appearances of supernatural strangeness and beauty.

Banishing these wild imaginings, I rode on in the direction of this strange object, but it was only when I came within a very short distance that I was able to distinguish its nature. It was a live oak of most stupendous dimensions, the very patriarch of the prairie, grown gray in the lapse of ages. Its lower limbs had shot out in an horizontal, or rather downward, slanting direction and reaching nearly to the ground formed a vast dome several hundred feet in diameter and full a hundred and thirty feet high. It had no appearance of a tree, for neither trunk nor branches were visible. It seemed a mountain of whitish-green scales, fringed with a long silvery moss, that hung like innumerable beards from every bough and twig. Nothing could better convey the idea of immense and incalculable age than the hoary beard and venerable appearance of this monarch of the woods. Spanish moss of a silvery gray covered the whole mass of wood and foliage from the topmost bough down to the very ground, short near the top of the tree but gradually increasing in length as it descended until it hung like a deep fringe from the lower branches. I separated the vegetable curtain with my hands and entered this august temple with the feeling of involuntary awe. The change from the bright sunlight to the comparative darkness beneath the leafy vault was so great that I at first could scarcely distinguish anything. When my eyes got accustomed to the gloom, however, nothing could be more beautiful than the effect of the sun's rays which in forcing their way through the silvered leaves and mosses took as many varieties of color as if they had passed through a window of painted glass and gave the rich, subdued, and solemn light of some old cathedral.

The trunk of the tree rose, free from all branches, full forty feet from the ground, rough and knotted, and of such enormous size that it might have been taken for a mass of rock, covered with moss and lichens, while many of its boughs were nearly as thick as the trunk of any tree I had every previously seen.

I was so absorbed in the contemplation of the vegetable giant that for a short space I almost forgot my troubles, but as I rode away from the tree they returned to me in full force, and my reflections were certainly of no very cheering or consolatory nature. I rode on, however, most perseveringly. The morning slipped away; it was noon; the sun stood high in the cloudless heavens. My hunger was now increased to an insupportable degree, and I felt as if something were gnawing within me, something like a crab tugging and riving at my stomach with his sharp claws. This feeling left me after a time and was replaced by a sort of squeamishness, a faint sickly sensation. But if hunger was bad, thirst was worse. For some hours I suffered martyrdom. At length, like the hunger, it died away, and was succeeded by a feeling of sickness. The thirty hours' fatigue and fasting I had endured were beginning to tell upon my naturally strong nerves: I felt my reasoning powers growing weaker and my presence of mind leaving me. A feeling of despondency came over me—a thousand wild fancies passed through my bewildered brain; at times my head grew dizzy, and I reeled in my saddle like a drunken man. These weak fits, as I may call them, did not last long, and each time that I recovered I spurred my mustang onward, but it was all in vain—ride as far and as fast as I would, nothing was visible but a boundless sea of grass.

At length I gave up all hope, except in that God whose almighty hand was so manifest in the beauteous works around me. I let the bridle reins fall on my horse's neck, clasped my hands together, and prayed as I had never before prayed, so heartily and earnestly. When I had finished my prayer I felt greatly comforted. It seemed to me that here in the wilderness, which man had not as yet polluted, I was nearer to God and that my petition would assuredly be heard. I gazed cheerfully around, persuaded that I should yet escape from the peril in which I stood. As I did so, with what astonishment and inexpressible delight did I perceive not ten paces off the track of a horse.

The effect of this discovery was like an electric shock to me and drew a cry of joy from my lips that made my mustang start and prick his ears. Tears of delight and gratitude to Heaven came into my eyes, and I could scarcely refrain from leaping off my horse and kissing the welcome signs that gave me assurance of succor. With renewed strength I galloped onward, and had I been a lover flying to rescue his mistress from an Indian war party, I could not have displayed more eagerness than I did in following up the trail of an unknown traveller. . . .

I had ridden on for three or four hours following the track I had so fortunately discovered when I came upon the trace of a second horseman, who appeared to have here joined the first traveller. It ran in a parallel direction to the one I was following.

Had it been possible to increase my joy, this discovery would have done so. I could now entertain no doubt that I had hit upon the way out of this terrible prairie. It struck me as rather singular that two travellers should have met in this immense plain which so few persons traversed, but that they had done so was certain, for there was the track of the two horses as plain as possible. The trail was fresh, too, and it was evidently not long since the horsemen had passed. It might still be possible to overtake them, and in this hope I rode on faster than ever, as fast, at least, as my mustang could carry me through the thick grass and flowers, which in many places were four or five feet high.

During the next three hours I passed over some ten or twelve miles of ground. Although the trail still lay plainly and broadly marked before me, I saw nothing of those who had left it. Still I persevered. I must overtake them sooner or later, provided I did not lose the track and that I was most careful not to do, keeping my eyes fixed upon the ground as I rode along and never deviating from the line which the travellers had followed.

In this manner the day passed away and evening approached. I

still felt hope and courage, but my physical strength began to give
way. The gnawing sensation of hunger increased. I was sick and
faint; my limbs became heavy, my blood seemed chilled in my
veins, and all my senses appeared to grow duller under the influence
of exhaustion, thirst, and hunger. My eyesight became misty, my
hearing less acute, the bridle reins felt cold and heavy in my
fingers.

Still I rode on. Sooner or later I must find an outlet; the prairie
must have an end somewhere. It is true that the whole of Southern
Texas is one vast prairie; but then there are rivers flowing through
it, and if I could reach one of those, I should not be far from the
abodes of men. By following the streams five or six miles up or
down, I should be sure to find a plantation.

As I was thus reasoning with and encouraging myself, I suddenly
perceived the traces of a third horse, running parallel to the two
which I had been so long following. This was indeed encouragement. I was certain that three travellers, arriving from different
points of the prairie and all going in the same direction, must have
some object, must be repairing to some village or clearing, and
where or what this was had now become indifferent to me so long
as I once more found myself among my fellow men. I spurred on
my mustang, which was beginning to flag a little in his pace with
the fatigue of our long ride.

The sun set behind the high trees of an island that bounded
my view westward, and there being little or no twilight in those
southerly latitudes, the broad day was almost instantaneously replaced by the darkness of night. I could proceed no farther without losing the track of the three horsemen, and as I happened to be
close to an island I fastened my mustang to a branch with the lasso
and threw myself on the grass under the trees.

This night, however, I had no fancy for tobacco. Neither the
cigars nor the *dulcissimus* tempted me. I tried to sleep but in vain.
Once or twice I began to doze but was roused again by violent
cramps and twitchings in all my limbs. There is nothing more horri-

ble than a night passed in the way I passed that one, faint and weak, enduring torture from hunger and thirst, striving after sleep, and never finding it. I can only compare the sensation of hunger I experienced to that of twenty pairs of pinchers tearing at my stomach.

With the first gray light of morning I got up and prepared for departure. It was a long business, however, to get my horse ready. The saddle, which at other times I could throw upon his back with two fingers, now seemed made of lead, and it was as much as I could do to lift it. I had still more difficulty to draw the girths tight, but at last I accomplished this and scrambling upon my beast rode off. Luckily my mustang's spirit was prettily well taken out of him by the two last days' work, for if he had been fresh the smallest spring on one side would have sufficed to throw me out of the saddle. As it was, I sat upon him like an automaton, hanging forward over his neck, sometimes grasping the mane, and almost unable to use either rein or spur.

I had ridden on for some hours in this helpless manner, when I came to a place where the three horsemen whose track I was following had apparently made a halt, perhaps passed the previous night. The grass was trampled and beaten down in a circumference of some fifty or sixty feet, and there was a confusion in the horse tracks as if they had ridden backward and forward. Fearful of losing the right trace, I was looking carefully about me to see in what direction they had recommenced their journey, when I noticed something white among the long grass. I got off my horse to pick it up. It was a piece of paper with my own name written upon it; and I recognized it as the back of a letter in which my tobacco had been wrapped and which I had thrown away at my halting place of the preceding night. I looked around, and recognized the island and the very tree under which I had slept, or endeavored to sleep. The horrible truth instantly flashed across me—the horse tracks I had been following were my own; since the preceding morning I had been riding in a *circle!*

I stood for a few moments thunderstruck by this discovery and then sank upon the ground in utter despair. At that moment I should have been thankful to any one who would have knocked me on the head as I lay. All I wished for was to die as speedily as possible.

I remained I know not how long lying in a desponding, half insensible state upon the grass. Several hours must have elapsed, for when I got up the sun was low in the western heavens. My head was so weak and wandering that I could not well explain to myself how it was that I had been thus riding after my own shadow. Yet the thing was clear enough. Without landmarks and in the monotonous scenery of the prairie, I might have gone on forever following my horse's track and going back when I thought I was going forward had it not been for the discovery of the tobacco paper. I was, as I subsequently learned, in the Jacinto prairie, one of the most beautiful in Texas, full sixty miles long and broad, but in which the most experienced hunters never risked themselves without a compass. It was little wonder, then, that I, a mere boy of two-and-twenty, just escaped from college, should have gone astray in it.

I now gave myself up for lost, and with the bridle twisted round my hand and holding on as well as I could by the saddle and mane, I let my horse choose his own road. It would perhaps have been better if I had done this sooner. The beast's instinct would probably have led him to some plantation. When he found himself left to his own guidance he threw up his head, snuffed the air three or four times, and then turning round, set off in a contrary direction to that he was before going, and at such a brisk pace that it was as much as I could do to keep upon him. Every jolt caused me so much pain that I was more than once tempted to let myself fall off his back.

At last night came, and thanks to the lasso which kept my horse in awe I managed to dismount and secure him. The whole night through I suffered from racking pains in my head, limbs, and body. I felt as if I had been broken on the wheel, not an inch of my whole person but ached and smarted. My hands were grown thin and transparent, my cheeks fallen in, my eyes deep sunk in their sockets. When I touched my face I could feel the change that had taken place, and as I did so I caught myself once or twice laughing like a child—I was becoming delirious.

In the morning I could scarcely rise from the ground, so utterly weakened and exhausted was I by my three days fasting, anxiety, and fatigue. I have heard say that a man in good health can live nine days without food. It may be so in a room or a prison, but assuredly not in a Texan prairie; I am quite certain that the fifth day would have seen the last of me.

I should never have been able to mount my mustang, but he had fortunately lain down, so I got into the saddle, and he rose up with me and started off of his own accord. As I rode along, the strangest visions seemed to pass before me. I saw the most beautiful cities that a painter's fancy ever conceived, with towers, cupolas, and columns, of which the summits lost themselves in the clouds; marble basins and fountains of bright sparkling water, rivers flowing with liquid gold and silver, and gardens in which the trees were bowed down with the most magnificent fruit, fruit that I had not strength enough to raise my hand and pluck. My limbs were heavy as lead, my tongue, lips, and gums, dry and parched. I breathed with the greatest difficulty and within me was a burning sensation, as if I had swallowed hot coals; my extremities, both hands and feet, did not appear to form a part of myself, but to be instruments of torture affixed to me, and causing me the most intense suffering.

I have confused recollection of a sort of rushing noise, the nature of which I was unable to determine, so nearly had all consciousness left me, then of finding myself among trees, the leaves and boughs of which scratched and beat against my face as I passed through them; then of a sudden and rapid descent with a broad bright surface of a river below me. I clutched at a branch, but my fingers had no strength to retain their grasp; there was a hissing, splashing noise, and the waters closed over my head.

I soon rose, and endeavored to strike out with my arms and legs, but in vain. I was too weak to swim, and again I went down. A thousand lights seemed to dance before my eyes: there was a noise in my brain as if a four-and-twenty pounder had been fired close to my ear. Just then a hard hand was wrung into my neckcloth, and I felt myself dragged out of the water. The next instant my senses left me.[4]

When I recovered from my state of insensibility and once more opened my eyes, I was lying on the bank of a small but deep river. My horse was grazing quietly a few hundred yards off and beside me stood a man with folded arms holding a wicker-covered flask in his hand. . . . I knew he was my deliverer, that he had saved my life; when my mustang, raging with thirst, had sprung head-foremost into the water . . . I must inevitably have been drowned, even had the river been less deep than it was; and that it was by his care and the whiskey he had made me swallow, and of which I still felt the flavor on my tongue that I had been recovered from the death-like swoon into which I had fallen. . . .

"Lost my way—four days—eaten nothing."

These words were all I could articulate. I was too weak to talk.

"Four days without eatin," cried the man, with a laugh like the sharpening of a saw, "and that in a Texas prairie, and with islands on all sides of you! Ha! I see how it is. You're a gentleman—that's plain enough. . . . You thought our Texas prairies was like the prairies in the States. Ha, ha! And so you didn't know how to help yourself. Did you see no bees in the air, no strawberries on the earth?"

"Bees? Strawberries?" repeated I.

"Yes, bees, which live in the hollow trees. Out of twenty trees there's sure to be one full of honey. So you saw no bees, eh? Perhaps you don't know the creturs when you see em. Ain't altogether so big as wild geese or turkeys. But you must know what strawberries are and that *they* don't grow upon trees."

. . . he disappeared among the trees . . . and presently emerged again, leading a ready saddled horse with him. He called to me to mount mine, but seeing that I was unable even to rise from the ground, he stepped up to me and with the greatest ease lifted me into the saddle with one hand, so light had I become during my long fast. Then taking the end of my lasso, he got upon his own horse and set off, leading my mustang after him.

NOTES TO SECTION I

1. Although cattle drives from Texas to northern states are much better known, cattle were driven from Texas to New Orleans long before the northern trails were established. James Taylor White of old Anahuac, Chambers County, made the first recorded drive to New Orleans during the days of the Texas Republic, over the trail that became known as the Opelousas Route—from Southeast Texas across the Trinity River at Liberty and the Calcasieu River above Lake Charles, Louisiana, up to Opelousas, and on to the Atchafalaya, where the cattle were put on steamers to be shipped to New Orleans. This route was used until the fall of New Orleans during the Civil War. Another trail ran from Central Texas to Shreveport, with branches to Natchitoches and Alexandria. See T. U. Taylor, *The Chisholm Trail and Other Routes* (San Antonio, 1936); Garnet M. and Herbert O. Brayer, *American Cattle Trails, 1540-1900* (Bayside, N.Y., 1952); and Wayne Gard, *The Chisholm Trail* (Norman, Okla., 1954).

2. A bridoon is the snaffle and rein of a military, or double, bridle (one having both snaffle and curb bits), which may be used independently.

3. Bengal fire, also called Bengal light, is a type of fireworks with a brilliant blue light, often used as a signal.

4. Part I, as it appeared in *Spirit*, ends here. The opening section of the second instalment is given to show how the narrator was rescued. The remainder of Part II presents the narrator's observations of a murderer who eventually confesses; it contains far less local color.

II
Varmints and Mustangs

II. Varmints and Mustangs

JUST AS *the land of Texas itself was both familiar and different to the early settlers and travelers, so were the wild animals found there. Animals of the eastern woodlands—bear, deer, turkey, wolves— existed in overwhelming numbers. But the traveler who perhaps had read about western animals or who had seen maps with "Wild Horses" scrawled across great empty spaces was hardly prepared for this first sight of vast herds of mustangs racing across the plains. Nor could words convey the fierce majesty of thousands of buffalo stampeding, sweeping all in front of them. Less spectacular but still intriguing were the wild cattle (descendants of Spanish cattle gone wild and later called Longhorns) that inhabited hundreds of miles of the thickets and inland prairies of the coastal region.*

Many early accounts try hard to capture the scope and magnificence of the herds of large animals, but the writers seem to feel more at home with the unusual denizens of prairie, desert, and plain—the horned toad, tarantula, centipede, and roadrunner (paisano *or chaparral cock*). *From the beginning, tales clustered about these unique creatures—tales that are a mixture of strange truth, fantasy, and folklore. And over the years these little animals, which readily adapted themselves to the presence of man, have continued to dominate his imagination and so remain to this day elements of the Texas myth.*

Animals and Things in Texas

ANONYMOUS

THIS TEXAS OF OURS is an astonishingly prolific country. Every field stands luxuriant, crowded so that it can scarce wave under the breeze, with corn, or sugar, or cotton. Every cabin is full and overflowing, through all its doors and windows, with white haired children. Every prairie abounds in deer, prairie hens, and cattle. Every river and creek is alive with fish. The whole land is electric with lizards, perpetually darting about among the grass like flashes of green lightning. We have too much prairie and too little forest for a great multitude or variety of birds.

But in horned frogs, scorpions, tarantulas, and centipedes, we beat the universe. Everybody has seen horned frogs. You see them in jars in the windows of apothecaries. You are entreated to purchase them by loafing boys on the levee at New Orleans. They have been neatly soldered up in soda boxes and mailed by young gentlemen in Texas to fair ones in the old States. The fair ones receive the neat package from the postoffice, are delighted with the prospect of a daguerreotype—perhaps jewelry—open the package eagerly, and faint as the frog in excellent health hops out, upon them. A horned frog is, simply, a very harmless frog with very portentous horns; it has horns because everything in its region—trees, shrubs, grass even has horns—and nature makes it in keeping with all around it. A menagerie would not be expensive. They are content to live upon air and can live, I am told, for several months without even that.

From *Spirit*, XXIII, 15 (May 28, 1853), 172. Reprinted from *Arthur's Home Gazette.*

The scorpions are precisely like those of Arabia, in the shape of a lobster exactly, only not more than some three inches long. You are very apt to put one upon your face in the towel which you apply thereto after washing. If you do, you will find the sting about equal to that of a wasp—nothing worse. They are far less poisonous than the scorpion of the East. In fact none, except newcomers, dread them at all.

But the tarantula! You remember the astonishing elasticity with which you sprang into the air, when you were on the point of putting your raised foot down upon a snake coiled in your path. You were frightened through every fiber of your body. Very probably the snake was as harmless as it was beautiful. Spring as high, be as utterly frightened as possible, when you just avoid stepping upon a tarantula, however. Filthy, loathsome, abominable and poisonous—crush it to atoms before you leave it. If you have never seen it, know henceforth that it is an enormous spider, concentrating in itself all the venom and spite and ugliness of all spiders living. Its body is some two inches long—black and bloated. It enjoys the possession of eight long, strong legs, a red mouth, and an abundance of stiff brown hair all over itself. When standing it covers an area of a saucer. Attack it with a stick and it rears on its hind legs, gnashes at the stick, and fights like a fiend. It even jumps forward a foot or two in its rage, and if it bites into a vein, the bite is death! I have been told of the battle fought by one on board a steamboat. Discovered at the lower end of the boat, it came hopping up the saloon, driving the whole body of passengers before it. It almost drove the whole company, crew and all, overboard.

The first one I saw was at the house of a friend. I spied it crawling slowly over the wall, meditating murder upon the children playing in the room. Excessively prudent in regard to my fingers, I at last, however, had it safely imprisoned in a glass jar, unhurt. There was a flaw in the glass as well as a hole through the cork by which it could breathe, but in ten minutes it was dead from rage! Soon after, I killed three upon my place crawling about, ground trodden every day by the bare feet of my little boy. Had he seen one of them, he would of course have picked it up as a remarkably promising toy, and I would have been childless.

I was sitting one day upon a log in the woods when I saw one slowly crawling out to enjoy the evening air and sunset scenery. He was the largest, most bloated one I ever saw. As I was about to kill him, I was struck with the conduct of a chance wasp. It too had seen the tarantula, and was flying slowly about it. The tarantula recognized it as a foe and throwing itself upon its hind legs breathed defiance. For some time the wasp flew around it, and then like a flash flew right against it and stung it under its bloated belly. The tarantula gnashed its red and venomed jaws, and threw its long hairy legs about in impotent rage, while the wasp flew round and round it, watching for another opportunity. Again and again did it dash its sting into the reptile and escape. After the sixth stab, the tarantula actually fell over on its back dead. The wasp, after making itself sure of the fact and inflicting a last sting to make matters sure, flew off happy in having done a duty assigned in its creation.[2] In an hour or more, a colony of ants had carried the tarantula down piecemeal and deposited it in their catacombs.

But the deadliest and most abhorrent of all our reptiles in Texas, is the centipede. This is a kind of worm from three to six inches long, exactly like a caterpillar. It is green, or brown, or yellow, some being found of each of those colors. As its name denotes, it has along each side a row of feet or horny claws rather. Imagine that you walk some night across your chamber floor with naked feet; you put your foot down upon a soft something, and instantly it coils around your foot in a ring, sticking every claw up to the body in your foot. The poison flows through each claw, and in two minutes you will have fainted with agony; in a few more you will be dead. The deadly thing cannot be torn away. It has to be cut off, and claw by claw picked out. Even if it crawls over the naked body of a sleeping person without sticking in his claws, the place will pain the person for years after—at least so I have been told.

I have often seen these things in which nature corks her deadly poison; yet I have heard of few cases in which they have killed or bitten anyone. The kind Being who makes the butterflies to be abundant, in the same loving kindness which makes them so beautiful and abundant, makes all the deadly creatures to be scarce.

A Pleasant Country for a Nervous Man

ANONYMOUS

A TEXAS CORRESPONDENT of an Eastern paper describes the domestic products of that favored land in glowing terms. If the half of his account be true, it must be a pleasant place for a nervous man:

The cattle are not the sole occupants of the prairie by any means. Droves of wild horses are not unfrequent, and deer are in countless numbers. The small brown wolf or cayeute [coyote] is quite common, and you occasionally get a glimpse of his large black brother. But Texas is the paradise of reptiles and creeping things. Rattle and moccasin snakes are too numerous to shake a stick at; the bite of the former is easily cured by drinking raw whiskey till it produces complete intoxication, but for the latter there is no cure. The tarantula is a pleasant institution to get into a quarrel with. He is a spider with a body about the size of a hen's egg and legs five or six inches long, covered with long coarse black hair. He lies in the cattle tracks, and if you see him, move out of his path, as his bite is absolutely certain death, and he never gets out of the way for anyone. Then there is the centipede, furnished with an unlimited number of legs, each leg armed with a claw and each claw inflicting a separate wound. If he walks over you at night, you will have cause to remember him for many months to come, as the wound is of a particularly poisonous nature and is very difficult to heal. The stinging lizard [scorpion] is a lesser evil, the sensation of its wound being likened to the application of a red hot iron to the person; but

From *Spirit*, XXX, 23 (July 21, 1855), 273.

one is too thankful to escape with life to consider these lesser evils any annoyance. But the insects! Flying, creeping, jumping, buzzing, stinging, they are everywhere. Ask for a cup of water, and the rejoinder in our camp is, "Will you have it with a bug or without?"

The horned frog is one of the greatest curiosities here and is perfectly harmless. It has none of the cold slimy qualities of his northern brother but is frequently made a pet of. Chamelions are innumerable, darting over the prairie in every direction with inconceivable swiftness and undergoing their peculiar changing of color, corresponding to the color of the object under which they may be. The woods on the banks of the bayous are perfectly alive with mocking birds singing most beautifully, and feathered game is abundant and very tame, as it is scarcely ever sought after. The only varieties that I have seen are the quail, partridge, snipe, mallard, plover, and prairie hen.

Texas Varmints

IN A SMALL GROVE of timber where I had halted to rest awhile, I saw for the first time a horned frog. I had heard of the tarantula and centipede of Texas, and supposing the harmless frog was one or the other I picked up a stick about ten feet long (not venturing to approach near such a poisonous reptile) and mashed him as flat as a pancake.

*　*　*

Today, for the first time, I saw what I know now was a tarantula, a very large and exceedingly venomous spider that haunts the dry and elevated prairies of Western Texas. They are not often seen in the timbered lands or in the immediate vicinity of settlements. The body of a full grown one is as large as a hen's egg and is covered with scattering hairs or bristles. They have two curved fangs protruding from the mouth, about as long and very similar in ap-

---

From John C. Duval, *Early Times in Texas* (Austin, 1892), pp. 89, 91, 100-101, 104-5, 113. John Crittenden Duval (1816-1897), born in Kentucky, left St. Joseph's College in Bardstown in 1835 to join a company organized by his brother, Captain B. H. Duval, to fight in the Texas Revolution. Later he studied engineering at the University of Virginia, and in 1840 he returned to Texas as a land surveyor. He was a member of John C. (Jack) Hays's company of Texas Rangers, serving with his close friend Bigfoot Wallace, and during the Civil War fought as a private in the Confederate Army. Many years later he died in Fort Worth. He was the author of *The Young Explorers* and *The Adventures of Bigfoot Wallace, The Texas Ranger and Hunter*.

pearance to those of the rattlesnake. When provoked they are very pugnacious, rising upon their hindlegs and springing towards the assailant five or six inches at a time in successive leaps. The Mexicans say their bite is certain death, and one can readily credit the assertion after seeing them.

* * *

Whilst passing through some tall grass, I came very near treading on a rattlesnake, the first I had seen in Texas, although some portions of the country I had passed over was much infested with them, but the season then was hardly far enough advanced to bring them out of the dens or holes in which they take up their winter quarters. Often since, when passing over some of the uninhabited plains between the Nueces and Rio Grande rivers, I have found them so numerous in particular localities that I was scarcely ever out of hearing of the sound of their rattles. They are not, however, nearly so vicious in Texas as they are in some other countries and seldom attempt to strike, unless attacked. I have slept with them, ridden and walked over them frequently, and instead of trying to bite me they always did their best to get out of the way—except on one occasion. I was stalking some deer one day on the prairie when I stepped upon a rattlesnake lying coiled up in the grass. I knew even before I saw it by the peculiar soft *squirmy* feel under my foot that I had put it on a snake, and I promptly "lit out" without waiting for orders. As I did not wish to shoot him for fear of alarming the deer, I drew the ramrod from my rifle and gave his head a smart blow with it. I then mashed his head by repeated blows with the breech of my gun, and thinking of course I had killed him I went on after the deer. Two days subsequently when passing the place again that same snake came very near biting me. I knew it was the same, for one of his eyes was out and his whole head bruised and bloody from the blows I had given it with the breech of my rifle. I really believe he recognized me as the author of all his ills, for when I attempted to go near him he would raise his head a foot or more from the ground and with his rattles going incessantly would glare at me with his one eye in the most vindictive way. I determined to make sure of him this time, and leveling my rifle at his head I took good aim and fired. The bullet knocked his head into fragments, and one of the pieces struck me on the forehead, making a slight wound. The idea immediately occurred to me that I had been struck by one of his fangs and that I was fated to be killed by this particular snake. However, after bathing the scratch in a pool of water and finding that my head had not swelled up as big as a bushel, I went on my way congratulating myself upon my second escape from my vindictive foe.

*   *   *

Whilst lying awake the next morning upon my bed of dry leaves, my attention was drawn to a rustling among them, and turning them over I found an ugly reptile about six inches long, which I thought then and know now was a centipede. Not fancying such a bedfellow, I quickly dispatched him with a stick. They resemble somewhat the reptile called the "thousand-leg worm," but they are much larger and flatter, and although they are well provided with legs, they have not quite a *thousand*. They are of a dark brown color on the back and the under side a dirty white. Their tail is forked and has a long sting in the end of each prong besides smaller stings on each foot, and to complete their means of inflicting wounds, the mouth is furnished with fangs. They are a disgusting looking varmint and are said to be very venomous. An old Texan speaking about them said: "When they wound you with their feet alone, it hurts considerable; when they sting you with their forked tail it's a great deal worse, but when they pop you with all their stings, and *bite* you too—say your prayers."

*   *   *

Today I came across a specimen of the jointed snake, the first I had ever seen. It was a small snake, not more than fifteen or twenty inches in length, and its skin had a vitrified or glassy appearance. It seemed to be rather sluggish and unwieldly, and when I struck it a slight tap with a small stick, to my great astonishment it broke into half a dozen pieces, each piece hopping off in a very lively way on its own hook. I have since heard it asserted that after a time the broken parts of the snake will come together and reunite and then crawl off as if nothing had happened to it; but I shall always be doubtful of the story until satisfactory vouchers of its truth, duly authenticated and sworn to, are produced.

Snakebite Remedies

BIGFOOT WALLACE

IN GOING through a thick chaparral today, my pony was bitten on the leg by a rattlesnake. An old hunter told me to chew up some tobacco and tie it on the wound, which I did and, except for a slight swelling, no bad results followed from the bite. (I have seen tobacco used frequently since as a remedy for the bite of a rattlesnake, and there is no doubt it is a good one but not equal to whiskey or brandy taken in large quantities.)

* * *

Just after we had encamped, one of our men named Thompson while staking out his horse was bitten on the hand by a rattlesnake. It was a small one, however, and he suffered but little from the effects of the bite. We scarified the wound with a penknife and applied some soda to it, and the next morning he was well enough to travel. I do not think the bite of the rattlesnake is as often fatal as people generally suppose. I have seen several men and a great many animals bitten by them and have never known death to ensue,

From John C. Duval, *The Adventures of Bigfoot Wallace* (Philadelphia, 1871), pp. 22-23, 27-28. W. A. A. (Bigfoot) Wallace (1817-1899) was born in Lexington, Virginia, and came to Texas in 1836. A volunteer in the Somervill and Mier expeditions, he fought with Jack Hays and the Texas Rangers in the Mexican War and in the 1850's was captain of his own Ranger company, fighting border bandits and Indians. Having lived in LaGrange, Austin, and San Antonio, he spent his last days in Frio County. He was buried in the State Cemetery in Austin.

except on one or two occasions. Still, I have no doubt there is great danger whenever the fangs of the snake strike a large vein or artery. I believe the bite of the tarantula is much more fatal. I have seen two or three persons bitten by them in Mexico, neither of whom recovered, although many remedies were used. The Mexicans say they will kill a horse in ten minutes.

Hunting Jack Rabbits

"BEAGLE"

JUST THINK OF IT, out here, a regular old-fashioned hare chase; none of your half-hour runs, but a regular three or four hours' chase that would try the bottom of the best English stud and kennels.

Ours are hares that will do to count. One taken on the occasion mentioned measured fifteeen and one-half inches in height, thirty-one inches from hind to fore feet on the stretch, seventeen and one-half inches from tail to nose, with an auditory apparatus that would do honor to any of the small donkey race, say six and one-half inches long, and two and one-half wide. What do you think of it? A regular Texas-grown hare and plenty of them, too, with speed that calls forth all the energies of the fleetest courser to overtake one in a mile. Some call them mule rabbits, some mustang rabbits, and others, more properly, I think, Jack rabbits. Scientifically speaking, they are of the *genus Lepus*; for their species, you must call on Buffon or Cuvier; perhaps "Frank Forester"[3] could inform you.

My friend Col. W., a pure gentleman of the old "South State" school, having some fine hounds that would make no bad show in any country, was heard to say that he would run Leader and Whistler (black and tans of pure blood, that would do your soul good) against any pure hound in Texas. Now, who but W. and J. E. of the Mission Valley would have thought of taking it as a challenge? Now don't think us such heathens that we have to have

From *Spirit*, XXVI, 47 (January 3, 1857), 553-54. The author is unidentified.

missionaries among us to teach us the ways of Christendom (a little teaching might not be amiss). . . .

Well, in due season, W. and J. E. called upon the Colonel with their hounds all trained and drawn for the race. And as fate or something else would have it, as usual when there is sport brewing, on the very evening before the trial was to come off, Choctaw John (my horse) and I dropped in at the Colonel's, and after the ceremony of greeting our friends and putting John into the pasture (tied to one end of a long rope, the other fastened to a tree,) I was introduced to Ace Pierce (honorable name, that,) and Spot, the choice of the Mission pack, leaving Rattler out, he being a sure slow track, to be pitted against Leader and Whistler. The morning came, a lovely one, too. At dawn all were mounted and ready for the signal from the horn to start; Jim on Old Rough (pure Canadian), William upon Alec (of Spanish origin, no mean pony, however,) Tom P. upon Old Yew, wirey as the devil, the Colonel upon Sure-find, a small brown Spanish horse, and your humble servant upon Choctaw John, never far in the rear at the end of a chase. Thus mounted and equipped, we took right off to Bill Wright's to give his trained hare a run, but not finding him at home, we gave his hare but little trouble, simply warming his blood for a half mile or so, and then left for other quarters down the Tonquaway, where, after some beating about and chasing a few brace of deer, we started a hare not more than thirty or forty feet from the foremost hounds, when, as if all the hounds in Christendom had been let loose, the whole country rung with the cry of hot pursuit— far sweeter music than all the orchestras of the world. Away went horsemen over field and wood at breakneck speed; for miles around could be heard the deep cry of hounds and the stentorian voices of hunters. About a mile and the hare is turned, tacks, and runs for life, leaving the fastest dogs far in the rear; soon a mott (small bunch of thick chapparel) is gained, and here the dogs are put to it for a moment. Soon all are off again, man and horse at top speed, up hill and down steep; there Leader turns him a second time; now

all are in sight and off at redoubled speed, the hounds straining
every muscle to lead their neighbors in the chase. Now, up a long
hill horseflesh is put to task; the best bottom sees the sport; Rough
and Choctaw John leading the way, Mack and Old Yew close in
with Kelley (Cook, rider,) and Sure-find at their heels. Now all turn
the crest of the hill, the hare is in full view, the whole pack thundering down within a few feet of him—Leader and Ace neck and
neck, Spot and Whistler close behind. Ye gods! what a cry from both
men and dogs. As they approach a little chapparel mott at the base
of the hill, the hare is turned a third time, Leader and Ace both in
at the turning, when Juno, the slowest of the pack, took off the hare.
Here ended the first day's sport, after a dead run of about four
miles. This hare did not give a fair trial of their powers of endurance, as it was a female, and *enceinte*, too.

We then repaired to the residence of our good friend the Colonel,
where we found a table well spread with viands, rich, and well-
fitted to the palates of hungry sportsmen, at the head of which sat
the Colonel's good lady, seasoning the repast with her smiles and
an occasional *jeu d'esprit* at the expense of the party. After supper
the Havanas went round, and each in his own peculiar style told
of the events of the day and expanded on the prospects of the morrow. The contest for speed of dogs not yet being decided, the
Colonel contended that his dogs were far ahead of the others. Bill
E. thought that Ace would come in on a long run. Bets were about
equal on either side. At a late hour all turned in preparatory of the
morrow's chase which bid fair to decide which were the better dogs.

Morning came and with it a smoking breakfast, prepared under
the direction of the good lady with an eye especial to the day's
sport. She, though not an eye-witness of the sport, felt a deep interest in the speed of the Colonel's favorite, as any good wife would.
At the sound of the horn all the canines were up, men, horses, and
dogs, eager for the chase. A short ride brought us to a small prairie
on Mustang Branch, surrounded by live oak openings—a lovely spot
for a chase. After beating for the game a short time, a fine one was

started. Off it went like a blue streak, and off went all the dogs, getting a good start, making the welkin ring through all the woods. Off go the horsemen, the object now being to keep in sight of the dogs, no very easy task on "common stock." Two of us managed to look on the chase through the first stretch, Old Rough leading and Choctaw John next. On, on went hare, hounds, and horses, for four miles, with Leader far in advance, Ace and Spot taking the second place behind him, and the others coming up as they could. The hare being somewhat warm with this little race, made a quick lateral dodge, where some deer squatted in the grass until the dogs came up. Here for a moment they were at fault but soon started the hare again right back down along a hollow. Oh! such running, and the woods now resound with the cry of deep-mouthed hounds and the almost savage whoops of the hunters. In the return chase it was impossible to keep in view of the hounds, but the Colonel and Cook taking a stand in the course were in at the turning, and report Leader at fifty yards ahead when the hare doubled and made back. After a pause for the balance to come up, the hare was again started. Thus to the third and fourth turnings Leader kept clear ahead, Whistler taking the hare some little distance from the fourth turn, the balance coming in just in time to save their distance. According to old English rules, Leader won the day, after a brisk run with little intermission of about three and a half hours; convincing all that Tonquaway can boast horses not surpassed, and hares not equalled, in the world. If any doubt this, just let us know, and we will give them a chance.

Rabbit Chase in Texas

ANONYMOUS

TO FEEL, enjoy, and appreciate a rabbit race in Texas, it must be seen. A man who has never seen a mule-eared rabbit race knows nothing about the glories of the chase. The mule-eared or mountain rabbit will weigh from six to nine pounds and the ears will measure from fourteen to sixteen inches from tip to tip. We run them on the prairie on horseback and with greyhounds. They run all the time in a road or cow path, if possible, and scorn the protection of fences, bushes, or timber. They run four and a half or five miles and over a dry road; a full grown old buck which is in good running order will make Lecomte's time the first mile and Lexington's the next.[4] Compared with *his* running a fox chase is a mere "butter-and-eggs" lick, and over the broad, undulating prairie, on a good horse, by taking advantage of the turns and forks in the cow paths, every jump he makes can be seen. . . .

Five or six of us in the party, well mounted, and four or five of the fastest dogs perhaps—Lucy, Snip, Vic, Jake, and Fanny. About three miles from the city [Austin] we reach the big prairie—high, dry, dotted over with little farms and stretching from the foot of

From *Spirit*, XXV, 5 (March 17, 1855), 54. A postscript to this sketch reads: "Some of 'the boys' have this moment returned from a wolf chase. They started two, neither of which ran less than twenty miles! A lady joined the party—the same who a year or two ago actually ran a wolf twelve miles *by herself* and dragged him home with her bridle rein. Fact!" This is one of the rare references to women in the otherwise masculine world of hunting as seen in newspaper sketches.

the mountains far away into the country. As we come into the prairie the sun is just rising, the morning is lovely as the blush of modesty, and the air is balmy as a maiden's breath. The riders separate and move at intervals of forty or fifty yards. The horses raise their heads, quicken their pace, and seem to know what's coming. Two or three fox hounds that we take along to jump em push out a little ahead, while the greyhounds follow behind them and keep a sharp look out, ever and anon bounding into the air, as a lark is flushed, until—hark! a clear shout from one of the boys, "There he goes!" The rabbit is up and all eyes are upon him. The dogs are near him in a moment. At first he bounds about in every direction, ears erect, and so badly frightened as hardly to know which way to run. In an instant, however, they crowd him, and he strikes a path, lays his ears back, looks about half as large as he did at first, and he who wants to see the sport mustn't stay long at one place. The rabbit takes the lead, the dogs close behind him, and the horsemen bring up the rear. We wish we could put down in writing the loud ringing chorus that goes up from the boys as we run the first mile of that race, but it's no use. For half a mile they push him hard, and a "green one" would think they had him. Now they press him to the very heels. Watch him! Lord, what running! A wild pigeon couldn't begin to keep up, as gradually he widens the gap till the dogs lose sight of him, and we wait for the fox-hounds which take the track and put him up again in a mile or a mile and a half from where last seen. He has been "squatted" for a few moments and moves stiffly but makes another gallant effort of two or perhaps three miles, and even then no short stock can see his death.

Such is a faint description of the finest chasing sport we ever saw or heard of! The excitement is wild and glorious, and the pleasure sometimes becomes almost maddening. We challenge the world for a dog (or anything else that hasn't got wings) that can overtake one of these rabbits on the first heat of a mile and a half, and we'll pledge him a beautiful track and no obstructions.

Game on the Lower Rio Grande

"J."

THROUGHOUT this vast region the beautiful prairies are interspersed with patches of chapparel of unequal extent and irregular shapes which often give to the scene a curious and picturesque appearance. This chapparel consists of thickets of naked thorns of several species, so thick, tangled, and impenetrable, as to laugh the best cultivated hedgerows to scorn. The bushes are leafless, the arms and thorns as white as if painted, and they glitter in the sun. Attached to the stems and scattered beneath to the depth of several inches, are myriads of shining white snail shells which render the ground almost as white as if it were shrouded with snow. Interspersed among these chapparels are various trees of other kinds, such as the musquito-ebony, wild-briar, cabbage-wood, and numerous others, valuable for fire wood, fencing, and other mechanical and domestic purposes. When these thickets are cleared away, the ground is exceedingly fertile and easily tilled—cotton, sugar, corn, and so forth all flourish there with the highest degree of perfection.

In these chapparels are found countless numbers of rabbits of the ordinary gray species as well as a large gray rabbit, much resembling the English hare in shape but far larger with enormous ears; the true zoological name I do not know, but they are vulgarly called the "jack-ass rabbit." They are fine eating, and I have shot

---

Printed as "Sporting Scenes in Texas," *Spirit*, XXII (November 13, 1852), 463, one of several pieces so entitled. "J." may have been an army officer.

them weighing fifty pound. Vast flocks of wild turkeys, some of them very large and all of them fat, inhabit these forbidden haunts. Quails, pigeons, paisanos, and it must be added, no small quantity of rattlesnakes and tarantulas find here a safe and inviting abode. In all parts of this region, deer in fine condition abound, also the peccary, or Mexican hog, one of the most game-blooded animals that exists. They will fight anything, man or beast, and some amusing stories are told of their driving hunters up a tree and there besieging them for hours. We have also a peculiar bird denominated the "chachalacha"[5] about half the size of an ordinary game cock, which is well worth describing. It is shaped much like a wild pigeon, of an ash color, black legs, black shining beak, strong and sharp—and with eyes of great brilliancy. In its native state it is wild and shy, but when caught is easily domesticated and becomes especially fond of those who feed and camp it. At daylight in the morning, whether wild or tame, they commence a furious reveille, repeating in a loud, dismal tone, a chaunt, from the sound of which they derive their name. This is prolonged for about half an hour—the woods all around you appear to be alive with these invisible songsters, when suddenly they stop and not another sound breaks from them during the whole day. The chachalacha will crossbreed with the common game fowl and produce not only a beautiful bird, but one of the greatest value of its *game qualities*. Their crosses are a little under size, but in spirit, endurance, activity, and vigor, they are unmatched. *They are the best fighting cocks on earth.* This is no fancy sketch; they have been tried frequently and never were known to skulk or yield; like the Old Guard, they can "die, but never surrender."

They are difficult to catch and have generally to be raised from the egg. I have known, even then, twenty dollars to be paid for a pair, so highly are they esteemed. I have often been surprised that breeders of game fowls have not turned their attention to these birds to renew and improve their stock. Perhaps they were not aware of their high and valuable qualities. Let them try this gallant little hero, and they will find a full confirmation of all I have urged in his behalf.

We have, likewise, another peculiar bird, called the "paisano" which is deemed of great value by the Mexicans and Indians on account of its hostility to the serpent tribe. It is larger and taller than the chachalacha, delicately and beautifully formed, black and white speckled in color and can run as fast as a fleet dog. Whenever one of them discovers a rattlesnake or any other serpent, no matter how large, it commences a fierce cry, which summons to its aid all the paisanos within hearing. They begin to run and fly about the snake in a circle, crying and chattering all the time till their victim becomes confused, when, quick as the lightning's flash, one of them and immediately others make a dash at the eyes of the snake, and with their sharp, unerring beaks, he is blinded in a moment. He then falls an easy prey to their united prowess. These battles are of frequent occurrence and are described by spectators as interesting in the extreme.

Wild Cattle of Texas

ANONYMOUS

THE SETTLERS who have recently opened farms near the source of the San Gabriel and Brushy find the country well stocked with a singular breed of wild cattle. Large droves of these cattle are found not only on the San Gabriel, Leona, and other tributaries of Little River, but also on the San Saba, the Llano, and many other tributaries of the upper Colorado, far above the settlements. They differ in form, color, and habits from all the varieties of domestic cattle in Texas. They are invariably of a dark-brown color, with a slight tinge of dusky yellow on the tip of the nose and on the belly. Their horns are remarkably large and stand out straight from the head. Although these cattle are generally much larger than the domestic cattle, they are more fleet and nimble and when pursued often outstrip horses that easily outrun the buffalo. Unlike the buffalo, they seldom venture far out into the prairies, but are generally found in or near the forests that skirt the streams in that section. Their meat is of an excellent flavor and is preferred by the settlers to the meat of the domestic cattle. It is said that their fat is so hard and compact that it will not melt in the hottest days of summer, and candles formed with it are far superior to those that are formed with the tallow of other cattle.

Some persons have supposed that it is possible that these cattle are a distinct race indigenous to America, and the immense skeletons of a species of fossil ox with straight horns that are often found

From *Littell's Living Age*, VIII (January-March, 1846), 178. Reprinted from the *Houston Telegraph*.

in the beds of the Brazos and Colorado would seem to strengthen this opinion. But as these cattle are now found only in the vicinity of the old missions, it is much more probable that they are the descendants of the cattle introduced by the early Spanish adventurers. . . . Several attempts have been made by the settlers on the San Gabriel to domesticate the wild cattle in that section, but they have thus far been unsuccessful. As they are far superior to the domestic cattle of the country, not only in size, strength, and agility but also in the flavor of their meat and the density of their fat, they might, if once domesticated, become a valuable acquisition to the agriculturists of this country.

The Horse Avalanche

"JOHN OF OXFORD"

IT WAS on the march to Victoria (I think the Col. stated) and before the orders came to reinforce Gen. Scott that the very remarkable and astonishing circumstance occurred, which I am about to relate and which I will endeavor to give as nearly as possible in his own words.

Our route lay immediately across an extensive prairie, along which our train of 600 wagons dragged its cumbrous length like some monster serpent gorged with prey, winding lazily to its lair. Save the deceptions of the mirage which full often cheated our weary troops into the hope of dimpling and refreshing waters soon to be reached and the consequent disappointment, nothing occurred for some time to vary the monotony of the march. At length, about midday or a little thereafter, a sound like muttering thunder, or rather like the low rumbling of an earthquake, drew all eyes toward the right from whence in the far distance was seen rapidly approaching a dark line, as if of clouds. Faster and faster and faster it came until to the astonishment and delight of all, with a rush that shook the very earth, 20,000 Mustangs sprang full in view.

> A mighty Piebald led the way,
> Fit leader to that mass of life!

From *Spirit*, XXVI, 27 (August 16, 1856), 313. Reprinted from the New Orleans *Picayune*. The unidentified author contributed sketches from Louisiana, Texas, and other southern states; he may have been a journalist.

Bounding forward in front of the now motionless multitude, the wild chief of the Pampas, his stately head high lifted, slowly approached our cavalcade with an air of mingled wonder and suspicion. After scanning it some time, as though calculating our strength, with a wild and angry snort he wheeled and darted back to his troop. A scene of momentary confusion now ensued; but in a far shorter time than would have been required to marshal one-fourth the number of men, the whole mass was thrown into the form of a wedge, the leader forming the *apex* and the other males of the troop the sides of the triangle, the feeble ones and colts being thrown into the center.

Before any one could form the most remote conjecture as to the cause of this singular movement, at a wild cry from their leader the column was put in motion, and then

> As the winds come, when forests are rended,
> As the waves rush, when navies are stranded,

full on the center of our devoted line they broke like an *avalanche*. For some moments from out the cloud of dust, came

> Mingled crash, and groan, and curse, and yell,
> As though within the realms of hell,
> All hands had broken loose.

When the dusty canopy was lifted, sixty wagons with teams and teamsters strewed the road, mingled in with everything—horse, foot, and dragoons—that came within the sweep of that living besom of destruction. Here and there a crushed and mangled mustang, struggling wildly to follow its fellows.

At the distance of some 130 or 200 yards, the drove stopped just in the order it had passed through with the exception that the mighty Piebald now brought up the rear. After gazing a few seconds in apparent exultation, a shrill neigh of defiance seemed to give the signal for retreat and the whole swept away like a vision. No dream, however. . . .

Except those who were with me, none I am sure saw ever such a sight, the like of which while life lasts I never expect to look upon again.

A Mustang Chase in Texas

"ESPERANCE"

A FRIEND and myself being in the western part of Texas some years ago, we found ourselves during the month of May in a section of country where the wild horse or mustangs were to be seen in great numbers. Having long wished for an opportunity of this kind, we sounded our friends and acquaintances in the neighborhood and found many were willing to join with us in giving them a chase. At the time appointed, we found our party to consist of two old veteran mustang hunters—who were to lead the way and show us the 'Elephant'⁶—five gentlemen who resided in the vicinity, and two greenhorns, viz. L. and myself. Our number was sufficiently large to protect ourselves from straggling parties of Indians, who might not be over scrupulous in observing the law of *meum* and *teum* in regard to our horses or scalps.

After a day's journey over a beautiful and interesting prairie country, we arrived about sundown and encamped on the northern boundary of the mustang range which was a bayou whose banks were shaded by the live oak and meskit [mesquite].

At the time I speak of, the prairies were in good order; there had been no rain for two weeks, the dead grass of the preceding year had been burnt up a month previous, and a fresh and green growth had sprung up about a foot high, making altogether one of the grandest and most extensive race grounds we could have wished for.

From *Spirit*, XIX, 34 (October 13, 1849), 403. "Esperance" may have been a newspaperman in Galveston; he contributed several sketches from that city.

After giving our horses sufficient rest and making some necessary preparations, on the third morning we prepared for the race.

At daylight we were all busy—each horse was brought up by his owner, well examined and rubbed down; of course great rivalry and much bantering existed amongst us, and from the many good horses present, there was little doubt but the contest would be one of interest. Many were the bets bandied about as to which would show the greatest speed and bottom and who the best riding and greatest success.

As I led my own well tried faithful Bolivar—whose slick coat, clean legs, and fiery eye well proclaimed his Archy blood—and as I smoothed down the silky hair of his well-formed compact body and recalled to mind what he *had* done and would do, I could not but exclaim with the old Saxon in *Ivanhoe,* to my boasting companions, "Lead I may not, but may posterity curse me if I follow not with the foremost." We were all soon mounted, each person having his lasso coiled up and tied to the pummel of his saddle. As we rode out of the skirt of wood where we had been encamped, a beautiful view presented itself to us. The sun was just rising, displaying like a vast carpet of green the noble prairie sprinkled with flowers of every hue and color—over whose bosom the eye might wander for miles, with not a tree, bush, or shrub to intercept the vision. The air was sweet and exhilarating; the smoke that arose from a few smouldering brands we had left ascended in a slow graceful column and hung in fanciful wreaths over the green tree tops around our camp. Every heart beat high with hope and excitement, each one well knew of the ridicule that would attach to him if the boasted speed of his horse should fail, or his skill in roping—and inwardly determined he would "do or die" that day.

In a few moments our camp was far behind, and we continued a direct course across the broad prairie before us. We proceeded on slowly for about an hour, occasionally starting up a herd of deer which on our approach would scamper away until lost to view in the distance. Very soon one of the party called a halt and directed our attention to some dark spots on the horizon; a spy glass was turned in that direction, and by its aid we distinctly saw a large body of horses quietly feeding unsuspicious of the approach of danger. Every man now dismounted, tightened the girth of his saddle, and prepared his rope for instant use. We then proceeded slowly on again in Indian file until the mustangs should discover us. As we gradually lessened the distance between us, we were astonished at their numbers. The prairie for a quarter of a mile in extent was covered with them of every color:

> But where are they the reins to guide,
> A thousand horse and none to ride.

Many mules which had escaped from travellers were here quietly feeding with the wild horse, no doubt rejoicing in their state of freedom. By approaching carefully we got within half a mile of the herd before they became aware of our presence. Suddenly one who appeared to be their leader, threw his head high in the air, snuffed the breeze, and with a shrill snort turned his gaze full upon us. In an instant every head was up, and with ears erect they looked wildly at us; a moment more and the leader, for such he was, wheeled to the right and dashed over the prairie followed by the whole herd:

> Away! away! and on they dash—
> Torrents less rapid, and less rash.

"Hurrah! Now's your time boys! Catch who can," shouted one of the old hunters as he darted by—his long grey hair streaming from his bare head behind and his rope swinging in open noose high in the air. "Huzza for the black leader," shouted L. and myself, and giving our horses the spur, we started like a whirlwind in pursuit. I have felt, and always do, a hunter's interest in the game afoot, but *now*, ye gods, how my blood leaped and boiled with excitement! Nought cared I or heeded, but the black leader who with great ease kept far in advance of the whole. We gained rapidly on the herd which jostling and running against each other, served to retard their flight. Now we were close to them, so close that I could easily have hurled my rope over the nearest head. Such, however, was not my intention, but spurring my horse I urged him on to greater speed. Still we gained, slowly indeed, but inch by inch we crept past them until at last we were thundering with the foremost. Now came the tug of war; the leader seeing himself so closely pursued exerted himself to his full strength which, when compared, his former speed was at a mere canter. On! on! we flew, the ground shaking and roaring behind beneath the tramp of feet; mile after mile did we keep the same headlong speed, and there was no perceptible decrease of the distance between us. A few moments more and we gained on him. With a shout of encouragement I urged my horse on; the generous animal at the sound of my voice strove his uttermost. The mustang at this time was scarce fifty feet from me. I now was sufficiently near to see him well: He was a large and well limbed black, his form perfect, and every movement served to show the strength and grace of the fine animal. His glossy hide spotted with flakes of foam sparkled in the sun; his tail, long and silky, would when standing have touched the ground, whilst his mane flew in jetty ringlets from his muscular neck. No time had I to make farther observations, for a cry from L., who was close behind me, directed my attention to a new object; a deep indentation of the prairie, scarce half a mile off, told us well that we were approaching the broadest and deepest part of a bayou that skirted the southern boundary of our hunting ground. For an instant as it burst into full view, the mustang checked his furious pace; that moment L. and myself, side by side, sprang forward within ten feet of him. I now prepared my rope with all haste, throwing down the rein. I swung my noose around my head several times and hurled it at him with all my force, but weak and exhausted my arm failed me, and the rope fell heavily on the wild horse's back. Nothing was wanting now to complete his terror, for gathering himself up as we gained the bank, he sprang nobly forward. For an instant his swarthy body, gleaming in the sun, was seen descending through the air; the next the water received him in its bosom. "Follow if you dare," shouted L., as he sprang fearlessly after. Mad with excitement, I hesitated not a moment and giving my horse the spur plunged over the bank also. Up! up! we came, and shaking the water from my head I looked for the wild horse; there he was scrambling up the opposite bank. On! on! through mud and water we gained the shore, but alas! the race was up; my horse taking but a few steps staggered and fell, bringing me to the ground. "Never mind," said L., who at this moment looked like a drowned rat,

> Although he's off and run away
> We will have him yet, another day.

We had done our best, but the wild horse won the race; he was still free. Long may you roam over the prairies, my noble black, and lead the same herd, worthy of such a leader; fleet indeed must be the horse and bold the rider that takes you fairly on your native plain.

The Bucking Mustangs

JOHN C. DUVAL

IN THE VICINITY of the place where we had halted, we noticed a
large corral in which several hundred head of mustangs were penned. We were all tired of trudging on foot and concluded we would
"press" into the service (a military term for appropriating property
belonging to others) a sufficient number of these mustangs to
mount the whole company. Accordingly we compelled the Mexicans to rope and equip with saddle and bridles about fifty of them.
We were all I suppose pretty good horsemen as the term is understood in the old States, but we knew that these mustangs were only
partially broken to the saddle. We anticipated having some fun
when we mounted them though nothing like as much as we really
got, for at the time we were totally ignorant of that peculiar trick
of mustangs called pitching by which they manage almost invariably to get rid of a green rider. When the mustangs with considerable
difficulty, after roping them closely to trees, had all been saddled
and bridled, at the word of command we mounted (except five or
six who failed to do so), and the next instant a scene of horses
kicking, rearing, and plunging ensued, of which only a confused
recollection remained upon my mind. In less time than it takes me
to tell of it, we were all put *hors de combat* (no pun intended).

As for the part I took individually in this equestrian performance,
I have only to say that I had hardly seated myself in the saddle,
when my unruly steed humped his back like a mad cat, reared up,
and then came down on his stiffened forelegs with such force that

From *Early Times in Texas*, pp. 32-34.

if "next week" had been lying on the ground ten or fifteen feet ahead of me, I would certainly have knocked out the middle. I was partially stunned by the fall but soon rose to my feet and was much relieved and consoled looking round to find that all the rest had been served in the same way, except one rider who managed to stick upon his horse in spite of all the animal's efforts to get rid of him. The Mexicans no doubt had purposely selected the wildest horses in the corral, and it is probable the most of them had never been backed half a dozen times even by the rancheros themselves who are unsurpassed by any people in horsemanship. I am confident that the padre and his flock enjoyed this equestrian performance much more than the actors, but as heretofore the laugh had been all on our side, we did not blame them for the pleasure they took in our discomfiture. However, we concluded to dispense with our unmanageable steeds, "unpressed" them by restoring them to their lawful owners, and resumed our march *on foot* for Goliad.

Riding a Mustang

JOHN C. DUVAL

I IMMEDIATELY HURRIED OFF to the only livery stable in the place [Houston] and asked the keeper if he could furnish me with a saddle-horse for an hour or two. He looked at me dubiously for a moment and then asked me if I could "stick a horse pretty well." Yes, said I, rather faintly, for I had not forgotten my former attempt at backing a mustang, "I believe I am a pretty fair rider." "All right," said he, "then I can accommodate you." Going into a shanty he called a livery stable, he soon returned dragging at the end of a rope a white-eyed vicious looking mustang with a decided Roman nose and with his shoulders and hips covered with Egyptian hieroglyphics. I didn't like the appearance of the brute at all, but I was determined to ride him at all hazards rather than admit I was "a-young-man-afraid-of-his-horses." I, therefore, walked up to him with the intention of mounting him, but on my near approach he plunged and cavorted at such a rate there was but little chance for anything less active than a monkey to get into the saddle. "Hold on a bit," said the man, "until I slip the blind over his eyes." "Blind," said I, "what is that?" "Why, you see, Cap.," said he (I was promoted to a Colonelcy in a short time) as he slipped a broad band attached to the bridle over the mustang's eyes, "you see, Cap., these Texas mustangs come from the ginerwine Arab stock, and among other good pints they has they won't let a stranger git on em tell

From *The Young Explorers, or, Continuation of the Adventures of Jack Dobell,* bound in one volume with *Early Times in Texas,* pp. 9-10.

75

they are blindfolded, which saves many a one on em from bein carried off betwixt two days."

The moment the blind was drawn over the mustang's eyes he stood as still as a statue; I stepped up, seized the bridle, and put my foot in the stirrup, but I suppose I showed some hesitation about mounting, for the man said encouragingly, "Oh! you needn't be affeard of him for Sol Larkins gin him a round this mornin, and I know from the look of his flanks that he's tuck most of the pitch out'n him for today—Sol's a hard rider, he is." I screwed up my nerves to their utmost tension, clinched my teeth, and sprang into the saddle. The man let go the bridle at the same time, but the mustang didn't budge an inch. "What's to be done now," said I, "this horse can't travel blindfolded?" "In course he can't," said the man, "raise up the blind." I reached forward and drew up the band from the mustang's eyes, fully expecting to find myself the next moment running a somersault over his head, but he went off as slowly and gently as a broken down tacky—which in fact he was. "Crackey!" exclaimed the man in affected astonishment as I rode off at a funeral gait; "Sol has tuck the pitch out'n that mustang and no mistake." I soon found he had taken everything else out of him in the way of get-up, for it was only by the persistent use of whip and heels that I was able to reach my destination in the course of time.

Riding Contest in San Antonio

JOHN C. DUVAL

IT WAS OUR INTENTION to leave San Antonio the next morning, but we heard that a great riding match was to come off the next day between some Rangers and rancheros and a party of forty or fifty Comanche warriors who had come in for the purpose of making another treaty—to be broken the first time they had a chance to lift the hair from some fellow's head or steal a herd of horses. We had often heard of the astonishing equestrian feats performed by the Texas Rangers, rancheros, and Comanches, and we were anxious to see the riding match between them. Uncle Seth told us they could beat the circus riders all hollow and that the sight would be worth the loss of a day. We determined therefore to remain another day at San Antonio and see the show.

The next morning we found the whole population of the city, men, women, and children, all preparing to leave for the scene of the great riding match which was to take place in the prairie (now grown up in mesquite and chaparral) just west of the San Pedro creek. Gaily-dressed "caballeros" were prancing along the streets on their gaudily-caparisoned steeds; Rangers mounted on their horses and dressed in buckskin hunting shirts, leggins, and slouched hats and with pistols and bowie knives stuck in their belts, galloped here and there among the crowd, occasionally charging "horse and any" into some barroom or grocery for a glass of "mescal" or "scorch gullet." All the strangers in the place and all the citizens with their

From *The Young Explorers*, pp. 67-74.

families crammed into all kinds of vehicles were hurrying in hot haste to reach the scene of action before the match began.

Mounting our horses and leaving Uncle Seth in charge of camp, who declined going, as he said he "had seen Injins often enough cuttin up their didoes on horseback," we followed the crowd until we came to the San Pedro, a little stream flowing through the western suburbs of the city. . . . It was indeed a strange and novel scene that presented itself to our view. Drawn up in line on one side of the arena and sitting like statues upon their horses were the Comanche warriors, decked out in their savage finery of paints, feathers, and beads, and looking with Indian stoicism upon all that was going on around them. Opposite to them, drawn up in single file also, were their old enemies upon many a bloody field, the Texas Rangers, and a few Mexican rancheros, dressed in their steeple-crown, broad-brim sombreros, showy scarfs, and slashed trowsers, holding gracefully in check the fiery mustangs on which they were mounted. After some preliminaries, the space selected for the riding was cleared of all non-contestants and the show began. A Mexican lad mounted on a paint (piebald) pony, with a spear in his hand, cantered off a couple of hundred yards and laid the spear flat on the ground. Immediately a Comanche brave started forth from their line, and plunging his spurs into his horse's flanks dashed off in a direction opposite to that where the spear was lying, for a hundred yards or so; then wheeling suddenly he came rushing back at full speed, and as he passed the spot where the spear had been placed, without checking his horse for an instant, he swerved from his saddle, seized the spear, and rising gracefully in his seat, continued his headlong course for some distance beyond, wheeled again and galloped back (dropping the spear as he returned at the same spot from which he had taken it) and resumed his place in the ranks. The same feat was then performed by a dozen or so each of the Rangers, rancheros, and Indians, which was about the number of the actual contestants for the prizes. A glove was then substituted in place of the spear, and in like manner it was picked up from the

ground by the riders, whilst going at full speed, and without checking their horses for an instant, with one exception, caused by the
stumbling of the horse just before he reached the spot where the
glove was lying. A board with a bull's eye marked upon it was then
set up at the point where the spear and glove had been placed. A
warrior with his bow in his hand and three or four arrows from his
quiver charged full speed towards the mark and in the little time he
was passing it planted two arrows in the board. The Rangers and
rancheros then took their turn, using their pistols instead of bows,
and all of them struck the board as they passed it and several the
bull's eye. A good many other extraordinary feats were performed,
such as hanging by one leg to the horn of the saddle in such a way
that the rider could not be seen by those he was supposed to be
charging and whilst in that position discharging pistols or shooting
arrows at an imaginary foe under the horse's neck; jumping from
the horse when at a gallop, running a few steps by his side, and
springing into the saddle again without checking him for a moment;
passing under the horse's neck and coming up into the saddle again
from the opposite side, etc.—all performed while the horse was running. No feats of horsemanship we had ever seen exhibited by the
most famous "knights of the ring" could compare with them. . . .

The last and most interesting and exciting performance of all was
the "breaking in" of several "wild steeds of the desert" that had
never been backed by man, as they had been recently captured.
These were tied "short up" to stakes firmly planted in the ground.
Young McMullen,[7] one of the Rangers, who had already been voted
by general acclamation the most daring and graceful rider on the
ground, was the first to perform this dangerous feat. Approaching
cautiously the most perfectly formed and powerful of these un-
broken steeds, he at length succeeded in spite of the furious struggles of the terrified animal in slipping a blind of thick cloth over its
eyes, and instantly as if transfixed by the wand of an enchanter the
horse ceased struggling and stood perfectly still. McMullen then
forced the bit in his mouth, girted the saddle securely upon him, and

placing his foot in the stirrup sprang upon his back. All this time the horse never moved, but the quivering of its well-formed, muscular limbs, showed that its terrors were still unabated. McMullen fixed himself firmly in his seat, and grasping the reins with his left hand he leaned forward and quickly drew off the blind he had placed over the horse's eyes. The instant it was drawn up, the wild horse snorting and absolutely screaming in its rage and terror, gave one tremendous bound and then darted off at headlong speed across the prairie; but instead of trying to check him, McMullen urged him on with whip and spurs until he had gone perhaps a mile, when he reined him round and brought him back within fifty yards of the point he had started from. Here, suddenly coming to a halt, the horse began to pitch or plunge in such a violent manner that none but the most perfect rider could possibly have kept his seat in the saddle. But McMullen stuck to him as if he had been part of the animal itself, and the horse in vain attempted in this way to get rid of his unwelcome burden. At length, frantic with rage and fright, the horse reared straight up and threw himself backwards upon the ground. A cry of horror broke from the lips of the spectators, for everyone supposed that McMullen would be crushed to death beneath the weight of his steed; but he was on the *qui vive* and sprang from under him just in time to save himself, and the moment the horse rose to his feet we saw him seated in the saddle as calm and composed as though he were bestriding the gentlest hack that ever bore a country curate to his church. Again the horse darted off at the top of his speed, and again McMullen urged him on as he did before with quirt and spurs for more than a mile, when we saw him turn and coming back towards us. In a few moments he came galloping up and after cantering slowly around the arena, he drew up his panting and foaming steed at the place he had started from, and the black eyes of many a senorita glanced admiringly towards the daring and handsome young Ranger. The "wild steed of the desert" had been effectually subdued. Several more were "broken in" by Indians and Mexicans, but a description of the feat would be merely a repetition of what has been said. At the conclusion, the distribution of prizes took place, consisting of handsomely mounted pistols, bowie knives, Spanish blankets, etc. The first prize was awarded by the judges to McMullen. The second to Long Quirt, a Comanche warrior; the third to H. L. Kinney, of Corpus Christi, and the fourth to Senor Don Rafael, a ranchero from the Rio Grande. Presents of various kinds were then distributed among the Comanches, which ended the show, and we returned to camp, well pleased with all we had seen.

NOTES TO SECTION II

1. The word "tarantula" derives from the Latin *Tarentum,* now *Taranto,* a place in southern Italy. It refers to any of several large venomous spiders. The true tarantula, however, is the European wolf spider whose bite was popularly believed to cause a nervous affliction characterized by melancholy, stupor, and an uncontrollable desire to dance, cured only by protracted dancing to appropriate music. A lively, passionate Neapolitan folk dance, the *tarantella,* performed by couples and accompanied by the tambourine, is supposed to be a remedy against the tarantula's bite. The tarantulas of Texas and the American tropics are large hairy spiders, *Eurypelma hentzii.*

2. Probably refers to the tarantula hawk or killer, a species of large wasp of the southwestern United States that captures tarantulas as food for its young.

3. "Frank Forester" was the pen name of Henry William Herbert (1807-1858), American author of sporting books and articles.

4. Lecomte and Lexington were two famous racehorses whose great period of rivalry was 1854-55. Lexington, the most illustrious thoroughbred of the time, earned $56,000 in winning six of seven races, losing one to Lecomte. Noted for his victory over Lexington, Lecomte also won many other races. See John Hervey, *Racing in America, 1665-1865* (New York, 1944), II, 271-300.

5. The Texas guan, a large tropical bird that somewhat resembles a turkey. The Spanish name "chachalacha" derives from the Nahuatl word meaning "the twittering of a bird."

6. "Seeing the elephant" was a popular phrase of the period. A. B. Longstreet used it in *Georgia Scenes* (1835) to describe a country yokel's impression of city sights. Journalist George W. Kendall, in *Santa Fe Expedition* (1844), I, 110, defined the oft-repeated phrase: "When a man is disappointed in anything he undertakes, when he has seen enough, when he gets sick and tired of any job he may have set himself about, he has 'seen the elephant.'"

7. John McMullen, later a lieutenant in Captain Ben McCulloch's company of Texas Rangers, came to Texas from Maryland in 1839. Fun-loving and brave, he often distinguished himself by saving the lives of others; for example, in 1846 at Independence Hall he rescued, under Mexican fire, a fellow Texan who had fallen from his horse. In 1849 he left Texas and went to California.

III
Texians

III. Texians

TEXIAN *(with an* i*) was the name given to the earliest settlers of the state. The word was commonly used during the Republic period, and it lingered in some instances long afterward. Texians were largely Anglo-Americans who lived in Texas under Mexican rule. Although they added a few Spanish words to their vocabularies and seasoned some of their customs with Spanish flavor, they resisted efforts to make them Mexican colonists. During the Revolution that threw off Mexican domination, the common cause united all Texians, whether originally Anglo-American, European, or in some cases Spanish, and gave a very special meaning to the name. But the flood of immigrants from the United States, France, Germany, Ireland, and Scotland soon after the Revolution tended to dissipate the old patriotic feeling. Then admission to the Union and the Mexican War strengthened the already dominant Anglo-American culture, and the new name "Texan" was indicative of the change.*

But the transition from "Texian" to "Texan" was not easy. An editorial entitled "Texian vs. Texan" in the Texas Monument, *February 5, 1851, spoke vehemently of "the wretched barbarism 'Texan.'" "When we hear a man say* Texan," *the irate editor wrote, "we involuntarily look to see if he has the lock-jaw, or if he has ice in his mouth. There is no excuse for a man to use such a word in a mild climate." He maintained that* Texian *is more euphonious than* Texan *and that "the genius of our language requires generally the termination* ian, *when it is necessary to give a name to the inhabitants of a country." Arguing that* Texian *"is the name for which we fought" and which shows "ourselves independent of all foreign dictation," he then concluded, "Let us stand up for the rights of the 'old Texian,' against the ruthless Goths and Vandals who are endeavoring to deprive him of that which has blazed so brilliantly from the folds of his banner over all his battle-fields."*

It was a losing battle; yet the distinction the editor of the Monument *wished to maintain is significant. The Texian was different. If he had come from the United States, he had brought with him some doubts, for the stay-at-homes had considered him foolhardy to leave the safety and comfort of home for an unknown land; if he had come from Europe, these doubts were multiplied. He was, therefore, on the defensive from the beginning. During the rapid transition from colony to Republic to state, he saw many fugitives from justice come into his land and heard the damning "G.T.T." ("Gone to Texas," that is, beyond the law) applied to all his fellow countrymen. No wonder, then, that the Texian developed certain characteristics that were later thought to be typical of a Texan: self-sufficiency, taciturnity, distrust of outsiders, handiness with a gun.*

In reality the Texian who came from the Anglo-American culture (and among Texians he was the greatest in number) probably did not differ greatly from his fellow American pioneers elsewhere, but characteristically he left little record of his own thoughts about these matters. Instead, he is to be seen in retrospect largely through the eyes of European travelers, visitors from the United States, and others who came to Texas determined to find the people different, and who saw what they were looking for.

Difficult Times

NOAH SMITHWICK

I SET OUT on foot for Dewitt's colony, ten miles further up the Lavaca. . . . Fulcher accompanied me up to the station. The beautiful rose color that tinged my visions of Texas while viewing it through Robertson's long-distance lens paled with each succeeding step. There were herds of fine, fat deer, and antelope enough to set one wild who had never killed anything bigger than a raccoon, but to my astonishment and disgust I could not kill one, though I was accounted a crack marksman; but I found it was one thing to shoot at a mark, the exact distance of which I knew, and another to hit game at an uncertain distance.

The colonists, consisting of a dozen families, were living—if such existence could be called living—huddled together for security against the Karankawas, who, though not openly hostile, were not friendly. The rude log cabins, windowless and floorless, have been so often described as the abode of the pioneer as to require no repetition here; suffice it to say that save as a partial protection against rain and sun they were absolutely devoid of comfort. Dewitt had at first established his headquarters at Gonzales, and the colonists had located their land in that vicinity, but the Indians stole their horses and otherwise annoyed them so much, notwithstanding the soldiers, that they abandoned the colony and moved down on the Lavaca, where they were just simply staying. The station being in the limits of the reserve, they made no pretense of improving it, not even to the extent of planting corn, one of the first things usually

From *The Evolution of a State*, pp. 15-16, 17-19.

attended to, for the Texas Indians, unlike their eastern brethren, scorned to till the soil, and the few Mexicans scattered through the country did so only to the extent of supplying their own wants; so when the colonists used up the breadstuff they brought with them they had to do without until they raised it. This, however, was no very difficult matter near the coast, where there were vast cane-brakes all along the rivers. The soil was rich and loose from the successive crops of cane that had decayed on it. In the fall, when the cane died down, it was burned off clean. The ground was then ready for planting, which was done in a very primitive manner, a sharpened stick being all the implement necessary. With this they made holes in the moist loam and dropped in grains of corn. When the young cane began to grow they went over it with a stick, simply knocking it down; the crop was then laid by. Game was plentiful the year round, so there was no need of starving. Men talked hope-fully of the future; children reveled in the novelty of the present; but the women—ah, there was where the situation bore heaviest. As one old lady remarked, Texas was "a heaven for men and dogs, but a hell for women and oxen." They—the women—talked sadly of the old homes and friends left behind, so very far behind it seemed then, of the hardships and bitter privations they were undergoing and the dangers that surrounded them. They had not even the solace of constant employment. The spinning wheel and loom had been left behind. There was, as yet, no use for them—there was nothing to spin. There was no house to keep in order; the meager fare was so simple as to require little time for preparation. There was no poultry, no dairy, no garden, no books, or paper as nowadays—and, if there had been, many of them could not read—no schools, no churches—nothing to break the dull monotony of their lives, save an occasional wrangle among the children and dogs. The men at least had the excitement of killing game and cutting bee trees.

It was July and the heat was intense. The only water obtainable was that of the sluggish river which crept along between low banks thickly set with tall trees, from the branches of which depended long streamers of Spanish moss swarming with mosquitoes and pregnant of malaria. Alligators, gaunt and grim—certainly the most hideous creatures God ever made—lay in wait among the moss and drift for any unwary creature that might come down to drink. Dogs, of which every well regulated family had several, were their special weakness, and many a thirsty canine drank and never thirsted more. . . . Their bellow was just such a hideous sound as might be expected to issue from the throat of such a hideous creature and was of itself enough to chase away sleep, unassisted by the tuneful mosquito, whose song, like the opera singer's, has a business ring in it. I had heard the bellowing nightly while in New Orleans, but heard amid the noises and lights of the city there lurked in it no suspicion of the horror it could produce when heard amid the gloom and solitude of the wilderness. Wolves and owls added their voices to the dismal serenade. I had heard them all my life, but I had yet to learn the terrible significance that might attach to the familiar howl and hoot. The whippoorwill's silvery notes filled in the interludes, but they seemed strangely out of tune amid such surroundings.

Newcomers were warmly welcomed and entertained with all the hospitality at the command of the colonists. Sleeping accommodations were limited to the mosquito bars, a provision not to be despised, since they were absolutely indispensable to sleep. The bill of fare, though far from epicurean, was an improvement on dried venison and honey, in that the venison was fresh and cooked, and Colonel Dewitt, my host, had bread, though some families were without. Flour was $10 a barrel. Trading vessels came in sometimes, but few people had money to buy anything more than coffee and tobacco, which were considered absolutely indispensable. Money was as scarce as bread. There was no controversy about "sound" money then. Pelts of any kind passed current and constituted the principal medium of exchange.

Children forgot—many of them had never known—what wheaten bread was like. Old Martin Varner used to tell a good story of his little son's first experience with a biscuit. The old man had managed to get together money or pelts enough to buy a barrel of flour. Mrs. Varner made a batch of biscuits, which, considering the resources of the country, were doubtless heavy as lead and hard as wood. When they were done Mrs. Varner set them on the table. The boy looked at them curiously, helped himself to one, and made for the door with it. In a few minutes he came back for another. Doubting the child's ability to eat it so quickly, the old man followed him to see what disposition he made of the second. The ingenious youngster had conceived a novel and not altogether illogical idea of their utility. He had punched holes through the center, inserted an axle, and triumphantly displayed a miniature Mexican cart. And I assure you, from my recollection of those pioneer biscuits, they were capable of sustaining a pretty heavy load. . . .

Game was the sole dependence of many families and I fixed up many an old gun that I wouldn't have picked up in the road, knowing that it was all that stood between a family and the gaunt wolf at the door, as well as the Indians. Domestic animals were so scarce that the possession of any considerable number gave notoriety and name to the possessor; thus there were "Cow" Cooper and "Hog" Mitchell. Failing to secure more choice game, there were always mustangs to fall back on. Over on the Brazos lived Jared E. Groce, a planter from South Carolina, who had over 100 slaves, with which force he set to work clearing ground and planting cotton and corn. He hired two men to kill game to feed them on, and the mustangs being the largest and easiest to kill, the Negroes lived on horse meat till corn came in.

Entertainment Among the First Colonists

NOAH SMITHWICK

ANOTHER TYPE of the old colonists but one that played a no less important part in the development of the country, was Thomas B. Bell, who lived up on the San Bernard above McNeal's. He came several times to my shop during my stay at McNeal's, and he being an intelligent, well-bred man, I took quite a fancy to him and gladly accepted an invitation to visit him. I found him domiciled in a little pole-cabin in the midst of a small clearing upon which was a crop of corn. His wife, every inch a lady, welcomed me with as much cordiality as if she were mistress of a mansion. There were two young children, and they, too, showed in their every manner the effects of gentle training. The whole family were dressed in buckskin, and when supper was announced we sat on stools around a clapboard table, upon which were arranged wooden platters. Beside each platter lay a fork made of a joint of cane. The knives were of various patterns ranging from butcher knives to pocket-knives. And for cups we had little wild cymlings [wild squash] scraped and scoured until they looked as white and clean as earthenware, and the milk with which the cups were filled was as pure and sweet as mortal had ever tasted. The repast was of the simplest, but served with as much grace as if it had been a feast, which, indeed, it became, seasoned with the kindly manners and pleasant conversation of those two entertainers. Not a word of apology was uttered during my stay of a day and night, and when I left them I did so with a hearty invitation to repeat my visit. It so happened

From *The Evolution of a State*, pp. 38-41.

that I never was at their place again, but was told that in the course of time the pole-cabin gave place to a handsome brick house and that the rude furnishings were replaced by the best the country boasted, but I'll venture to say that the host and hostess still retained their old hospitality unchanged by change of fortune.

They were a social people, these old Three Hundred, though no one seems to have noted the evidence of it. There were a number of weddings and other social gatherings during my sojourn in that section, the most notable one perhaps being the marriage of Nicholas McNutt to Miss Cartwright. There was a large number of invited guests, both the families occupying a high social position. Jesse Cartwright, father of the bride, was a man in comfortable circumstances and himself and family people of good breeding. They were among the very first of Austin's colonists, Cartwright being a member of the first ayuntamiento organized in Texas. The bridegroom was the son of the widow McNutt, also among the early arrivals. The family, consisting of mother, two sons, and three young daughters, came from Louisiana, where they had been very wealthy, but having suffered reverses they came to Texas to recoup their fortunes. Bred up in luxury, as they evidently had been, it was a rough road to fortune they chose, but they adapted themselves to the situation and made the best of it. . . . Miss Mary Allen, daughter of Martin Allen, a very pretty girl and a great belle by the way, was the bridesmaid, and John McNutt, brother of the bridegroom, was groomsman. There being no priest in the vicinity, Thomas Dukes, the "big" alcalde, was summoned from San Felipe. The alcalde tied the nuptial knot in good American style, but the contracting parties had in addition to sign a bond to avail themselves of the priest's services to legalize the marriage at the earliest opportunity. . . . The next thing in order was the wedding supper, which was the best the market afforded. That being disposed of, the floor was cleared for dancing. It mattered not that the floor was made of puncheons. When young folks danced those days, they danced; they didn't glide around; they "shuffled" and "double

shuffled," "wired," and "cut the pigeon's wing," making the splinters
fly. There were some of the boys, however, who were not provided
with shoes, and moccasins were not adapted to that kind of dancing
floor, and moreover they couldn't make noise enough, but their
more fortunate brethren were not at all selfish or disposed to put
on airs, so, when they had danced a turn, they generously exchanged
footgear with the moccasined contingent and gave them the ring,
and just literally kicked every splinter off that floor before morning.
The fiddle, manipulated by Jesse Thompson's man Mose, being
rather too weak to make itself heard above the din of clattering
feet, we had in another fellow with a clevis and pin to strengthen
the orchestra, and we had a most enjoyable time. . . .

Another dancing party in which I participated was at Martin
Varner's, near Columbia. When we were all assembled and ready
to begin business, it was found that Mose, the only fiddler around,
had failed to come on time, so we called in an old darky belonging
to Colonel Zeno Philips, who performed on a clevis as an accom-
paniment to his singing, while another Negro scraped on a cotton
hoe with a case knife. The favorite chorus was:

> O git up gals in de mawnin',
> O git up gals in de mawnin',
> O git up gals in de mawnin',
> Jes at de break ob day,

at the conclusion of which the performer gave an extra blow to the
clevis while the dancers responded with a series of dexterous rat-tat-
tats with heel and toe.

A Settler in Texas

"H."

A MAN by name of Yeamans brought me in a wagon from Deckrose Point to his house, fifty-five miles up the peninsula. This man, with twenty-five other persons, including his father and mother, grandfather and grandmother, left the most western part of New York in 1829 under the invitation of the Austin Grant. They embarked on board a flatboat on the Alleghany River, came to Wheeling on the Ohio, took a steamboat, and reached New Orleans in December. By this time their party had increased to fifty souls, the additions being made by young men, adventurers to the new country, who, aside from the promising garden they were to reach, were allured by the company they were to go in, a good share of the original twenty-five being young ladies. At New Orleans they chartered a little schooner for three hundred dollars to take them to Matagorda Bay, for there then was no town in that section. They were shipwrecked off Aransas Pass; their provisions and water became exhausted, they suffered greatly from cold, and otherwise they were sorely tormented. After two months they landed or reached what is now the town of Matagorda and found three men who had pitched their tents at that place and who wept for joy at this new accession.

This Mr. Yeamans and his party set about surveying (that was his profession) and improving and in a short time had a smart town. He tells me that out of the fifty not more than one third are living and most of them had come to their end by violent deaths. He had

From *Littell's Living Age*, XIII (April-June, 1847), 569-70. Reprinted from the *Journal of Commerce*. The author is unidentified.

two brothers butchered in the Fannin massacre. His family were pious. He has worn out three rifles, for his country and in procuring wild food for his and his family's living. He has been in camp for months, has chased and been chased by Mexicans and Indians, and has met them face to face. The female portion of his family has often been compelled to fly to the woods for protection from the savage, with no earthly protection but their own sex. Still, he doesn't seem to think his lot has been a hard one as he contrasts it with those who have been his neighbors. Surrounded as he has been with the vileness and profanity of the camp and mingling, as he necessarily has done, with all sorts of human depravity, he tells me no day has passed during the eighteen years without his offering up a prayer of supplication and thanksgiving to God. He is quite unlike the "old settlers," though many of them are excellent people. Alas! how few are left, how few of the Austin Colony have been spared the tomahawk and scalping knife, if they escaped the Mexican's duplicity and consequent murder. The pioneers to any country seldom reap their reward. It is those who come after them. This man lives on the peninsula nine miles below Caney and has a rancho with a few hundred head of cattle. He keeps a small sail-boat to run with passengers from his house to Matagorda, sixteen miles across the bay; he makes a little butter, sells now and then a steer for beef, but is still poor, and makes not more than two hundred dollars a year. He says he has a brother in the section where he was raised, a merchant, that writes him he clears five hundred dollars per annum and has never seen any trouble. "And now, (he says,) would it not seem that I am a great fool for suffering so much as I have?"

His wife's brother brought me to Velasco on horseback. After I felt sufficiently acquainted, said I, "What *might* be your name?"

Said he, "Smith."

"Smith?"

"Yes, Smith!"

"How is that? are you not a Dutchman?"

"Yes, and a great many of our people are named Smith."

"Well, I never heard of one before. Pray how do you spell it?"

"I don't know how in Dutch, but think 'tis S-c-h-m-i-d-t-h, *Smith!*"

"Good," said I, and perhaps smiled aloud.

"You need not laugh," said he, looking grave, very grave, "for I know 'tis so." So you see this accounts for a "right smart chance" of the Smith family. He is a jolly good fellow anyhow, and his Dutch ma makes the best kind of cornbread.

Just the other side of the San Bernard, night approaching with terrible thunder and lightning, we stopped for the night at Hugh's Tavern. When we drove up to the door and hailed, a volley of twenty-nine dogs greeted us with yells and a thunder that really outdid the real thunder. For myself I was fearful of being torn in pieces, but we were soon relieved by their master appearing with whip in hand and dispersing the animals. This house is kept by two young men twenty-two and twenty-five years of age with not a soul of the gentler sex within several miles of them. Their house has two rooms, in one of which are two beds for themselves and patrons. They had no candle or lamp, seeming to consider such a matter unnecessary. On retiring, I found by feeling that the bed was literally covered with sand and dust which the recent wind had thrust through the logs, and during the night my temples were kept perfectly cool by a brisk northwest wind coming through the same opening. These young men have near five hundred head of fine stock with horses and mules. They are both fine looking, one of them remarkably so, and extremely hospitable. What a chance for some of our city belles! At night they made coffee—a beverage always at hand in this country—and in the morning fried us a fine piece of a fat doe, killed within a few rods of their rancho the day previous by the unerring rifle of the youngest. Though they had hundreds of milch cows, not a particle of milk or butter was thought of for their table.

Not long since I stopped to camp for dinner and to rest my horse not far from the Brazos river on a beautiful, green, luxuriant prairie, on which and in sight were feeding a thousand fine domestic oxen and cows with their young calves and at a little greater distance were ten thousand large handsome wild geese; and also comprehended in the same view was a large herd of fat deer with large stately bucks all enjoying the tender grass in the greatest apparent security. As soon as we had stripped our horses and given them a chance, we turned to with our bacon, cornbread, and coffee. At this moment up came dashing across the plain a regular old Kentuck who had been in Texas seventeen years. Said he, "Strangers! where mout you be from?" We told him. Says he, "Maybe ye havn't seen a hoss critter like the one I'm on?"

"No."

"Rot him," says he; "he's a heap of trouble to a feller, though I don't blame him, for them'ar geese and deer eat and pison up right smart of the grass."

"Why don't you shoot and eat them?" said I.

" 'Cause they ain' no account, no how."

"Don't your men hunt them at all?"

"No," said he.

"Why, what do you live on?"

"Hog and homony," said he, "and dog; anything else, barring coffee, and I will have a smart chance of that, if I have to run to my neighbor's fort." I asked him how near he had any neighbors. "Oh plenty," said he, "right near. One ten miles and one thirteen miles." He was barefooted and had on a shirt that might have been worn without washing six months, and like its possessor looked dirty and hideous—disgustingly so. Such is living or staying in Texas with many of the settlers, who are well off, but have no ambition above the brute. Vastly different is it with the larger class, who both live and dress well.

The Shingle Family

PERCY B. ST. JOHN

ONE OF THE EARLIEST settlers in Galveston county, under General
Austin, was Jeremiah Shingle, his wife, daughter, and grownup son.
Now the male Shingles were a desperate set; they could hit a cent
at a hundred and fifty paces, wield an American axe of the most
huge caliber, and lay a tree, a nigger, or an Indian low in "a'most
half less than no time." They were citizens of the free and enlightened republic which boasts itself the smartest nation in all creation,
and like most Yankees transplanted from their native localities to
the rank soil of Texas were lazy, reckless, and rude beyond the con-
ception of anything European. They disdained the culture of the
fertile earth, thousands of acres of which they owned, and after
erecting a miserable shanty in which more wood was expended
than would have sufficed to build an hotel of the first magnitude,
the father and son shouldered their rifles, with which wandering
the woods they laid low as much game as sufficed to keep the family
in food, clothing, and powder, and above all, the real Monongahela
whiskey. Old Jerry Shingle was a thorough toper, and yet he carried
it well withal, at five-and-fifty being hearty and hale as many a man
of forty. His son Ezekiel, or, as he was commonly called, Zick, unfortunately added to all these characteristics that of being an arrant
bully. Secure in his rifle, bowie knife, and huge stature, he scorned
the most distant attempt at courtesy of manner. It will readily,

From *Littell's Living Age*, IV (January-March, 1845), 506-7. Reprinted from the *United Service Magazine*. No information on the
author could be found.

therefore, be believed, that in a new country where women were scarce it was not very easy for Zick to find a partner. Now young Shingle's highest ambition was a log hut of his own; but as he could not raise the money to buy a nigger helper who would wash, bake, and brew, a wife was an indispensable requisite to begin house-keeping. Years, however, passed, and Zick found not his mate. His sister, too, was unmarried from no fault of her own, however, but from the dislike all the neighbors entertained of having Zick for a brother-in-law.

At length the Indians located themselves in the spot above de-scribed. The consequence was a great increase in the difficulty of procuring game. The Shingles, therefore, hated the Waccos, whom, on the principle ever actuating their class, they looked upon despite their natural right as interlopers. Both old Shingle and Zick had henceforth to go further and fare worse. That is, to procure game they had to scour new regions, and being lazy their family was forced to be content with a less ample supply of provisions. A deadly hatred was, therefore, nourished in secret against the Waccos, whom, how-ever, they blinded to their dislike by an outward show of friendship, waiting until a favorable opportunity should offer itself for wreaking their vengeance upon their innocent foes. Suddenly, however, a change came over the spirit of Zick. Among the maidens who dwelt within the wigwams of their enemies was one who once seen was not easily forgotten. Peoria was the daughter of a great chief and destined to be the bride of one equal in renown. This girl, Zick, having once set eyes upon, determined should become his squaw and lost no opportunity of pushing himself into her good graces. Henceforth he was ever within the Wacco inclosure, joined in their hunting parties, smoked the pipe in the council hall, ventured a compliment to the girls, and, in fact, became a regular spy upon the movements of the Indian girl. A white wife and a black helper, being equally unattainable, a redskin squaw was decided upon.

Early one morning Zick tracked his mistress to a grove near the village round which the hunter lingered until Peoria had had time to perform her matutinal ablutions, when hearing her light step about to leave the shelter and seek the camp, he advanced into the thicket and stood motionless before her. Leaning on his long rifle and taking also the precaution of supporting his back against a tree, Zick looked the maiden full in the face. Both were silent for a few minutes; the girl was the first to speak in her own tongue.

"What does Long Rifle want with a redskin girl?"

"Long Rifle thinks the Forest Rose more beautiful than—" Zick was at a loss for a simile but he looked unutterable things.

The girl laughed and said, "My white brother is very tall, but his words are few."

"Well, I jist arn't the chap for a long lockrum," replied the hunter, relapsing into his own rich lingo; "it goes considerable agin the grain; but for shootin, or treein a coon, or sich like matters, I'm a Yankee, that's all, and they're ginerally allowed to stump the univarse in thim things."

"Long Rifle can shoot—his eye is very quick," replied the girl emphatically, the matter being one ever held among her people of the highest importance.

"Well, I arn't availed of any in these parts can chaw me up; or if he does, he must be a knowin old shaver and rise considerable airly of a morning, but that arn't the chop just now. Long Rifle can wipe it up considerable hard, you may depend; but Forest Rose, do ye see—I must blart it out—my wigwam is empty, I want a squaw, a wife, and I can't altogether say that I've seen any one comes up to my cipher afore—" Here Zick stopped.

"Long Rifle was speaking," replied the girl quietly.

"Well, I tell you what Peoria, or Red Rose, don't get my dander up; I feel most particularly ugly, I do. Don't you cipher me. Skin is skin, whether it be white or black, red or pink, and, do you see, if you will just take half my wigwam, it shall be the warmest in these parts, that's a fact. I'm about a right up an down hunter, a real first chop of a feller, and can shoot more deer, trap more turkeys, and send a ball further than a'most or many about these diggens."

"My brother's skin is white, but his heart is red; the skin of Peoria is red, and her heart is very red. A brave waits for the Forest Rose; he hears her voice, and it is very sweet!"

"Well, I tell you what, girl, you make me feel ugly, but we'll settle this in tu tus. Jumping Jim—"

"The Leaping Panther," interposed the girl proudly.

"Well, I do feel ryled and kinder sore, that's a fact. What's in his name? I know he's a'most an almighty villain, and he'd better clear out next hitch."

"The Leaping Panther is a great warrior."

"Well, I reckon he's pretty considerable smart, but that's nothin. I say, Peoria, my wigwam is empty, I want a squaw, I take a fancy to you, and the Red Rose comes with me."

With these words the young man caught the Indian girl in his arms, threw her on his brawny shoulder, and carrying his silent victim as if she had been a child, turned for his rifle, which while speaking he had leaned against a tree. In its place stood the Leaping Panther, his eyes flashing fire, his deerskin wrapper thrown back, his tomahawk loose, and his hands holding the rifle of the now help-less hunter.

"My white brother is very good," said the Indian, scornfully, "but the Forest Rose has long feet; she can walk."

"A pretty prime superfine scoundrel," muttered the discomfitted Zick, and then he added aloud, "You have the vantige, Ingian, you may depend, and it looks wickedly ugly for me. What chop shall we make! You keep the rifle—it's an uphill one—and I'll keep the gal."

"The Leaping Panther has many medicine guns, but he has no squaw. The Forest Rose must come."

"It's an etarnal pity," muttered Zick, "but he's got his dander up, and tu guns—I can't catch him nohow. Ingian, give me the gun—here's the gal. I reckon we won't quarrel for nothing."

"The white man's life is in my hands," said the Indian, proudly, "but he has smoked in the wigwam of my fathers. Go! There are two paths, one of peace, one of war. The warpath leads to the big wigwam—when the great light goes to rest, the wampum belt will be with the pale faces."

Zick took his rifle, which the Indian had first discharged, and the odds being still against him, suffered both Leaping Panther and Peoria to disappear.

"A riglar ugly customer that, you may depend, and a pretty kettle of fish I have got to cook, I conclude. Well, I must be active; thim Ingians 'ull be a'ter scalping every soul of us afore long. Once they begin, they hold on most especial fast, you may depend."

Zick was right. Once the Waccos had a quarrel with one white man, there was very little doubt that it would spread to all around. Aware that his neighbors were all burning for an excuse to attack the Indians, Zick hurried home, told old Shingle to get his horse out and start one way, while he caught a grey old mustang, and dashed on to Austinia, where he knew a dozen men could be raised in an hour for any wild harum-scarum purpose whatsoever. The recent retreat of Santa Anna, and the dispersion of the Texan volunteers, had spread over the land a host of wild and untamable spirits to whom fighting, especially with Indians, was a perfect treat.

The Wedding

ANONYMOUS

DURING A RESIDENCE in America, no observing person can fail to have remarked, whether he travel in Canada, the United States, or Texas, the vast number of Irish families everywhere to be met with. They bear such distinctly-marked peculiarities that no mistake can occur in attributing to them their native soil. It has been my lot to visit many of the settlements of these wanderers from the green isle, but nowhere did I meet any family which so singularly interested me as one which a few months back was residing within the limits of the young republic of Texas, consisting of the father, mother, a son, and two daughters. Old Rock, or as he is generally called, Captain Rock—a name doubtless assumed—emigrated to America seventeen years ago, his family then consisting of two daughters, for the son was born afterwards in the land of his adoption. For seven years, the sturdy Irishman (originally well informed and well educated, though his early history was never known) contended with the difficulties incident to new settlers with various success in different parts of the Union, when he was induced to join the first band of adventurers who under General Austin obtained leave from the Mexican government to locate themselves in Texas. The family obtained a grant of land as a matter of course, but Old Rock did not fancy settled agricultural pursuits. To have round him a well-stocked farm, cleared and productive fields, and herds of cattle would have required a degree of perseverance and patient personal

From *Littell's Living Age*, I (April-August, 1844), 503-6. Reprinted from *Chambers' Edinburgh Journal*.

labor of which he was incapable. He preferred the life of a wandering squatter upon which he at once entered and which he has never since deserted. Building a boat, Old Rock embarked in it on one of the Texian rivers with his family, an old gun, and a small stock of ammunition and following the windings of the stream did not stop until he came to an abandoned log hut, or frame-house, where he thought he might find temporary accommodation.

Of these deserted houses Texas has many, their abundance arising from various causes—death from fever, the terrible civil war, or, oftener still, from men having hastily chosen a location and built thereon before it was found out that the spot was undesirable and unproductive. Rock was not nice. If the neighborhood supplied game, he was satisfied. Sometimes an acre of sweet potatoes, Indian corn, and pumpkins might be put under cultivation; otherwise, the family lived entirely upon venison, wild fowl, fish and oysters, and—it was whispered—pork upon occasion. A reported fondness for this latter article was one of the causes of Old Rock's frequent migrations. No sooner did he pitch himself in any neighborhood than it was said pork was at a premium. Pigs certainly disappeared most mysteriously; but though all threw the blame upon Rock, he ever averred the panthers, wolves, and stray hunters, to have been the real culprits. However this might be, after some months' residence in any particular spot, the family usually received a polite notice to quit and find another dwelling-place. Eighteen several times had the Hibernian patriarch removed his tent at the bidding of his fellows; any neglect of such orders was usually followed by the infliction of that summary justice called lynch law.

When I became acquainted with the family early in the autumn of 1842, they were residing on one of the tributaries which pour into Galveston bay—known as Dick's Creek. The son was sixteen, a small-made lad who entirely supported the family by means of his gun, being one of the most expert hunters I ever met with in the backwoods. Every article not produced by themselves, their clothing being entirely of deer skin, was obtained by bartering venison hams

which they always carefully preserved for this purpose. Rock and
his wife were now old; the former, though yet sturdy, moving about
only in his boat and smoking over his fire; the latter doing all the
cooking. Mary and Betsy Rock, the daughters, it would be vain to
attempt faithfully to delineate. Fat, brown, and healthy, dressed in
petticoats and spencers of deerskin, they were the most original pair
it was ever my lot to encounter. They could neither read nor write,
but could hunt and fish most excellently well; two adventurous days
they were that I spent in their company. They had never seen an
Englishman before since they were grown up, and my pictures of
life at home enraptured them. With the younger daughter, Mary—
the other was engaged to be married to a Yankee—I became a prodigious favorite, and many a hunt in canoe and in the prairie had
we together. But to my story. After leaving them with a faithful
promise of paying another visit, I found myself six weeks after again
at the door of the once elegant farmhouse where I had left them.
To my surprise it was half-burnt and desolate. This disappointed
me much, for I had brought up several appropriate presents for
both my young friends. Pursuing my way, however, up the river, I
halted at a farmhouse, where I found several persons collected who
quickly informed me that the family had been "mobbed" off the
creek with threats of being shot if they settled within ten miles of
the spot. Where they had gone to no one knew nor seemed to care;
and these parties being the very extempore administrators of justice
who had warned them off, I soon departed and gained the house of
my friend Captain Tod, where I purposed ruralizing during some
weeks. From Tod I learned that two fat pigs had lately disappeared;
and suspicion most unjustly, as it afterwards turned out, having
fallen on the Rocks, the squatter and his family had to seek a new
resting place. On hearing this, I gave up all idea of ever again
seeing my fair friends.

Three days passed in the usual occupations of a hunting party
when on the afternoon of the fourth day I was left alone in the log
hut to amuse myself over certain lately arrived English papers,

while my companions were employed in searching the country round for some cattle which my friend the captain was desirous of selling. About an hour before sunset, footsteps, which I supposesd to be those of one of the returning party of cowboys, were heard behind the hut, then at its side, and in a minute more the latch was raised and in walked—Tim Rock. The young hunter, having satisfied himself that I was really there, advanced close to me and answered my greetings. My first inquiries were after his sisters. "Why," said he, "sister Bet is to be married tomorrow, and sister Mary has sent me to invite you to the wedding." "How," said I, in some surprise, "did your sister know I was here?" Tim laughed and replied that when I stopped with my boat's crew at the farmhouse, he was on the opposite bank in the big timber hunting but dared not communicate with me in consequence of what had occurred. After a few more words of explanation, I shouldered my gun, my packet of presents for the young ladies, and, leaving a line in pencil for my friends, followed Tim through the forest until we reached overhanging trees and bushes, and found a moderate-sized canoe. It was almost dark when I stepped into the boat, but still I saw that it already contained a human being; so my hand mechanically sought the butt of my pistol. "You won't shoot me, sir," said the rich, full, merry voice of Mary Rock to my infinite surprise. Tim laughed heartily at my mistaking her for an Indian, and then, cautioning me to speak low, until all the houses on the river were passed, we placed ourselves in the craft and commenced our voyage. I, knowing the bayou to a nicety, acted as steersman. Mary sat next with a paddle, and Tim in the bow with another. It seemed that, determined to have me at the wedding, the brother and sister with the consent of their friends had started to fetch me, feeling certain that I would come after the promises I had made to that effect. It seemed that they had judged rightly, for here was I in company with two of the rudest settlers in the wilderness embarked in a frail canoe to go I knew not whither—nor did I much care. This roving spirit it was, indeed, which initiated me into my secrets and

mysteries of the wood and prairies which escape the more sober
and methodical.

The record of that night's journey would in itself be a curious
chapter in western economy, but more important matters forbid.
Suffice it to remark that after sixteen miles' journey down a river
by moonlight and as many more across the rough and sea-like bay
of Galveston, enlivened by merry jocund talk all the way, we
arrived about dawn at the new settlement of the Rock family. It
was a large deserted barn or warehouse near Clare Creek. The family were already up and stirring and engaged in active preparation for the important ceremony; and to my surprise the supply of
eatables and drinkables was both varied and great—all, however,
being presents from the bridegroom, one Luke, a wealthy land-
owner for Texas, in possession of much cleared ground and many
hundred head of cattle. It may be a matter of surprise that a man
well to do in the world should have chosen a bride so every way
rude and uneducated; but in Texas women are scarce, and then the
lover might have looked far before he could have found a more
cheerful and good-natured companion, more willing to learn, more
likely to be loving, faithful, and true, than Betsy Rock. The blushing
bride received me in a cotton gown, shoes and stockings, and other
articles of civilized clothing previously unknown to her and in
which she felt sufficiently awkward. But Luke had sent them, and
Betsy wished to appear somebody on her wedding day. My presents were all, therefore, except a bead necklace, employed in
decorating Mary, who secreting herself behind a screen with her
sister almost convulsed me with laughter by appearing a few minutes after in a man's red hunting-shirt, a cotton petticoat, white
stockings and moccasins, the body of a silk dress sent to her by a
Galveston lady, and a cap and bonnet. Never was London or
Parisian belle prouder than was this little rosycheeked light-hearted
Texian beauty.

About eight o'clock the visitors began to arrive. First came a
boatful of men and women from Galveston, bringing with them a

Negro fiddler, without whom little could have been done. Then came Dr. Worcester and his lady from St. Leon in a canoe; after them Colonel Brown from Anahuac in his dugout; and about nine the bridegroom and four male and an equal number of female companions on horseback, the ladies riding either before or behind the gentlemen on pillions. Ere ten, there were thirty odd persons assembled, when a most substantial breakfast was set down to, chiefly consisting of game, though pork, beef, coffee, and, rarer still, bread, proved that Luke had had a hand in it. This meal being over, the boat in which the party from Galveston had come up and which was an open craft for sailing or pulling was put in requisition to convey the bride and bridegroom to the nearest magistrate, there to plight their troth. The distance to be run was six miles with a fair wind going, but dead against us on our return. The party consisted of Luke, who was a young man of powerful frame but rather unpleasant features; the bride and bride's maid (Mary Rock officiating in this capacity), papa of course, myself as captain, and eight men to pull us back. The breeze was fresh, the craft a smart sailer, the canvass was rap full, and all therefore being in our favor, we reached West Point, the residence of Mr. Parr, the magistrate, in less than an hour. We found our Texian Solon about to start in chase of a herd of deer, just reported by his son as visible, and being therefore in a hurry the necessary formalities were gone through, the fee paid, and the usual document in the possession of the husband in ten minutes. The eye of the old squatter was moistened as he gave his child away, some natural tears *she* shed but dried them soon, and presently everybody was as merry as ever.

No sooner were the formalities concluded than we returned to the boat, and to our great delight found that, close-hauled, we could almost make the desired spot. The wind had shifted a point, and ere ten minutes we were again clean full, the tide with us, and the boat walking the waters at a noble rate. All looked upon this as a good omen and were proportionably merrier; none more so than my own particular friend Mary, who in her finery was an object of much good-humored joking from the men who surrounded her. About one o'clock Mr. and Mrs. Charles Luke were presented by Old Rock to the assembled company at the barn, and after an embrace from her mother the bride led the way accompanied by her lord and master to the dinner table. The woods, prairies, and water, as well as the Galveston market, had all liberally contributed their share of provender. Wild turkeys, ducks, geese, haunches of venison were displayed beside roast beef, pork, red-fish, Irish and sweet potatoes, pumpkin and apple pie, and an abundant supply of whiskey, brandy, and Hollands, without which a *fete* in Texas is nothing thought of. An hour was consumed in eating and drinking, when Sambo was summoned to take his share in the day's proceedings. Tables, such as they were, were cleared away, the floor swept, partners chosen, and, despite the remonstrance of one of the faculty present, Dr. Worcester, against dancing so shortly after a heavy meal, all present, the dissentient included, began to foot it most nimble. Never was there seen such dancing since the world began, never such laughing, such screaming, such fiddling. Every one took off shoes and stocking. I was compelled to do so, to save the toes of my especial partner, Mary, and to the rapid music of the old Negro reels and country dances were rattled off at a most surprising rate. All talked and joked and laughed, such couples as were tired retreating to seek refreshments, but the dancing never ceased, except at rare intervals, when Sambo gave in from sheer fatigue and thirst. Such was the state of things until about nine o'clock when a sudden diminution in our number was noticed by all present. Mary had before let me into the secret, and the bride and bridegroom were missed as well as the four couples who had accompanied Luke. Rushing into the open air, we descried the husband and wife on their fine black horse galloping beneath the pale moon across the prairie, escorted by their friends. A loud shout was given them, and those who remained returned to the house to renew the dancing which was kept up until a late hour. It was four days after my departure ere I regained my companions at Todville.

Such was the wedding of one of thoses hardy pioneers of civilization, whose descendants may yet be members of a great and powerful nation. I saw Luke and his wife as well as Mary on many subsequent occasions, but I never learned that the American backwoodsman repented his union with the wild Irish Diana, who had hunted deer on Murtany Island with the English stranger, could paddle a canoe with more ease than she could use the needle, and shot a duck with more facility than write her name. Luke, however, is teaching her more useful accomplishments, and Betsy ere her children—one of whom I have already seen—are of an age to require instruction will doubtless be able to render it. I hope, however, my picture will send over no one to wed Mary for though I have for the meantime returned to civilization, I cannot yet resign a certain faint notion that there might be worse lives than that of a Texian settler with such an associate.

A License to Marry

ANONYMOUS

IN THE EARLY DAYS of Texan independence and youth, an eccentric genius, still living and reigning, was clerk of one of the western counties. The village was quite secluded in the prairies, and the Squire pastured his cows on the broad acres around, bringing them home at night and letting them go to grass in the morning. He kept a bell on one of them to help him in finding them; but as he was letting them loose, he perceived that the clapper of the bell was lost out, and, being unable to find it, he made a substitute by making fast in the bell his office key. Not till he reached his office did it occur to him that he should want the key, but now finding himself locked out, he betook himself to other matters, proposing to recover the key at night. About noon a rough-and-ready young Texan in buckskin dress came riding into town, inquired for the clerk, scared him up, and asked for a marriage license.

"Sorry I can't accommodate you today, but it's no go."

"Why not? I'm going to be spliced tonight, and I must have it whether or no."

"But, the fact is," said the clerk, "my office is locked up, and *my cow is gone away with the key!*"

"The cow!—what does the cow want of the key?"

So the old fellow told the whole story, and the two set off for the prairie to find the cattle and get the key. But the more they

---

From *Spirit*, XXVII, 50 (January 23, 1858), 593. Reprinted from the "Editor's Drawer" in *Harper's*.

looked the less they found and finally had to give it up. A bright thought struck the Clerk of the County.

"I'll fix you out!" said he, and Young Texas jumped a rod, so tickled was he to know that he was to be fixed out of the fix he was in. They proceeded to a store close by the office, and there the country scribe indited the following autograph:

"*Republic of Texas:* To all who shall see this present, greeting: Whereas I, Clerk of this County, having this morning unthoughtedly tied my office key as a clapper in my cow's bell; and whereas the said cow has gone astray to parts unknown, bearing with her the said key, and therefore the said key is *non inventus est*—that is, can't be had: And whereas one Abner Barnes has made application to me for marriage license, and the said Abner persists that he cannot wait until the cow comes back with the key, but is compelled, by the violence of his feelings and the arrangements already made, to get married: Therefore these presents are to command any person legally authorized to celebrate the rites of matrimony to join the said Abner Barnes to Rebecca Downs; and for so doing this shall be your sufficient authority.

"Given under my hand and private seal, on the doorstep of my office—the seal of the office being locked up, and my cow having gone away with the key—this fourth day of October, A. D. 1838.

                                        Henry Osborne, Clerk."

Stag Parties and a Charivari

NOAH SMITHWICK

SO GREAT was the dearth of female society in San Felipe that during my whole residence there—'28 to '31—there was not a ball or party of any kind in which ladies participated. There being so little opportunity for social intercourse with the gentler sex, the sterner element should not be too severely censured if they sought diversion of a lower order. And if our stag parties were a bit convivial, they would probably compare favorably in that regard with the swell club dinners in the cities. Godwin B. Cotton was the host in many a merry bout; love feasts, he called them. Collecting a jovial set of fellows, he served them up a sumptuous supper in his bachelor apartments at which every guest was expected to contribute to the general enjoyment according to his ability. Judge Williamson was one of the leading spirits on these occasions. Having a natural bent toward the stage, Willie was equally at home conducting a revival meeting or a minstrel show, in which latter performance his wooden leg played an important part; said member being utilized to beat time to his singing. One of his best choruses was:

> Rose, Rose; coal black Rose;
> I nebber see a nigger dat I lub like Rose,

a measure admirably adapted to the banjo which he handled like a professional.

Some sang, some told stories and some danced. Luke La Sascie, a

---

From *The Evolution of a State*, pp. 70-71.

Louisiana Frenchman—and by the way a brilliant lawyer—was our champion storyteller, with Cotton and Doctor Peebles worthy competitors. I, being reckoned the most nimble-footed man in the place, usually paid my dues in jigs and hornpipes, Willie patting Juba for me. Many a night was I dragged out of bed after a hard day's work in the shop to help out an impromptu "jag."

The biggest time we ever had was on the occasion of a double wedding, the brides being a couple of grass widows who were domiciled together just out of town, their comfortable home and reputed bank account proving an irresistible attraction to a couple of good-looking young scamps who were hanging about, hence the wedding. The boys all got together and went out to charivari them. It was my first experience in that kind of a performance and was unquestionably the most outrageous din I ever heard—cowbells, cowhorns, tin pans, and in fact everything that contained noise were called into requisition; and with their discordant sounds mingled hoots, howls, and caterwaulings enough to make the hair rise on one's head. But all our efforts to bring out the happy quartette proved abortive. We overdid the thing and frightened them out of their wits; so after exhausting every device short of breaking in the door and dragging them forth, we adjourned to town to wind up. Austin never participated in these jamborees, nor did the Bordens. Sam Williams sometimes looked in, took a glass, and cracked a joke.

A True Texas Gal

"FINCK, THE ROVER"

DURING A PORTION of the three years I spent on the Texas frontier, I
served as one of Jack Hays's Rangers. On one occasion I was employed to carry an express from San Antonio to a company stationed
on the Rio Borgane [?], which is one of the tributaries of the
Brazos, about the falls.[1] My route lay from Austin, some two hundred miles through a country almost entirely without inhabitants
with no roads or guides; and, pursuing a small Indian path which
was frequently crossed by buffalo trails more clearly defined than
those of the Indians, it was not to be wondered at that I got lost
and wandered about for some time without knowing where I was
or whither I was going. Whilst in this agreeable predicament, meditating upon the pleasant prospect of sleeping out all night in a
country infested with hungry wolves which would no doubt like to
make a supper of my lean carcass, and with savage Indians who
would consider my yellow scalp a beautiful ornament to wear at
their war dances, I happened to come upon a trial which looked,
as Sam Slick[2] would say, as if it would "lead somewhere, if not somewhere else." So I followed the path which led through a rugged
pass in the Colorado hills and soon emerged into a delightful prairie
valley some four or five miles in extent, through which meandered
a beautiful stream. The banks of this stream were studded here and
there with a luxuriant growth of hackberry, live oak, and pecan. To
my delight, I soon discovered a little cabin far down the valley, and

From *Spirit*, XX, 15 (June 1, 1850). Reprinted from the New
Orleans *Delta*. "Finck, the Rover" is unidentified.

I lost no time in steering my course for it. As I approached the cabin, I observed a great quantity of skulls of various animals and the scalps and hides of buffaloes, bears, panthers, catamounts, wolves, deer, and so forth which convinced me that I was in the neighborhood of one of the frontier hunters. I rode up to the little fence which surrounded the cabin and hallooed. No person answered. I hallooed again, when out came a bonnie lass dressed up in a medley of fabrics from striped calico to dressed buffalo skins, with her hair matted and flowing down her back as free as the mane of a mustang. I do not believe that a comb had ever invaded its sacred precincts. Oh! for the pen of Hogarth to describe her figure. She was a perfect Venus in form, and did not

> Have recourse to artificial bustles
> To compensate the loss of nature's muscles.

But to my story. Our heroine threw wide open the door of the cabin, and with the air of an empress, exclaimed, "Hello, yourself!— how do you like to be called hello? Won't you get down?"

Here were two questions asked at once, and I concluded to answer the easiest one and let the other pass. I replied, "No, I thank you, Miss. Where is the gentleman of the house?" At the word *gentleman,* she turned up her nose in derision and answered rather pettishly, "We don't have no gentlemen here, but Dad is around here somewhere, though; but I guess I can tell you anything you want to know."

"Well," says I, "I wish to get directions how to go to Georgetown."

"Oh, I can tell you that, sure. You must go down by the Cuppin and jest under the hill, you'll see a big waggin-road turn off, but don't notice that; and torectly you'll see a double file horse track turn off, take that—it's the Georgetown road."

"Well, how far is it to Georgetown?" inquired I, confused and bewildered by her directions.

"Oh," said she, "it is but a little ways, seven or ten miles, I reckon, but it ain't fur, for I have been thar with Daddy a huntin many a mornin before breakfast. Are you goin to live a Georgetown?"

"No, Miss," said I, "I am carrying an express back to Ross's[3] company, on the Brazos."

"Wall, are you? Why I have got a brother in that ar company."

"Have you indeed?" said I, "and do you want to send any word to your brother?"

"Nothin perticler—but you can tell him we are all well, and his old hound slut has got nine of the purtiest pups in the world and is doin as well as could be expected."

I could stand no more, so wheeling my horse, I rode away in double quick time, whistling the popular air of "Buffalo Gals."

Giving Directions

JOHN C. DUVAL

MR. PITT and I remained at Goliad several days, and then recrossing the river we took our course towards the uppermost settlement on the Lavaca, where his relative, Col. Rivers, lived, following as closely as we could a "way bill" that had been given us by an old frontiersman. We fortunately encountered no Indians, although we passed several trails on the way. We traveled but short distances each day as Mr. Pitt had not entirely recovered from the severe spell of sickness he had at Houston, and it was not until the morning of the fourth day after leaving Goliad that we came to outskirts of the settlement on the Lavaca. Riding up to the first house we saw, we asked a woman who was standing on the porch how far it was to Col. Rivers' place. "Why, bless my soul," said she, "you must be strangers in these parts." We told her we were. "Kin folks of Col. Rivers, I reckon?" Mr. Pitt owned up to the soft impeachment. "Well, do tell," said she, "and where be ye from, now?" Having answered this and half a dozen more leading questions, Mr. Pitt inquired again how far it was to Col. Rivers' place. "Why," said she, "he's our nighest neighbor. We kin e'en a'most hear the chickens crowing over there of a right still mornin—its only five short miles." "Will you be kind enough, madam," said Mr. Pitt, "to give us the direction how to find the way there?" "To be sure," said she. "Do you see that lone tree out yander in the perara [prairie]?" Mr. Pitt said he did. "Well," said she, "keep right straight on to that tree, and arter you pass it 'bout fifty or maybe so a hundred yards, you

From *The Young Explorers,* pp. 36-38.

will come to a cow trail, but don't you take that; go right straight across it, and purty soon you'll come to another; follow that till you git to whar it splits, then take the right hand, or ruther, I should say, the left hand split, and it'll carry you into the road to Thompson's Mill. Mind though, you take the left hand split." "I thought it was the right hand?" said Mr. Pitt. "Did I say the right hand? Well I meant the left hand, anyhow," said she, "and when you git to the mill road follow that till it splits—but you keep the straight forward split to whar it strikes the bottom, and there it sprangles off, so I can't say adzackly which split you do take. Howsomever, 'taint fur, anyway, from there to Col. Rivers', and I reckon you won't go wrong."

Mr. Pitt thanked the good lady for her precise and definite direction, and we were about to turn our course towards the lone tree, when she stopped us with another question. "Anything strange," said she, "from beyant?" "Strange!" replied Mr. Pitt, "haven't you heard the news?" "Good laws!" she exclaimed. "No, I haven't. We don't see a body in these parts in a coon's age." "And in fact, then, you haven't heard the news," said Mr. Pitt. "No," said she, "I tell you I hain't," and her eyes fairly sparkled with eager expectation. "Git down, young gentlemen, and 'skin a tater', and then you can tell me all about it." "Can't stop," replied Mr. Pitt, "only long enough to tell you the news. Party split is running so high in the trans-Atlantic States upon the question of the next presidential canvass, it is supposed that thousands and tens of thousands will have great difficulty in exercising the constitutional right of suffrage."

"Good laws!" exclaimed the old lady, "you don't tell me so?" "Yes," said Mr. Pitt, riding off, "it's true as gospel." "Do stop a bit, young gentlemen," said the old lady, who hadn't understood a word of Mr. Pitt's news, but who was convinced from the dolorous expression of his countenance that something dreadful had happened somewhere, "stop and tell me all about it." "Yes," said Mr. Pitt, riding on, and pretending not to hear what she said, "it's a fact, certain," leaving the old lady in a paroxysm of unsatisfied curiosity.

When out of hearing I said, "It was too cruel, Pitt, to excite the old lady's curiosity as you have and then leave as you have without gratifying it, particularly when she was so kind to invite us to 'light and skin a tater'." "Not a bit of it," replied Mr. Pitt, "she deserved it all, and more too, for asking us so many questions and for not giving us definite directions about our way." "But the fact is," added Mr. Pitt, "I have known a great many women who were intelligent, smart, and all that, but I have never seen one yet who could give directions how to go from one place to another, though they had traveled the road dozens of times; it's a curious idiosyncrasy of woman kind." "Oh, bosh," I replied, "the old lady's directions are perfectly plain from the lone tree yonder to where the road 'sprangles out' in the bottom, and we won't have the least difficulty in following them." "I hope not," said Mr. Pitt, "for I am tired of camp fare and would greatly prefer a good supper and a comfortable bed tonight."

Hungry for News

THE NEXT MORNING after a cold snack for breakfast, as we did not think it prudent to build a fire, we mounted our horses and took the way back to our trail. Shortly after we came to it we struck a heavily timbered bottom, near the edge of which we saw a house about a half a mile to our left. Towards it we directed our course, but before we had gone more than two hundred yards we saw a man on horseback with a deer tied behind his saddle come out of the timber a short distance ahead of us. The moment he observed us he started off in a gallop towards the house, but finding we did not pursue him he halted until we got near enough for him to see we were white men and then turned to meet us. As he rode up, he said, "Hello! strangers, which way are you traveling?" We told him we were going to a settlement at the head of the Lavaca, providing the Indians didn't bag us before we got there. "Well," said he, "it's expressly against orders for anyone to pass Cayote Ranch without stopping, so you may as well hold up your hands and come along with me." "If that's Cayote Ranch," said I, pointing to the house, "we were just going there." "Oh well, that's all right," said he, "and you can drop your hands," and we then rode on together to the house. When we came to the gate in front of the house, a crowd of little darkies and dogs ran out to meet us, and our companion greeted them all by their names; but there were such a number of them crowded together and their names were so similar, I couldn't tell which belonged to the darkies and which to the dogs.

From *The Young Explorers*, pp. 22-25.

121

Dismounting, we entered the house and had scarcely taken the seats offered us, when an old Negro woman came in carrying a coffeepot and a half dozen cups on a waiter. Evidently she thought it useless to ask if we would take coffee, for she proceeded at once to fill the cups and hand them around. When she handed one to me, by the way of a joke, I told her I never drank coffee, and the expression of astonishment depicted upon her wrinkled phiz could not have been greater if I had suddenly disappeared through the floor. But seeing me smile she said, "Shaw, chile, I know you'se jokin," and poured me out a cup which I emptied with "ease and elegance." At that day it was the universal custom in Texas to present a cup of hot coffee to the visitor as soon as he entered the house, and even yet, especially in thinly populated parts of the country, the coffee-pot is kept continually on the fire. So generally was the beverage used that the expression "as common as coffee for breakfast" was as common among the old settlers as coffee itself.

Whilst we were discussing the beverage, our host informed us that he had but lately settled at that place, having moved out there only a few months previously from the red lands in Eastern Texas, which, he said, were getting to be too thickly populated to suit him. He told us we were the first strangers he had seen in several weeks, and consequently he was entirely ignorant of everything that had occurred in the States for that length of time. Mr. Pitt drew a couple of *late* New Orleans papers from his pocket (they were not more than six weeks old) and gave them to our host, saying he would find all the *late* news in them. He eagerly clutched the papers, and I have no doubt he read them faithfully through without skipping a single advertisement. Newspapers in those days were much scarcer in Western Texas than—Indians, for instance, and I don't believe our host would have bartered either of those Mr. Pitt gave him for anything of less value than a sack of coffee.

When we had finished our coffee, Mr. Pitt got up and said we had better be moving on, but our host flew off the handle at once and told us "the motion" had to be "laid on the table" indefinitely

as it was entirely against "parliamentary rules" for anyone to leave
Cayote Ranch until they had broken bread with him. "It's a fact,
though," he added, "that very often there is no bread to break on
this ranch, for it is twenty miles to the nearest horse mill, but we
have a hand mill and there's always plenty of grits. I'll tell you a
a little anecdote," continued our host, "to satisfy you there is no
prospect of your leaving Cayote until tomorrow, at any rate. I had
been at this place about three weeks without seeing a living soul
except my own family and Sol Smith, my nearest neighbor, who
lives six miles below on Burnt Root, and I was getting powerful
hungry for news, as you may suppose. One morning I had a kind
of presentiment that a traveler would come along that day, so I
picked up Old Bess, my double-barrel shotgun, and went out to
the corner of my fence near which the trail passes, and took a stand
for him. In about an hour sure enough I saw my man coming
jogging along the trail. I knew he was a green one from the States,
because he had his gun in a leather case tied to the horn of his
saddle, and no old frontiersman ever carries his in that way unless
he is with a strong crowd. I hid behind a large pecan tree and
waited till I saw he had passed the fork leading to Cayote, when
I stepped out and leveling Old Bess at him I ordered him to halt.
'My God!' he exclaimed, 'do you intend to murder me?' 'Oh no,' said
I, 'not if you obey orders and report yourself at once to headquarters according to regulation.' 'And where's that,' said he. 'Cayote
Ranch, yonder,' said I, 'so march,' and he marched whilst I followed
him with Old Bess at a present. As soon as I had got my man safely
in the house I began on him, but as I suspected he was green from
the States and chock full of news, and as he was a slow talker and
the weather was bad besides, he didn't get away from Cayote for
a week. So you see, gentlemen," continued our host, "there's no
show for you to leave here until tomorrow at any rate, for Old Bess
(pointing to the double-barrel on a rack) is in prime order with
twenty-one blue whistlers in each barrel."[4]

We laughed and told our host there would be no necessity at all to take Old Bess from the rack as we would willingly remain until morning. "But," said I, "I think it only fair to tell you that I am a very dangerous kind of character to tamper with in this way. My best girl used to say that I was like a hog—that she had to pull my ears off to get me to visit her and then pull my tail off to get me away."

Our host laughed heartily at my little joke and said, "All right, I've got you by the ears now, and if you stay here a month I'm sure I shan't change eends. Tomorrow," continued our host, "if you insist on leaving, I will ride with you to the Bernard which is pretty full and dangerous to cross for one who doesn't know the ford." This settled the question, and thanking our host for his hospitable and *pressing* invitation to make ourselves at home we proceeded to do so without ceremony. Though rather behind the times as to recent events, we found our landlord was pretty well posted otherwise, and he gave us much valuable information in regard to matters and things on the frontiers.

"Mushmillions" and "Cowcumbers"

BIGFOOT WALLACE

OCTOBER 17th [1837]—Made an early start again and went fifteen miles, when we halted to rest on a little creek called by the hunters "Burnt Boot." The country passed over high and rolling and about "half-and-half" prairie and woodland. Here is the last white settlement, I am told, we shall see for many a long day. A man by the name of Benson lives here and supports himself and family by hunting and trapping and cultivating a small patch of land. I went up to his house to see if anything in the way of vegetables could be had. Benson was out hunting, but his wife, a tall, raw-boned, hard-favored woman, as soon as she saw me coming, stepped to the door with a gun in her hand and told me to "stand"—and I stood! A half-dozen little cotton-headed children, who were playing in the yard, discovered me at this moment, and they "squandered" and squatted in the bushes like a gang of partridges.

"Who are you?" asked Mrs. Benson, pointing her gun right at me, "and what do you want here?"

"I am from the settlements below, ma'am," said I, as polite as possible, but keeping a tree between the good lady and myself all the time; for women, you know, are very awkward about handling firearms; "and," I continued, "I want to buy some vegetables, if you have any to sell."

"Well," she answered, "come in. We hain't no vegetables left now," she continued, as I walked into the cabin and took a seat on a bench, "except cowcumbers and mushmillions, and, maybe so, a

From Duval, *The Adventures of Bigfoot Wallace,* pp. 19-21.

few collards, the dratted varmints are so uncommon bad on em; but if you want any of them, you can go in the truckpatch and help yourself."

"You seem," I ventured to remark, "from the way you handled your gun to be a little suspicious of strangers in these parts."

"Yes," she said, "I am, and good reason to be so, too! Only last Saturday was a week ago some Tonk Ingens, dressed up like white folks, walked into Squire Henry's house, not more than two miles from here, and killed and sculped the whole family; but, as luck would have it, there was nobody at home, except the baby and an old nigger woman that nussed it. And which way are you travelling to?" she asked.

I told her we were going up on the headwaters of the Brazos to survey land. "Well," says she, "you'll be luckier than most everybody else that has gone up there, if you'll need more than six feet apiece before you get back. If I was your mammy, young man, you shouldn't go one foot on sich a wild-goose chase,"—and she looked so determined, I do believe, if she had been my mammy, I should never have got nearer than "Burnt Boot" to the head of the Brazos.

After some further questioning on the part of the old lady, she showed me the way into the truckpatch and filled my wallet with "mushmillions" and "cowcumbers," for which I thanked her, as she would take no pay, and started back to camp.

"Goodby, young man!" she called after me; "I feel mighty sorry for your poor mammy, for you'll never see her again."

"Well," I answered, "if I don't and you do, you must be sure and give her my kindest regards."

"You oudacious young scamp," she replied, "put out from here fast. I'll insure you against everything but hanging, which you are certain to come to."

The "mushmillions and cowcumbers" were a treat to the boys, as well as the account I gave them of the way in which the old lady had made me dodge behind the tree, when she levelled her gun at me.

A Case of Supposition

ANONYMOUS

A TEXAN who was returning home after the battle of Buena Vista, having got separated from his companions and had his horse stolen by the Indians, was obliged to take it afoot. Walking along leisurely one Sunday morning, with his rifle on his shoulder, looking out for game to make a breakfast on, without knowing what day of the week it was, he suddenly came to a small stream on the confines of Texas, not knowing that he had as yet reached the border of his native State. Perceiving that the stream abounded in fish, he took a hook and line from his pocket, and procuring some worms for bait, he sat down patiently on the bank, wrapped in a brown study, thinking of his little farm at home, when a preacher who was on a circuit rode suddenly up and thus accosted him:

"Hallo, stranger! what are you doing here?"

"Fishing for my breakfast," replied the imperturbable Texan, without deigning to look around at his interrogator.

"Well, do you know you are violating the Sabbath?" said the preacher, in a drawling, psalm-singing tone.

"No," said the Texan, turning around and looking up at the preacher for the first time with an air of surprise, which the preacher took for consternation. "I must be somewhar near the white settlement, then?"

"Yes, you are," replied the preacher, "and violating the Lord's

---

From *Spirit*, XIX, 39 (November 17, 1849), 460. Reprinted from the New Orleans *Picayune*.

Day, for which you will have to answer hereafter on the great day of judgment."

The Texan looked up with a supplicating air, and the preacher, thinking his penitent mood a good time to make him a convert, continued:

"Do you know, my young friend, that you are sitting on the verge of the broad stream of iniquity, and that without you leave here and turn into the home paths of virtue that you will be lost? Where do you think you would go to now," said the preacher, warming with his own eloquence, "supposing the angel Gabriel was to blow his horn?"

The Texan coolly hauled in his line, and, putting it in his pocket rose to his feet, and, fronting the preacher, said, "You ask me whar I think I would go to *if* the angel Gabriel should blow his horn?"

"Yes," replied the preacher.

"Well, you see, wherever thar is an *if* the case admits of an argument—now you're *supposin'* ain't you? Well, now, maybe you know what a bee gum is? Maybe you've hearn tell of these big black bar hereabouts, and maybe you've seen Injins? Well, now, supposin you was after a bee gum, and one of these black bar was after you, and a smart chance of redskins were after the bar. Now, what would you do—keep the tree from the bar, jine the bar agin the Injins, jine the Injins agin the bar, or grease and slope?"

The preacher gave the Texan one look, and rode along!

Mrs. Houstoun's Yacht Voyage to Texas

ANONYMOUS

THE NAME of Houston will be as conspicuous in the annals of Texas as the names of Romulus and Numa⁵ in those of Rome, should Texas maintain an independent existence, but whether the husband of our fair and lively tourist is any connexion of the conqueror of Santa Anna and the president of the republic, we do not know. Mrs. Houstoun, however, is an Englishwoman, Mr. Houstoun a sportsman; and they determined to undertake a yacht voyage to the New World, the wife in search of health and the husband of game. Accordingly, about the middle of last September, they started from Blackwall in the schooner *Dolphin;* encountered the usual gale "in the Bay of Biscay O"; called at Madeira, Barbadoes, and Jamaica; twice visited both New Orleans and Galveston, the seaport of Texas; made a steamboat trip up the Buffalo Bayou river to Houston, a city that is to be; and looked in at Cuba and Bermuda as they returned home. This consummation occurred in May last, and now in the two volumes before us we have a very animated and pleasant account of what appears to have been a very pleasant excursion. . . .

[Mrs. Houstoun says] The city of Houston was our headquarters during our stay up the country; and greatly did we regret that the state of the prairie owing to the constant and heavy rains prevented our travelling as far as Washington which city we had intended to have visited. The scarcity and indifference of the accommodations would not have deterred us from such an undertaking, but in a

From *Littell's Living Age,* II (August-October, 1844), 476-78. Reprinted from the *Spectator.*

country where roads do not exist it is difficult not to lose one's way. The danger is considerably increased when the trail of previous travellers is obliterated by the rains, for "plumbing the track", the Texan term for tracing a road, is at all times a slow and tedious operation. Between Houston and Washington there is a certain space of two miles which, when we were in the country, was not traversed in less time than four hours so deep was the mire.

Even at Galveston, the first city in the country, things do not seem vastly better for a little excursion.

The only "drive" is on the sea-beach; and a most beautiful beach it is—so hard and smooth with its fine sand that you scarcely hear your horse's foot fall as he trots, or rather runs along, a light carriage behind him and the broad prairie spreading far before. Occasionally you are—I was going to say stopped but I should have been wrong—no one is stopped in this country by anything short of a bowie knife or a rifle ball; but your progress is delayed by an interesting bayou, through which you have to wade, or swim, as the case may be. There is neither time nor spare cash to erect bridges, and indeed were the expense to be incurred, the probability is they would be washed away by the first rain or by a more than usually high tide. Bridges, then, being out of the question, nothing is left you but to make the best of such means of transport as are within your reach. If you fortunately chance to meet with any person who has lately crossed, you ask, "Well, sir, is it swimming?" Should the answer be in the affirmative and you happen to be on horseback, equipped for a journey with your plunder (luggage) about you, you "up saddle-bags" and boldly plunge into the stream. Should your route lie along the shore, the safest plan is to go a good way out to sea—on, on—till you find yourself well out among the breakers. I confess that at first this struck me as rather alarming proceeding, but in fact it is much the safest plan; there is always a bar of sand formed across the mouth of these bayous, and if you can hit that the depth of water is much lessened.

Nor does there seem much in the social state of Texas to counterbalance the material evils. Mrs. Houstoun admits three drawbacks to British emigration—a total insecurity of titles to land, the *smartness* of the Texans, who when they deal with a Britisher generally end by completely "shaving" him, that is, possessing themselves of all his substance, and the want of adaptability in the British character to qualify our settlers to meet the new and endless demands upon ingenuity. She says there are a great many lawyers in Texas, and a vast many laws—the Assembly having been industrious enough in this kind of work. Mrs. Houstoun makes it a ground of panegyric that there is little law among them—which seems to be true enough.

At present, however, the Texan people go on remarkably well with their primitive system of administering justice. During the months we remained in Galveston Harbor, there was no single instance of malicious crime—no street fights, no apparent drunkenness or tumult. It is true that on New Year's day one man was shot; and doubtless this fact would to those ignorant of the details furnish a strong argument in favor of the popular opinion of the prevalence of crime in Texas. The circumstances were as follows. Some children were quarrelling in the street; from words they came to blows; when their respective parents who had been drinking together thought proper to interfere. "I say, sir, you call your children away, sir!" This gentle remonstrance not being duly attended to, the speaker went forthwith for his rifle and was in the act of presenting it at the head of his foe (probably only as a means of intimidation) when he received his deathwound from the other's pistol. No notice whatever was taken of this *misdemeanor*.

At seven o'clock in the morning we arrived at the pretty town of Houston; it is built on high land, and the banks which are covered with evergreens rise abruptly from the river. There are plenty of inns at Houston, such as they are. We took up our quarters at the "Houston House," a large shambling wooden building, kept by a Captain or Colonel Baldwin, one of the most civil, obliging people I ever saw. We had a sittingroom which was weatherproof, though to keep out the intense cold was impossible. It was said that our landlord was anxious to add to the comforts of his house, but he had a great many bad debts. It was, he told us, a losing concern altogether; more went out than came in. Only that morning, having asked a gentleman to pay his bill, the reply was, "If you come to insult me again, sir, by——I'll shoot you, sir!"

The First and Last Chance

JOHN C. DUVAL

AT THAT DAY there was truly a hard set congregated in Houston. It seemed to me that the sole business of most of them was drinking liquor and playing cards, varied now and then by a little recreation in the way of target shooting at each other with their double-barrel guns and derringers. I was walking leisurely along Main Street, when I heard the reports of two or three pistols in rapid succession, and shortly afterwards I noticed a small crowd collected in front of a shanty, over the door of which was a board with the following legend inscribed on one side: "The First Chance" and on the other "The Last Chance," thus appropriately soliciting the custom of thirsty wayfarers, coming into or going out of town.

I stepped up to one of the crowd collected around this "juicery" and inquired if anything unusual had happened. "No," said he, "nothing more'n common. Bob Sprowls and Arkansaw Jake had a little misunderstanding 'bout a game of poker just now, and Jake 'upped him' with a derringer, that's all." "And where is Sprowls now?" said I. "Well, some of his friends carried him off to the drug-store to see if the doctor could do anything for him, but I reckon he can't do much for a fellow that's got a half ounce bullet through his lights." "And where is Arkansaw Jake now?" I asked. "Have they arrested him?" "Arrested thunderation!" replied my informant, "you must be green from the States—he's in there," pointing to the door of the "juicery." "Seth Blake has taken Sprowls' hand, and they are finishing the game—and by the by, my young man," he continued,

From *The Young Explorers*, p. 7.

"you'd better get out of the range of that door, for I hearn Arkansaw
Jake jes now tell Seth he was renigging, and I reckon 'twont be long
afore another derringer goes off."

NOTES TO SECTION III

1. The Falls of the Brazos are located near the present town of Marlin,
Falls County. In the days of steamboats the falls were the head of navigation,
and an early town located there was called Bucksnort.

2. Sam Slick is the main character in a series of books of popular humor
by Thomas Chandler Haliburton (1796-1865), Canadian jurist, author, and
compiler of *Traits of American Humor*, a three-volume anthology of humorous
sketches. Beginning in 1837 with *The Clockmaker; Or, The Sayings and Doings of Samuel Slick*, Haliburton wrote five volumes featuring Sam Slick. Most
of his books were reissued many times, making the name of his Yankee a house-
hold word. (Walter Blair, *Native American Humor* [New York, 1937], pp.
183-84.)

3. Lawrence Sullivan Ross (1838-98) was a captain in the Texas Rangers;
among his more important feats was the capture of Cynthia Ann Parker. Ross
fought in the Texas Brigade in the Civil War, was governor of Texas (1887-
91), and was president of Texas A & M College from 1891 until his death.

4. A similar story is told in Joseph G. Baldwin's *Flush Times of Alabama
and Mississippi* (1853) about a Virginian who migrated to the Alabama
frontier, where people were scarce. He would wait beside a difficult stream
crossing and take travelers home with him at gun point in order to have some-
one to talk to.

5. Numa was the legendary second king of Rome who initiated fire-
worship.

IV
Heroes, Big and Small

IV. Heroes, Big and Small

SOME EARLY TEXAS HEROES *were more widely praised outside Texas than at home—Sam Houston, for example. Despite his being universally acclaimed in the United States as the Hero of San Jacinto, he had his troubles with his fellow Texians. One wonders why Austin, Fannin, and Bonham have not been more kindly treated in popular stories; it may be that the feeling of sacredness that has surrounded some of the founding fathers and heroes of the Alamo has prevented the clustering around their names of the flesh-and-blood stories by means of which popular heroes are made. They could not be treated humorously, as could Bigfoot Wallace, say, or Three-Legged Willie.*

So it was in the reports of outsiders that early Texas heroes first begin to assume the roles they were later to play in the development of the Texas myth.

Booth and Samuel Houston

ANONYMOUS

ONE EVENING during the winter of 1834 as Booth,[1] the celebrated tragedian, was walking up Pennsylvania Avenue in the city of Washington, he accosted an old friend from the west whom he had not seen for many years. After mutual expressions of surprise and salutation, these two singular men walked arm in arm to Brown's Hotel, where both had taken lodgings. In the whole country, perhaps, there could not be found two other more passionately fond of excitement, more remarkable in their habits, or more noted for their eccentricities. Retiring to a private room, they sat down to recount the story of their past lives, and as they industriously circulated the bottle many a loud shout echoed through that hall and startled the watchmen in the street as they went their silent rounds. As the night wore on their excitement increased until at the close of a thrilling story relating to his strange career, his companion exclaimed: "Now, Booth, let's have a speech to liberty—one of those apostrophes to Old Roman freedom with which you startle audiences!"

Had Booth been inclined to refuse, he knew that his friend when the mood was on him would not be denied any request, however absurd or difficult the performance. But the tragedian had himself entered into the spirit of his companion, and nothing loath he rehearsed with magic power many of those electric passages in defence of liberty with which the English drama abounds. His friend,

From the *Richmond* (La.) *Compiler*, I, 31 (February 1, 1842), 1. Reprinted from the St. Louis *Reporter*.

138

whose memory as well as habits partook of the Indian character, caught up the words and with equal force, clearness, and accuracy went through each speech in regular succession. Thus they proceeded for a time and then again sat down upon the floor of that chamber to renew their potations and the story of their personal adventures. Booth drank and listened whilst the other told of his own elevation in his native state, of his disgust at civic honors, of his home in the distant forest, of the uncontrolled freedom of the redmen, of their stoic fortitude and matchless heroism. Warmed by the recollection of those thrilling scenes, he sprang at last to his feet, and, in the tone of one amid the battle's din, fighting against fearful odds, exclaimed, "Now, Booth, once more for liberty!"

The tragedian dared not disobey. He ran through with all his usual energy the tale of Mexican thraldom, the Spanish conquest of that land, the dangers incurred by the invading army, their commander's exhortation before the battle, and the stubborn bravery of the native chiefs. Before him stood, at that lone hour, listening with an intensity of thought and feeling which shone through his eyes and which lightened o'er his face, strained every muscle, and started the sweat in great drops from his lofty brow, one who had all the spirit of a Cortes and ambition of a Pizzarro. Quick as thought he took up the task and repeated the words just uttered by Booth with the most critical precision of tone and manner.

The scene was one of no small moment, it may be, to a nation's history. As he became excited in the recitation, his spirit seemed to take fire—and with an air so strange, so determined, so frightful that it seemed the voice of one inspired, he exclaimed at the close of a masterly extemporaneous rhapsody, "Yes! yes! I am made to revel yet in the halls of the Montezumas."

Booth's companion on that night is now President of Texas, the hero of San Jacinto. And who can say that the words uttered by him in that hour of excitement are destined never to be fulfilled. Sam Houston, if ever "coming events cast their shadows before," *will* yet revel in the halls of the Montezumas.

Sam Houston

ANONYMOUS

THE "Hero of San Jacinto" is not much troubled with *mauvaise honte*. He is a fine looking man and would not be taken for more than fifty years of age although he must be near sixty. In his rollicking speech on Friday night in the Park, he told some capital stories and laid bait for complimentary notices with singular adroitness. "I have come to this city," said he, "the companion of men far more distinguished in the history of my country than myself."

Here, of course, there were loud cries of "No!" "no!" "*no!*"

"Well, gentlemen," said the Senator from Texas, "as you please. There was once a boy who came home drunk to his mother, and when she scolded him, he vowed that 'they had *forced* it down him.' 'Pshaw!' said his mother, 'I don't believe it.' 'Well, mother,' said he, 'they were *going* to force it down me, and so, seeing that, I took it freely.'

"Now, gentlemen," said Gen. Houston, "seeing that you *will* force this distinction down me, *I'll take it freely!*"

The story was admirably eked out with staggering and hiccoughing, as "natural as life." Gen. Houston would make a first rate comedian, should all other trades fail.

From the New Orleans *Picayune*, XII, 135 (June 29, 1848), 2. Reprinted from the *New York Sunday Times*.

James Bowie, the Napoleon of Duelists

ANONYMOUS

FOUR YEARS AGO, when Theodore Parker, the eminent theophilan-thropic preacher of Boston, visited Europe, having a letter of intro-duction for that purpose, he called on Thomas Carlyle. The English solitaire plied the American with innumerable questions relating to our customs and habits of social existence on this side of the great water, but manifested the keenest curiosity concerning the people of the backwoods. Parker drew, for the other's amusement, a vivid sketch of the achievements of Bowie, the famous arch-duelist of Texas. Carlyle listened with sparkling eyes to the close of the narra-tive and then burst into exclamations of involuntary enthusiasm: "By Hercules! the man was greater than Caesar or Cromwell—nay, nearly equal to Odin or Thor. The Texans ought to build him an altar!"

The burning sympathizer with the heroic in all its phases rubbed his hands together, chuckled in an ecstacy of savage glee and made Parker repeat his story of bloody anecdotes. Finally he put the ques-tion, "But by what miracle could it happen that the brave fellow escaped the capital penalty of the law after such countless viola-tions?"

To this interrogatory, Parker, as he himself confessed, could re-turn no satisfactory answer; and as ten thousand readers have per-haps pondered the same problem without conceiving a rational

From *Spirit*, XX, 21 (July 13, 1850), 243-44. Reprinted from the *New York Sunday Times*.

solution, it may not be uninteresting to explain it briefly, especially as a clear elucidation can be detailed in a few words.

Let it be remembered, then, that although the great system of common law, that perfection of human reason for the Anglo-Saxon race, prevails throughout all the states of the West, wholly as to its definition of crimes and partially as to the mode and measure of punishment annexed to each; nevertheless, in its practical application to given cases, it is controlled by the power of a far mightier law—the omnipotent law of public opinion; because in most Western courts juries are absolute judges of both the law and the fact, and their interpretations often evince direct antagonism with the *dicta* of my Lord Coke and the classic comments of Blackstone.[2]

On the subject of homicide in particular, public opinion has passed the bounds of all books of jurisprudence and settled as an immutable statute this extraordinary axiom: It is justifiable to kill in fair combat, everybody and anybody who ought to be killed!

In Bowie's numerous rencontres, he always kept within the prescribed rule of latitudinarian rule, and hence he was always acquitted by frontier juries, and frequently with *addenda* to their verdicts highly complimentary to his character as a chivalrous gentleman. In truth, most of his desperate engagements grew out of his innate and invincible disposition to espouse the cause of the weak against the mighty. One illustration, by incident, will present this peculiarity in the strongest light and may besides reveal a thorough knowledge of the heart and soul of the man.

On the evening of the fourth of June, 1835, the steamboat *Rob Roy* started from St. Louis to New Orleans with a full crowd of passengers. Immediately after getting under good headway (to adopt a favorite backwood phrase), one person attracted universal attention by the annoying eagerness with which he endeavored to make up a party at cards. Indeed, his oft-repeated and persevering efforts to that end soon became insulting and unendurable, and yet his appearance was such as to deter the bravest on board from administering the chastisement which he so richly deserved. He was a huge mass of mighty bone and muscle, with swarthy features bearing the impress of many a scar; piercing black eyes that seemed to possess the power of blasting the beholder—cold, gleaming eyes, such as haunt the memory painfully; a rank luxuriance of coal black hair; immense whiskers and moustache. This savage-looking figure was habited in the costliest clothing and adorned with a profusion of jewelry, while the outlines of several murderous weapons were plainly distinguished beneath his gaudy vest and superfine coat. Nor did he need these to render him an object of terror. A connoisseur in the science of belligerent gymnastics would have confidently pronounced him a match for any five men on the deck without any aid from lead or cold steel.

At length, after many failures, he prevailed upon a wealthy young merchant of Natchez to join him in a game of poker. They sat down beside a small table near the bar and were soon absorbed in that most perilous of excitements, of which the two alluring ingredients are the vanity and pride of individual skill and the uncertainty of general hazard. At first the stakes were small and the run of cards seemed wholly in favor of the merchant, but presently they bet more freely, and gold eagles and hundred dollar notes were showered down with extravagant ardor; and then the current of fortune changed—ebbed away from the young merchant and flowed to the professional gambler in a stream like the ocean's tide. As usually happens in such cases, his want of success only piqued and maddened the loser, and he sought to recover himself by venturing such desperate ventures as could not but deepen and confirm his ruin. And thus they continued during a whole summer night.

The intensity of their excitement became equivalent to insanity. Every nerve was strung, every energy of the brain was taxed to the utmost—teeth were set hard as those of antagonists in the tug of mortal strife—the sweat rolled from their brows like great drops of rain.

The passengers formed a circle around the players and looked on with that interest which such extraordinary concentration of intellect

and passion never fails to inspire, even in bosoms that shudder at
its success. The merchant and the gambler attracted all eyes and
kept many awake and gazing till morning. Among the latter was
one presenting a countenance so piteous that it might have melted
hearts of marble to tears. A pale and exquisitely beautiful face
peeped incessantly from the half-opened door of the ladies' cabin,
weeping all the while, as if impressed by some dreadful sensation of
irremediable sorrow. It was the merchant's lovely wife, weeping her
farewell to departing hope.

There was one spectator, also, whose appearance and action excited almost as much curiosity as the players did themselves. He
was a tall, spare man of about thirty with handsome features,
golden hair, keen blue eyes of preternatural brightness, and his firm
thin lips wore a perpetual smile—mysterious smile of the strangest,
the most inscrutable meaning. With the exception of his red calico
shirt, this person was dressed wholly in buckskin, ornamented with
long swaying tassels, and wild figures wrought out of variegated
beads, after the fashion of some Western Indians. He stood close
beside the card table and held in his left hand a sheet of paper, in
his right a large pencil, with which he ever and anon dashed off a
few words, as if engaged in tracing the progress of the game.

Still the merchant and the gambler persevered in their physical
and mental toil. The dial of the stars with its thousand fingers of
golden fire pointed to the world-shadows of midnight, but still they
did not pause. It still was "shuffle and cut, and pass ante up, and I
call you, and rake down the pile." Toward the morning a tremendous storm arose. The red lightning flashed awfully—the hail
poured like a frozen cataract—the great river roared till it rivalled
the loudest thunder of Heaven, and the very pilot at the wheel was
alarmed. But the mad players heard it not. What was the tumult of
the raging elements to those whose destiny hung upon the turning
of a card? And the smiling blue-eyed stranger in buckskin still stood
by them with his pencil and paper, calmly noticing the develop-
ments of the game.

Finally the storm passed, as the beautiful daybreak came out like a thing of glory in the grey east. Then the infatuated merchant, distracted with his heavy losses, dared the climax of folly. He staked five thousand dollars, comprising his last cent of money in the world, on two pairs of kings. The whiskered gambler called him; they showed hands; the blackleg had two pairs of aces and raked the board. The merchant dropped to the floor as if he had been shot through the brain, and that beautiful young wife flew to his side and fell shrieking upon his bosom. They were both borne away insensible to the ladies' cabin.

As he deposited the winnings in his pocket, the gambler emitted a hoarse laugh that sounded frightful as the chuckle of a fiend, but he instantly lost color as a low, calm voice remarked in his ear, "Villain, you play a strong hand at many different games, but here stands one who can beat you at all of them!"

He turned, met the glance of those keen blue eyes so preternaturally bright, and shuddered. But he immediately regained his presence of mind—for he was a coward—and then he frowned until his shaggy brows met like the coil of a serpent, and demanded sternly, "Beggar, who are you to banter a gentleman thus rudely?"

"I am James Bowie of Texas," the other answered with a ringing laugh, "and you are John Lafitte, a bastard of the old pirate!"[3]

The gambler reeled in his chair as if he had been struck with a thunderbolt, but recovering again from the shock in a moment, asked in a firm tone, "What game do you wish with me?"

"*Poker* first, and *pistols* afterwards, if you play foul," replied Bowie.

"Very well," rejoined the other, and they took their seats at the table. For a time the success seemed about equally balanced, the gain and loss being alternate. At last the gambler ventured one of his skillful manoeuvres in dealing. Bowie smiled strangely as his quick eye detected the trick. He said nothing, however, but looked at his hand and bet five thousand dollars, staking the money in ten large bills. The gambler went five thousand dollars higher, which resulted in a "call." Bowie held four jacks, but with his habitual fiendish chuckle his antagonist showed four queens, exclaiming as he did so, "By heaven! the pile is mine!"

"Not yet," shouted Bowie, as with both hands he raked a heap of notes to the tune of twenty thousand dollars into his own pocket. Choking and purple with rage and shame, the gambler roared, "To the hurricane deck, and let pistols be trumps this turn!"

"Good as gold!" replied Bowie, and the two hastily ascended the stairs and assumed the separate positions—the gambler over the stern and Bowie over the bow.

At that instant the sun was just rising in a cloudless sky. Nature looked sublime. The woods and waters appeared as parts of one divine picture with the boundless blue of heaven for its background. The broad-bosomed river rolled away like an immense sheet of burnished silver, speckled here and there with the flash of golden bubbles; shining fishes gamboled in the sparkling wave; and all the bright birds—those sweet singers, whose life is a dream and that dream only music—chanted their wild anthem to the new day; while the two great duelists, the most deadly ever known in the Southwest, stood with cocked pistols, eye to eye, and their fingers fixed on the hair-triggers, prepared and waiting to slay and be slain.

"I am ready. You give the word," cried Bowie in his clear, ringing voice and with that inseparable smile of strange meaning on his lips.

"I am ready. Fire!" shouted the gambler in tones murderous as death.

The two pistols roared simultaneously. Bowie did not move, though he barely escaped with his life, for the bullet of his foe had cut away one of the golden locks of his yellow hair. The gambler was shot through the heart and dropping on the brink of the deck had almost tumbled into the river. He was buried by the squatters at the next wood-yard. And thus perished, justly, a bastard son of the great pirate Lafitte.

There never was a jury empanelled in the West who would have brought in a verdict against any man for killing him and more especially under the circumstances because public opinion pronounced that he ought to be killed. And such were the desperadoes that Bowie commonly exterminated.

The generous victor immediately proceeded to the ladies' cabin and restored the winnings of the gambler to the young merchant and his beautiful wife who both received the boon as a gift from Heaven with much gratitude and joy.

If we should write a volume concerning the exploits of James Bowie, his character could not be rendered more transparent than it is revealed in the foregoing anecdote. He was always the same— the friend of the feeble, the protector of the oppressed, and the sworn enemy of tyrants. He was brave without fear, generous beyond precedent; and though he had faults, gigantic ones, too, he atoned for all the errors of a stormy life by the splendor of his magnificent death. His tomb is the Alamo, his epitaph the word "Texas," and his fame will fill a humble though safe niche in the Temple of Freedom through all time. He can never be forgotten till the bowels of the earth cease to furnish metal for the fabrication of those bright blades of steel which bear his imperishable name.

Colonel James Bowie

ANONYMOUS

COL. BOWIE was undoubtedly a man of vigorous intellect as well as of firm and flintlike nerve. His character is one of bold and captivating individuality and would form a magnificent study for some native novelist. We say "some," meaning only a few, and we will mention Simms[4] as one; there are also "some" that we hope will never mar so excellent a subject. From the wild forest life to which his bold and daring nature led him and the deeds and scenes in which he constantly appeared as the master-spirit, an untractable and coarse disposition is apt to be imputed to him, yet directly the opposite of this was one of Col. Bowie's most distinguishing traits of character. His manners in social intercourse were bland and gentle, so much so as to heighten materially the interest of his character. He spoke with slow and impressive intonation, nicely *ar-tic-u-la-ting ev-e-ry* syllable he uttered and with strict yet easy politeness observing every form of delicacy and good-breeding. In society he was stared at as a lion; but acquaintance attracted a gentler interest towards him, and it was curious as well as pleasant to find how the lord of the forest had known the embrace of the lamb. The following anecdote relates immediately to Rezin, but, being here giving as told by the Colonel himself, it will be found to convey a very vivid and just idea of both men's characters.

In one of the Texan wilds a brave little band of which the Colonel and Rezin were as usual the leading men fell into an engagement with a vastly superior number of mounted Camanches. Upon de-

From the New Orleans *Picayune*, V, 108 (June 2, 1841), 2.

tecting his red enemies, Colonel Bowie so manoeuvred his men as completely to conceal his inferiority of force, and, securing a position for defense, he very coolly awaited the moment for action. A favorable chance for execution soon occurred, and a few American rifles began to blaze away upon the savages in such a manner as to convince them that the party told about double its actual number. Still the Camanches were appearing in all directions flying about in great force, and the condition of the little American party became extremely critical. Once knowing the possession of advantage, these Indians are sufficiently warlike and daring to be of very respectable consideration as enemies, even to Americans, though until they obtain this confidence they will seldom venture upon much hazard. Now, every moment seemed to convey information to the Camanches of the miserable weakness of Bowie's party, and the Colonel disposed his men with the coolest caution in expectation of an overwhelming assault.

In such ticklish emergencies it is customary for a hunter to pat his good rifle affectionately and say, "I'm sure of at least *one* man before I fall!" but it seems Rezin Bowie had made up his mind for *two*. Rezin possessed the best rifle in camp—a weapon which was considered by connoisseurs a perfect prince of shooting irons and with which its owner was as sure of his mark as of lifting food direct to his mouth. At this position of the opponents, the Colonel observed his brother reclining behind a log with his favorite rifle in rest across it, his eye to the sight, the hair trigger sprung, and his finger in place for sending out the well-directed leaden messenger.

Looking in the direction of Rezin's aim, the Colonel saw two mounted Camanches (important chiefs, as appeared by the gleaming of their ornaments in the sun) dashing about, farther, then nearer apart, and seeming to be a pair of the most daring warriors, endeavoring to learn the true condition of the American party. They were beyond the reach of any ordinary rifle, where they took care to keep, but the Colonel knew that Rezin's beautiful weapon was equal to the distance and wondered why he delayed firing.

"Brother Rezin," said the Colonel in the smooth and deliberate manner which we have attempted to describe; "Brother Rezin, do you not see those two red rascals wheeling about there near each other? Why don't you pull one of them down from his horse?"

"Don't hurry me, brother James," returned Rezin, keeping his eye steady upon the sight and speaking slowly like the Colonel. "If I pull *one* of the red rascals down, brother, the other red rascal will get out of my reach; but wait till they *lap*, and then I'll pull them both down, brother James."

"They *did* lap, gentlemen," said Colonel Bowie (and these were the brave fellow's own words as he used to tell the story); "they *did* lap—Rezin pulled the trigger—and, as I an hon-est gen-tle-man, they *both fell from their horses!*"

The engagement with the Indians terminated with some loss to Bowie's party, but the two brothers lived to pass through many perilous adventures after that.

Deaf Smith

ANONYMOUS

ABOUT TWO YEARS after the Texan revolution, a difficulty occurred between the new government and a portion of the people which threatened the most serious consequences, even the bloodshed and horrors of civil war. Briefly, the cause was this: The constitution had fixed the city of Austin as the permanent capital where the public archives were to be kept with the reservation, however, of a power in the president to order their temporary removal in case of danger from the inroads of a foreign enemy or the force of a sudden insurrection.

Conceiving that the exceptional emergency had arrived as the Comanches frequently committed ravages within sight of the capital itself, Houston, who then resided at Washington-on-the-Brazos, dispatched an order commanding his subordinate functionaries to send the state records to the latter place where he declared to be, *pro tempore,* the seat of government.

It is impossible to describe the stormy excitement which the promulgation of this *fiat* raised in Austin. The keepers of hotels, boardinghouses, groceries, and faro banks were thunderstruck, maddened to frenzy; for the measure would be a death blow to their pros-

From *Littell's Living Age,* XXIV (January-March, 1850), 604-6. Reprinted from *Noah's Weekly Messenger. Deaf* was then pronounced *deef,* as it still is among country people in the Texas Panhandle where Deaf Smith County is located. Erastus (Deaf) Smith (1787-1837), born in New York, was a scout during the Texas Revolution. Houston placed him in command of a company. Smith later lived at Richmond, Fort Bend County, where he died.

perity in business; and accordingly they determined at once to take the necessary steps to avert the danger by opposing the execution of Houston's mandate. They called a mass meeting of the citizens and farmers of the circumjacent country who were all more or less interested in the question, and after many fiery speeches against the asserted tyranny of the administration, it was unanimously resolved to prevent the removal of the archives by open and armed resistance. To that end they organized a company of four hundred men, one moiety of whom, relieving the other at regular periods of duty, should keep constant guard around the statehouse until the peril passed by. The commander of this force was one Colonel Morton, who had achieved considerable renown in the war for independence and had still more recently displayed desperate bravery in two desperate duels, in both of which he had cut his antagonist nearly to pieces with the bowie knife. Indeed, from the notoriety of his character for revenge as well as courage, it was thought that President Houston would renounce his purpose touching the archives so soon as he should learn who was the leader of the opposition.

Morton, on his part, whose vanity fully equalled his personal prowess, encouraged and justified the prevailing opinion by his boastful threats. He swore that if the president did succeed in removing the records by the march of an overpowering force, he would then himself hunt him down like a wolf and shoot him with little ceremony, or stab him in his bed, or waylay him in his walks of recreation. He even wrote the hero of San Jacinto to that effect. The latter replied in a note of laconic brevity: "If the people of Austin do not send the archives, I shall certainly come and take them, and if Colonel Morton can kill me, he is welcome to my ear-cap."

On the reception of this answer, the guard was doubled around the statehouse. Chosen sentinels were stationed along the road leading to the capital, the military paraded the streets from morning till night, and a select caucus held permanent session in the city hall. In short, everything betokened a coming tempest.

One day, while matters were in this precarious condition, the caucus at the city hall was surprised by the sudden appearance of a stranger, whose mode of entering was as extraordinary as his looks and dress. He did not knock at the closed door—he did not seek admission there at all; but climbing unseen a small bushy-topped live oak which grew beside the wall, he leaped without sound or warning through a lofty window. He was clothed altogether in buckskin, carried a long and very heavy rifle in his hand, wore at the button of his left suspender a large bowie knife, and had in his leathern belt a couple of pistols half the length of his gun. He was tall, straight as an arrow, active as a panther in his motions, with dark complexion and luxuriant jetty hair, with a severe, iron-like countenance that seemed never to have known a smile, and eyes of intense, vivid black, wild and rolling, and piercing as the point of a dagger. His strange advent inspired a thrill of involuntary fear, and many present unconsciously grasped the handles of their sidearms.

"Who are you that thus presumes to intrude among gentlemen without invitation?" demanded Colonel Morton, ferociously essaying to cow down the stranger with his eye. The latter returned his stare with compound interest and laid his long, bony finger on his lip as a sign—but of what the spectators could not imagine.

"Who are you? Speak! or I will cut an answer out of your heart!" shouted Morton, almost distracted with rage by the cool, sneering gaze of the other, who now removed his finger from his lip and laid it on the hilt of his monstrous knife.

The fiery colonel then drew his dagger and was in the act of advancing upon the stranger, when several caught him and held him back, remonstrating. "Let him alone, Morton, for God's sake. Do you not perceive that he is crazy?"

At that moment Judge Webb, a man of shrewd intellect and courteous manners, stepped forward and addressed the intruder in a most respectful manner: "My good friend, I presume you have made a mistake in the house. This is a private meeting where none but members are admitted." The stranger did not appear to comprehend the words, but he could not fail to understand the mild

and deprecatory manner. His rigid features relaxed, and moving to
a table in the center of the hall where there were materials and im-
plements for writing, he seized a pen and traced one line: "I am
deaf." He then held it up before the spectators as a sort of natural
apology for his want of politeness.

Judge Webb took the paper and wrote a question. "Dear sir, will
you be so obliging as to inform us what is your business with the
present meeting?" The other responded by delivering a letter inscribed on the back, "To the citizens of Austin." They broke the seal
and read it aloud. It was from Houston and showed the usual terse
brevity of his style: "Fellow Citizens: Though in error and deceived
by the arts of traitors I will give you three days more to decide
whether you will surrender the public archives. At the end of that
time you will please let me know your decision.

                                                        Sam Houston."

After the reading, the deaf man waited a few seconds as if for a
reply and then turned and was about to leave the hall when Colonel
Morton interposed and sternly beckoned him back to the table. The
stranger obeyed, and Morton wrote: "You were brave enough to
insult me by your threatening looks ten minutes ago; are you brave
enough now to give me satisfaction?"

The stranger penned his reply: "I am at your service!"

Morton wrote again: "Who will be your second?"

The stranger rejoined: "I am too generous to seek an advantage
and too brave to fear any on the part of others; therefore I never
need the aid of a second."

Morton penned: "Name your terms."

The stranger traced without a moment's hesitation: "Time, sunset
this evening; place, the left bank of the Colorado, opposite Austin;
weapons, rifles; distance, a hundred yards. Do not fail to be in time!"
He then took three steps across the floor and disappeared through
the window as he had entered.

"What!" exclaimed Judge Webb, "is it possible, Colonel Morton,
that you intend to fight that man? He is a mute, if not a positive

maniac. Such a meeting, I fear, will sadly tarnish the lustre of your laurels."

"You are mistaken," replied Morton with a smile. "That mute is a hero, whose fame stands in the record of a dozen battles and at least half as many bloody duels. Besides, he is the favorite emissary and bosom friend of Houston. If I have the good fortune to kill him, I think it will tempt the president to retract his vow against venturing any more on the field of honor."

"You know the man, then. Who is he? Who is he?" asked twenty voices together.

"Deaf Smith," answered Morton, coolly.

"Why no. That cannot be. Deaf Smith was slain at San Jacinto," remarked Judge Webb.

"There, again, you honor is mistaken," said Morton. "The story of Smith's death was a mere fiction, got up by Houston to save the life of his favorite from the sworn vengeance of certain Texans, in whose conduct he had acted as a spy. I fathomed the artifice twelve months since."

"If what you say be true, you are a madman yourself!" exclaimed Webb. "Deaf Smith was never known to miss his mark. He has often brought down ravens in their most rapid flight and killed Comanches and Mexicans at a distance of two hundred and fifty yards!"

"Say no more," answered Colonel Morton in tones of deep determination; "the thing is already settled. I have already agreed to meet him. There can be no disgrace in falling before such a shot, and if I succeed my triumph will confer the greater glory!"

Such was the general habit of thought and feeling prevalent throughout Texas at that period.

Towards evening a vast crowd assembled at the place appointed to witness the hostile meeting, and so great was the popular recklessness as to affairs of the sort that numerous and considerable sums were wagered on the result. At length the red orb of the summer sun touched the curved rim of the western horizon, covering it all with crimson and gold and filling the air with a flood of burning glory; and then the two mortal antagonists, armed with long, ponderous rifles, took their station, back to back, and at a preconcerted signal—the waving of a white handkerchief—walked slowly and steadily off in opposite directions, counting their steps until each had measured fifty. They both completed the given number about the same instant, and then they wheeled, each to aim and fire when he chose. As the distance was great, both paused for some seconds—long enough for the beholders to flash their eyes from one to the other and mark the striking contrast betwixt them. The face of Col. Morton was calm and smiling, but the smile it bore had a most murderous meaning. On the contrary, the countenance of Deaf Smith was as stern and passionless as ever. A side view of his features might have been mistaken for a profile done in cast iron. The one, too, was dressed in the richest cloth, the other in smoke-tinted leather. But that made no difference in Texas then; for the heirs of heroic courage were all considered peers—the class of inferiors embraced none but cowards.

Presently two rifles exploded with simultaneous roars. Colonel Morton gave a prodigious bound upwards and dropped to the earth a corpse. Deaf Smith stood erect and immediately began to reload his rifle. Having finished his brief task, he hastened away into the adjacent forest.

Three days afterwards General Houston, accompanied by Deaf Smith and ten more men, appeared in Austin and without further opposition removed the state papers.

The history of the hero of the foregoing anecdote was one of the most extraordinary ever known in the West. He made his advent in Texas at an early period and continued to reside there until his death, which happened some two years ago. Although he had many warm personal friends, no one could ever ascertain either the land of his birth or a single gleam of his previous biography. When he was questioned on the subject, he laid his finger on his lip, and if pressed more urgently his brow writhed and his dark eye seemed to shoot sparks of livid fire. He could write with astonishing correctness and facility, considering his situation; and although denied the exquisite pleasure and priceless advantages of the sense of hearing, nature had given him ample compensation by an eye quick and far-seeing as an eagle's and a smell keen and incredible as that of a raven. He could discover objects moving miles away in the far off prairie when others could perceive nothing but earth and sky, and the Rangers used to declare that he could catch the scent of a Mexican or Indian at as great a distance as a buzzard could distinguish the odor of a dead carcass.

It was these qualities which fitted him so well for a spy, in which capacity he rendered invaluable services to Houston's army during the war of independence. He always went alone and generally obtained the information desired. His habits in private life were equally singular. He could never be persuaded to sleep under the roof of a house or even to use a tent-cloth. Wrapped in his blanket he loved to lie out in the open air under the blue canopy of pure ether and count the stars, or gaze with a yearning look at the melancholy moon. When not employed as a spy or guide, he subsisted by hunting, being often absent on solitary excursions for weeks or even months together in the wilderness. He was a genuine son of nature, a grown up child of the woods and prairie which he worshipped with a sort of pagan adoration. Excluded by his infirmities from cordial fellowship with his kind, he made the inanimate things of the earth his friends and entered by the heart's own adoption into brotherhood with the luminaries of heaven. Wherever there was land or water, barren mountains or tangled brakes of wild waving cane, there was Deaf Smith's home, and there he was happy; but in the streets of great cities, in all the great thoroughfares of men, wherever there was flattery or fawning, base cunning or craven fear, there was Deaf Smith an alien and an exile.

Strange soul! he hath departed on the long journey, away among those high bright stars which were his night lamps. . . . He is dead; therefore let his errors rest in oblivion and his virtues be remembered with hope.

Three-Legged Willie

JUDGE WILLIAMSON, or Three-Legged Willie as he was familiarly called, was one of the early judges of Texas. In his court a lawyer by the name of Charlton started a point of law, and the Court refused to admit the Counsel's statement as sufficient proof.

"Your law, Sir," said the Judge; "give us the book and page, Sir."

"This is my law, Sir," said Charlton, pulling out a pistol; "and this, Sir, is my book," drawing a bowie-knife. "And that is the page," pointing the pistol toward the court.

"Your law is not good, Sir," said the unruffled Judge; "the proper authority is *Colt on revolvers.*" He brought a six shooter instantly to bear on the head of the counsel, who dodged the point of the argument, and turned to the jury.

On another occasion the Judge concluded the trial of a man for murder by sentencing him to be hung that very day. A petition was immediately signed by the bar, jury and people, praying that longer time might be granted the poor prisoner. The Judge replied to the petition that the man had been found guilty, the jail was very

From *Spirit*, XXX, 44 (December 15, 1855), 520. Reprinted from the "Editor's Drawer" in *Harper's*. Robert McAlpin Williamson, a first cousin of Sam Houston, was known as Three-Legged Willie because he was crippled and wore a wooden leg strapped to the bent natural one. He came to Texas in 1827 and distinguished himself as a lawyer, district judge, and member of the Texas National Supreme Court. He was the first major of the Texas Rangers and a close friend of William Barret Travis. (Duncan W. Robinson, *Texas Three-Legged Willie* [Austin, 1948], i-iv) unsafe, and, besides, it was so very uncomfortable he did not think any man ought to be required to stay in it any longer than was necessary. The man was hung!

Old Singletire:
The Man That Was Not Annexed

ROBERT PATTERSON

A GOOD STORY is told of this bold frontiersman who had made himself notorious and given his character the *bend sinister* by frequent depredations on both sides of the boundary line between Texas and the United States. The old fellow had migrated thither from parts unknown years since, knew every foot of country for fifty miles on either side in his vicinity, and had communication by runners with many "birds of the same feather" then common in the region.

The old fellow saw with sorrow and regret the rapid influx of population within the last ten years and was compelled gradually to narrow his sphere of *usefulness,* for, said he, "People's a gettin to thick up the woods and spilin the huntin—and then tha aint no chance for a fellar to *speculate* upon travellers as tha used to be when tha wan't any body to watch a fellar. Why, tha is gettin to be so *civylizated* that a fellar can't drink a barrel of double-rectified 'thout havin em all abusin him about it, and then ef he doas happen jist by accident to drap half an ounce of lead into a fellar, why tha is all up in arms about it. Now t'other day when I wanted to mark Joe Sliteses' ears like tha marks their hogs, 'case he called me a vill-*yan,* they wanted to *jewdicate* me afore the court. But cuss em for a set of blasted fools they aint a goin to fool Old Singletire

---

From *Spirit,* XV, 25 (August 16, 1845), 287. Robert Patterson was the editor of the *Concordia Intelligencer,* Vidalia, La., one of the better newspapers of the day and the one on which Thomas Bangs Thorpe was probably working when he wrote his classic hunting tale, "The Big Bear of Arkansas."

ef he is a gittin old and aint as quick on the trigger as he used to was.

"Blast their skins, I don't care ef tha *does* annexate Texas! I'll show em somethin—tho' tha thinks tha is got me slick when tha git the two countries wedged up into one—but I'll fix em, I'll quit and go to Arkansas, whar a decent white man kin live 'thout being pestered, and bused and *jewdicated!*"

"Old Single," as he was called for short, had several years previous to the late discussion of the annexation question with singular 'cuteness ascertained the precise line dividing the two territories and built his cabin thereon in such a position that when lying down *he slept one half in the United States and the other half in Texas,* for he lay at right angles with the line.

The authorities of both sides had frequently found him in that position, but as their separate claims lay severally on the *entire* individual, they were not content to arrest *one half of him* at a time. A great deal of courtesy was at times exhibited by the officers, each pressing the other to break the forms of international law by pulling "Old Single" bodily over either side of the line. Each was up to trap and feared the other wished to trick him and declined the effort which might cause a rupture between Texas and the Union.

On one occasion they were exceedingly pressing on the subject, at first politely so then teasing each other and then daring by taunt and jeer and jibe until they worked themselves into such furious excitement that "Old Single," their pretended victim, had to command and preserve the peace. "Gentle-*men*," said he, "you may fun and fret and quarrel jist as much as you please in my house, but when tha is any lickin to be done 'bout these diggins, why 'Old Single' is *thar sure;* ef you strikes you *dies.* Show your sense, make friends, and let's *licker.* You," nodding to one, "hand me a gourd of water; and you," to another, "pass that bottle and I'll drink to your better 'quaintance."

The day passed, "Old Single" crossed the line, and one of the *beauties* on each side of his cot, all going it like forty at twenty-deck poker—a sociable game as Sol Smith says—and as remarked our informant, "the old man was a perfect *Cumanche horse* at any game whar tha was *curds.*"

For the last three months "Old Single" had been mightily distressed—*"mighty oneasy bout annexation"*—for he knew he would be compelled to travel—well, the news of the action of Texas on this great question was received in "Old Single's" vicinity on the 29th of June, the day it reached Fort Jessup. Next morning "the boys" from Boston and De Kalb, a couple of border villages, after a glory gathering about annexation determined to storm "Old Single" and *"rout"* him. They accordingly, *en masse a-la-regulator,* started off for his cabin and on arriving near it held a consultation. It was determined that bloodshed was useless—as it was certain to occur if violence was resorted to—and that a flag of truce should be sent into the fortress, offering terms.

The old man was found in a gloomy mood with a pack strapped to his back in woodsman style. "Old *Centersplit,*" his friend of thirty years' standing, his rifle, his favorite—his all—was laid across his knees, and he was in deep thought, his eyes resting on vacancy. As the delegation entered, he looked up. "Well, boys," he said, "the time is *cum* and Texas and you is annixated, *but I aint* and I *aint a goin to be nuther! So take care how you raise my dander. I can shoot sum yet!"*

The party explained, and it was agreed that the old fellow should take up the march *upon the line* for the nearest point on Red River, the party escorting him at twenty paces distant on either side, that the last mile should be run, and that if he struck the water's edge first he should go free; if otherwise, he was to be taken and rendered up a victim to the offended dignity of the laws. *"Agreed,"* said "Old Single," "It's a bargain. Boys, tha is a *gallon* in that barrel, let's finish it in a friendly way and then travel." The thing was done, the travel accomplished, and the race, fast and furious, was being done. The old fellow led the crowd, hallooing at his topmost voice as he gained the river, "Hoopee! Hurrah! *I aint annixated! I'm off. I aint no whar—nuther in the States nor Texas, but in Arkansas!!"* He swam to the opposite shore, fired a volley, gave three cheers, and retired victorious.

A Texian Hunter

"SADI"

THE LATE B. Bailey, one of the earliest settlers in Texas, was a man of singular habits, but of strong and energetic mind. Many anecdotes are told of him during his residence there, and many a silent and lonely circle by the camp fire in the forest has been amused and enlivened by the thrilling story of his adventures. He was a great hunter and a successful Indian fighter, as Big Prairie and Caney Creek could tell. He always went armed with a rifle, pistols, and large hunting knife and loved the deep solitude of the woods far better than the conventional usages of society. His death happened, as near as I recollect, in 1832, and he was buried, according to request, near Brazoria in a standing position—with his rifle by his side—his pouch (with a hundred and fifty bullets) slung over his shoulder, and his favorite pistols (a beautiful pair) belted around him.

I have been told by a gentleman of strict veracity that as early as twelve years ago he saw in the Bible of Mr. B. a written request to be buried in this manner. This gentleman had the curiosity to ask him the reason of this singular whim. Bailey merely remarked, "You know I never yet was caught unarmed by Indian or wild beast. I am a rude man and know not whom I may meet in another world. I wish to be prepared, as usual, *for all enemies.*"

From the New Orleans *Picayune*, II, 198 (September 23, 1838), 2.

Brit Bailey

NOAH SMITHWICK

A NOTED MEMBER of Austin's colony was Captain James B. Bailey, better known as "Brit" Bailey, his arrival even antedating that of Austin himself. But as up to that period foreigners could not procure title to land, Bailey had only a squatter's claim. Still he felt that the priority of his claim should be respected; therefore he rose in rebellion when notified that his claim was within the limits of Austin's grant and that in order to secure it he would have to comply with the regulations governing the real colonists. A compromise was effected, however, and Captain Bailey lived and died on his original claim. When he was in his last sickness, realizing that the end was near, he said to his wife:

"I have never stooped to any man, and when I am in my grave I don't want it said, 'There lies old Brit Bailey.' Bury me so that the world must say, 'There stands Bailey.' And bury me with my face to the setting sun. I have been all my life traveling westward and I want to face that way when I die."

His widow, in compliance with his request, had a deep hole dug like a well, into which the coffin was lowered, feet first, facing the setting sun.

From *The Evolution of a State,* pp. 72-73.

NOTES TO SECTION IV

1. London-born Junius Brutus Booth (1796-1852) achieved fame as a Shakespearean actor in the United States. He made several tours through the South and West, and once acted in and managed the Camp Street Theater in New Orleans. He was the father of two sons who were also actors—Edwin (1833-1893) and John Wilkes (1838-1865), the assassin of Lincoln.

2. Sir Edward Coke (1552-1634) was a famous English jurist whose works served as a model for law students. Sir William Blackstone (1723-1780) was noted for his volumes on English common law.

3. Jean Lafitte (1780-1826), born in France, engaged in privateering in the Gulf of Mexico and became a legendary figure in his lifetime. From 1808 to 1814 he operated from Barataria; later he made Galveston his headquarters. About 1820 he left for Yucatan, where he supposedly died. No mention is made of his having a bastard son.

4. William Gilmore Simms (1806-1870) was an American novelist whose romances have been compared to those of Sir Walter Scott and James Fenimore Cooper; many of his novels deal with Indian and frontier life. Best known of these are *The Yemassee* (1835), *The Partisan* (1835), and *Woodcraft* (1854).

V
Rangers and Soldiers

V. Rangers and Soldiers

A VITAL STRAIN *in the development of the Texas myth was the story of the Texas Rangers. The citizen-soldier, the frontier Indian fighter, and the home-guard volunteer had long been familiar to Americans before the emergence of this body of mounted men in Texas, but the Rangers appeared at a time when newspapers were reaching more readers than ever before and when readers were ready to accept the dramatic actions of these men as characteristic of all Texans. Joseph Leach in his book* The Typical Texan *devotes a great deal of space to the emergence of the Rangers; he says:*

During the early months of the Mexican War when the biggest group of Rangers were active, American papers pictured them as the most mettlesome men then fighting. . . . They were determined fighters who usually got what they went after. They were also widely known as the most incorrigible and unconventional lot American military disciplinarians ever had to put up with. (p. 47)

Leach goes on to point out that, though their leaders—Hays, Walker, and others—received a great deal of attention, no one of them was as influential in the formation of the image of the Texan as were the Big Three—Crockett, Houston, and Bigfoot Wallace. It is significant, perhaps, that the Rangers were popular for being fighters while at the same time they were admired for resisting military discipline, two seemingly contradictory traits that Americans generally have esteemed.

In contrast to the dramatic life of the Texas Rangers, soldiering

169

in the U.S. Army on the frontier in Texas appears to have been dull and tedious; thus the action and excitement of the Mexican War must have been a welcome relief. American soldiers in that first of our foreign wars found much to laugh about, and many of them went home from Texas soon to forget the mud and misery of camps on the Rio Grande, but not the stories about Texas and Texans.

Colonel Jack Hays

ANONYMOUS

Is this the scourge of France?
Is this the Talbot so much fear'd abroad?
That with his name the mothers style their babes?
I see, report is fabulous and false:
I thought I should have seen some Hercules,
A second Hector, for his grim aspect,
And large proportion of his strong-knit limbs.

AMID the countless multitude attracted to Washington from curiosity, business, or pleasure during the last few weeks—in the throng of distinguished and remarkable men of whom undoubtedly there were many to be seen—probably no man was the object of deeper interest than Col. Jack Hays, the world renowned Texan ranger. He was indeed the observed of all observers. It may be safely asserted that no man in America since the great John Smith explored the primeval forests of Virginia and held communion with the "noble savage" Powhatan, has run a career of such boldness, daring, and adventure. His frontier defense of the Texan Republic constitutes one of the most remarkable pages in the history of the American

From *Spirit*, XXIII, 6 (March 26, 1853), 65. Reprinted from the *Richmond* (Va.) *Examiner*. Born in Tennessee, John Coffee Hays at the age of fifteen went to live for a time with his uncle, Robert Cage, in Yazoo County, Mississippi. Because his uncle opposed a military career for him, he ran away, studied surveying, and worked as a surveyor in Mississippi for two years before going to Texas. As an officer in the Texas Rangers, he became one of the most widely known members of that group. (James K. Greer, *Colonel Jack Hays* [New York, 1952]) character. For importance of results, brought about by apparently utterly inadequate means, his services stand preeminent—for daring and endurance, for privation, suffering, and hard fighting, this soldier with his little band of followers stands without a parallel scarcely in the history of warfare.

It will hardly be credited by after time that this man with forty followers was required and did successfully defend from the ravages of a most powerful savage horde an exposed and defenseless frontier country of hundreds of miles in extent. That he accomplished still more than a simple defense of the frontier and, carrying the terror of his name far across the border country, drove the terrible Camanche to interpose for his own safety forests and prairies, rivers and plains, between him and the unerring revolver of his relentless pursuer. But the story of his warfare, even amongst his own countrymen, appears almost fabulous, when we remember that, superadded to the border defense against the Indian, was also imposed upon this little band the duty of keeping watch upon the wily Mexican foe, of meeting and fighting them in all numbers and under all circumstances, whenever they crossed the border—assisted only by such hardy frontier men as could be collected from their fields and firesides upon an emergency. This campaigning was continued and ran through a period, if we remember rightly, of nearly eight years.

There was no well appointed commissariat to supply this devoted little band with the necessaries even which pertained to a common life of drudgery; no marquees, no camp equipage, no ordnance, no wagons, no grooms—none of the pride, pomp, and circumstance of glorious war garnished the return of the daring frontier man and his brother in arms. Their covering was the firmament, and their beds the earth—their food was such game as they killed upon their march, and as for bread they had none. Not even the ammunition which they used was at all times furnished by the government; they purchased it with the skin of the wild beast which they killed for their food. And amid all this were perpetually recurring desperate and bloody conflicts with the foe. And seldom did that grim array return from a scout without an empty saddle or so which told the tale of their daring and their dangers.

The world is familiar with the services of Col. Hays in the war with Mexico. Everybody remembers the praises bestowed upon him as the Murat of the army by the glorious and lamented Gen. Worth. But an opinion expressed by that gallant officer relative to Col. Hays is certainly calculated to mislead. Worth said that Hays, when in front of the enemy, was the tallest man in the saddle belonging to the American army. Far otherwise is it with him when seen amongst a crowd of his countrymen. If you expect to see "a second Hector from his grim aspect," you will be disappointed—you will only see a slender, well proportioned, tightly-knit man of scarcely middle size, remarkable, certainly, for the formation of his head and the quiet, penetrating fire of his eye—but modest to an extent truly surprising for anyone, certainly for one who has not only "seen the elephant," but has for a great part of his life lived with them.

Col. Hays has paid a short visit to our city, but remained only long enough to pay a visit of respect and courtesy to the venerable mother of one of his most esteemed companions in arms, the late Major Chevallie. He returns home shortly to California, and few, we venture to say, who have seen him but would be glad to know that the best fortune of that golden land may be his.

The Texas Rangers in Mexico

SAMUEL C. REID

RETURNING, we met Mr. Kendall of the Picayune who introduced us to Capt. Benjamin McCulloch, the celebrated partisan scout. Capt. McCulloch is a man of rather delicate frame, of about five feet ten inches in height, with light hair and complexion. His features are regular and pleasing, though, from long exposure on the frontier, they have a weather-beaten cast. His quick and bright blue eye, with a mouth of thin compressed lips, indicate the cool, calculating, as well as the brave and daring energy of the man. Being told that we were anxious to join his company after running his eye over us, he asked, "Have you a good *horse*, sir? for," said he, "I have refused a great many because their horses would not do for our service." Our horse was then inspected, and being pronounced "a good horse" we were immediately made a "Texas Ranger." Capt. McCulloch had just come in from a scout towards Linares, and a detachment of his company had been left at Reynoso under the command of Lieut. McMullen; and it was expected that we would move up to Reynoso in a few days.

From Samuel C. Reid, *The Scouting Expeditions of McCulloch's Texas Rangers* (Philadelphia, 1847), pp. 23-25, 33-34, 42-43, 56-58, 59-60, 60-61, 73, 86, 136, 99-101, 63-65, 15. Born in New York in 1818, Reid was a lawyer who served with the Texas Rangers under Captain McCulloch during the Mexican War. During the Civil War he was a Confederate war correspondent for several newspapers. After 1865 he resumed his law practice and wrote a number of books dealing with legal and historical subjects. (*Appleton's Cyclopaedia of American Biography*, V, 216-17)

Benjamin McCulloch was born in Rutherford County, state of Tennessee, about the year 1814. His father, Alexander McCulloch, was aid-de-camp to General Coffee and fought under General Jackson at the battles of Talladega, Tallahassee, and Horse-shoe during the Creek war. While McCulloch was very young, his father emigrated to Alabama, and Benjamin was sent back to Tennessee to school where he remained until he was about fourteen years old. Shortly after, however, his father moved back to the western district of Tennessee and settled in Dyer County. There, Ben was kept hunting until he was near twenty-one. At that time the bears were so bad that hogs could not be raised on their account, and the settlers principally depended upon bear meat for subsistence. In those days, if a man's gun snapped he lost his breakfast, for hunting bears in the cane requires much caution. McCulloch, however, generally killed as many as eighty bears in the course of a season and never less than twenty during a winter.

When about twenty-one, being fond of a life of adventure, he determined to go on an expedition to the Rocky Mountains and left his home for St. Louis to join a company of trappers. Arriving too late, he was disappointed when he tried to get in with a party of Santa Fe traders; in this he likewise failed, the complement of men having been made up. He then visited the lead mines in Wisconsin Territory and remained during the summer at Dodgeville.

In September, McCulloch returned home and soon after his arrival, called on Colonel David Crockett, who was making up an expedition to go to Texas to take part in the revolution that had then broken out in Mexico; the whole southwest at that time was alive with feelings of sympathy for the Texians, and men were daily flocking to their standard. McCulloch agreed to accompany Colonel Crockett to Texas. Nacogdoches had been appointed the place of rendezvous from which the expedition was to start, and the Christmas of 1835 was named the day for the meeting—when, as "old Davy" said, they were to make their Christmas dinner off the hump of a buffalo! Unfortunately, however, McCulloch did not arrive until early in January, and finding the party was gone, he proceeded on by himself to the River Brazos, where he was taken very ill and did not recover until after the fall of the Alamo. McCulloch's disappointment was very great at not being able to join the gallant band of patriots at the time but which afterwards proved very fortunate for him; for Colonel Travis, after having sustained a siege for thirteen days with only one hundred and eighty Texians against Santa Anna's army, fell with his brave little band, having previously killed nine hundred of the enemy.

After his recovery, McCulloch descended the Brazos River in a boat to Gross Plant [Groce's Retreat] where the Texian army had assembled under General Houston. There he was induced to join the artillery by their making him captain of a gun. This he gallantly served at the battle of San Jacinto where Santa Anna was made prisoner and his army of 1500 killed or captured.

McCulloch settled in Gonzales County and was afterwards employed on the frontier of Texas in surveying and locating lands and serving in the wild border scouts against the Indians and Mexicans, which service he entered before the celebrated Hays. He also distinguished himself in a fight with the Indians who burnt Linnville, called the battle of Plum Creek. He was likewise at the taking of Mier, but not agreeing with the plans of the expedition afterwards, he returned home before the fight and thus escaped from the cruel hardships and imprisonment of that command, which had surrendered to the perfidious Ampudia. He was in almost all the expeditions of the time and engaged in nearly all of the fights.

*   *   *

At Camargo we were welcomed by many friends and were soon conducted to the camp of the Rangers, which lay at the upper end of the town. Our mess, in company with three others, occupied a long tent open at both ends, formerly used for an hospital—an old concern which had served to keep out the sun and rain—while the rest occupied the vacant and ruined huts around. Many of the men had just come in from grazing their horses and were now occupied in grooming them; others were cooking over fires, and preparing supper. At sundown we were invited by our mess to take a cup of coffee out of a tin pot and were reminded by them after our hearty meal that *our cook-day* would come on Monday. Rations of corn and oats were then served out for our horses—the guard was paraded, and the sentinels posted. It was a fine evening, and the Rangers sat round in groups listening to the songs and stories of their comrades. There is no place like camp for studying character. Men are there seen in their true light, and from the intimate association every trait which is noble and good or otherwise is sure to manifest itself. There can be no deceit or affectation practised there to advantage. And whatever may be the rank or station of men in life, in camp all find their level. The aristocracy of wealth which governs in large cities among civilians of the present day is not respected or courted in the camp of a soldier. There, bravery and intelligence outrank it. At 9 o'clock the men retired, our beds consisting merely of a blanket spread on the ground with a sack of corn or oats for a pillow, or *heading* as the *boys* called it, and save those who were on guard, all was soon hushed in sleep.

❀   ❀   ❀

Matamoras! Matamoras! was shouted along the line as we came in sight of the town we had so ardently desired to see. And far in the distance with its white walls and turrets gleaming in the sunlight, with the American flag floating proudly over it, we beheld the first Mexican town captured by American arms. Mexican towns are all magnificent at a distance; but you must not approach too closely unless you wish to find in many of them all your beautiful dreams of Moorish palaces and Oriental gardens, orange groves, and shady avenues immediately fade away, and in their place cherish recollections of rude mud-built houses, plastered and whitewashed; windows without glass, hot dusty streets, and a dirty, lazy, and most unpoetical-looking set of inhabitants.

As we approached the river bank, drums were beating and fifes
blowing, and on all sides were noise and excitement; flags fluttering,
arms gleaming, teamsters cursing at their unruly animals; soldiers
drilling, dogs barking, and Mexican hucksters bawling their goods
at their voices' tops. Pursuing our way through the various groups
which lined the roadside, we rode by several companies, who presented arms as we passed, and returning their salute we proceeded
to our quarters which were almost directly under the walls of Fort
Brown. Here we found Walker's and Price's companies of Rangers
encamped, and here we *constructed* our tents for the present—constructed, we say, because the government never furnished us, during
our whole term of service, with a patch of canvass large enough
to keep out a drop of rain, because they thought the Texian troops
were accustomed to and could endure more hardships than any
other troops in the field—why, we do not know. One thing is certain,
they gave us as ample an opportunity to evince our greatest powers
of endurance and fortitude as the disciples of Diogenes could
have desired, had they been placed in our room and stead. We were
left to shift for ourselves, wholly unprovided with tents, camp
equipage, or cooking utensils. Had we been allowed to appropriate
to our own use the unoccupied houses of the enemy, we would have
asked no favors from friend or foe, but while the strictest injunctions were laid upon us in regard to the property of the Mexicans,
we were charitably left to brave unsheltered as much of the sun and
rain as heaven pleased to send upon us. The consequence was that,
wherever we were encamped for any length of time, we were
obliged to construct rude shelters out of poles, cane, rushes, or any
other material which the vicinity afforded. And the Rangers' camp
frequently looked more like a collection of huts in a Hottentot ham-
let or a group of rude wigwams in an Indian village than the regular cantonment of volunteers in the service of the United States.

✢   ✢   ✢

We had been encamped in the old "cottongin shed" about two

weeks when Lieut. McMullen told us one evening about sundown that he wanted twenty men to saddle up for special and secret service. The horses were ready in a twinkling, and we were all eager to learn what the object of this night expedition could be. All was anxiety and expectation until about 8 o'clock when we were ordered to move in silence. Not a word was spoken as we filed out of the yard and took our position in the line. "Fall into double file—keep strict silence, and follow me," said our lieutenant in a low voice as he rode on in the advance. We followed without uttering a word. When we had rode on in this manner for about a mile and were entirely clear of all the houses of the town, we were halted, and Lieut. McMullen explained to us the nature of the duty he wished us to perform. "It is reported, boys," said he, "that Canales with some of his officers are at this moment at a fandango which is held at a rancho about six miles from town. My object is to capture them, if possible. To insure success, silence and caution are necessary. When we approach the rancho, it will be necessary for some of you to dismount and hold the horses of the others while the rest surround the house. Commence counting there in front!—every fifth man will be detailed to take care of the horses!" As soon as the names of the men upon whom this duty devolved were made known, we moved on again in silence. It was now necessary to procure a guide as none of us knew the ranch at which the fandango was held, except by name. Fortunately, we picked up a little Mexican boy on the road who agreed to be our pilot for the consideration of one dollar, paid in hand. The money was given to him, and he jumped up behind one of the men to direct us in the route we wished to pursue.

Splashing onward through mud and water for five miles farther, we came in sight of the lights of the ranch. The boy here requested to be put down as he did not wish his people to know that he had guided their enemies upon them. The little fellow slipped off in the darkness of the night, and we hastened on to the place of the merrymaking.

The scene which presented itself as we approached was unique and beautiful. The dance was held in the open air; and the bright fires kindled at different points, the candles and torches moving to and fro, the animated groups of revellers clustered on every side, the white robes of the girls prettily contrasting in the firelight with the dusky apparel of their partners; while gay forms, replete with life and motion, bounded in the lively dance, or floated in the graceful waltz in sweet accord with the spirit-stirring strains of music which the night breeze wafted to our ears—all made a scene that was, at the distance we viewed it, beautiful indeed.

"Halt!—dismount!—creep up cautiously, men, and surround the house—and when I call you, come up quickly and firmly at the charge." McMullen loosened his pistols in his belt as he gave this command and strolled quite carelessly into the midst of the astonished dancers. Our places were quickly taken, and before the revellers dreamed of danger they found their scene of festivity suddenly surrounded with a ring of Texian rifles. Never was a scene of rejoicing more quickly turned into one of dismay and confusion. The women shrieked and fluttered about like a flock of frightened doves upon the sudden appearance of a hawk; the men shouted in alarm, "The Americans are upon us!" and bolted right and left to make their escape, but on all sides they were met by the muzzle of a gun and a gruff voice saying, "Stand back, or I'll shoot you down." The party was completely entrapped and finding no chance to escape now gathered around an old drunken fellow who was dancing in their midst, singing as he danced and occasionally crying out, "We are poor honest people—what have we to fear from our enemies." While this scene was being enacted out of doors, McMullen was busily engaged in the house, turning over tables, looking under beds, and examining carefully every nook and corner that could possibly conceal a fugitive. None were found, however, and after scanning closely the members of the party out doors, we were forced to conclude that either our information was false or that Canales and his friends had left the fandango before we arrived. The fact was the most reasonable presumption. We asked no questions, for we did not expect a truthful answer.

The party, therefore, could only guess the cause of our unexpected visit until Lieut. McMullen told them that he was passing the rancho with his men when the sound of music made us stop to see how they were enjoying themselves. They appeared perfectly satisfied with the explanation and insisted that we should join the dance and partake of the refreshments. Two or three of the best dancers in our squad laid aside their guns and picking out the prettiest girls for their partners took their places in the set; the rest of us looked on with our rifles in our hands. We had seen some pretty *tall* dancing in our time, but we think the feats we witnessed that night were a little ahead of anything in that line we ever saw before. The men had not had an opportunity of enjoying themselves by tripping on the "light fantastic toe" for some time past, and on this occasion they determined, as they said, to "spread themselves." The step of every Negro dance that was ever known was called into requisition and admirably executed. They performed the "double shuffle," the "Virginny breakdown," the "Kentucky heel tap," the "pigeon wing," the "back balance lick," the "Arkansas hoedown" with unbounded applause and irresistible effect. We laughed heartily at their grotesque figures and comical movements, and the Mexicans were perfectly enraptured with their activity and skill. The rogues stepped about like *lions* after the dance was finished and appeared to enjoy the admiration they had excited amazingly. The Mexican girls were so much captivated that they entirely slighted their old lovers and were quarreling with one another as to who next should dance with "los buenos Americanos."

"Come, boys," said McMullen, after two or three more dances were over, "this is enough fun for one night. Mount! and return to quarters." So taking one glass of *muscal* more all round, we bade the party "adios" and hied merrily homeward, regretting that our information in regard to Canales had proved untrue but not sorry that we had been induced to hunt for him at a fandago.

*   *   *

Well knowing the manner in which the Mexicans observed [the Festival of San Juan], we determined to have our share of the fun. So carefully grooming our horses early in the morning, plaiting their manes, and expending upon their appearance all the finery we could muster, we mounted and rode in a body to the main plaza in [Reynosa]. The exercises of the day were much interrupted by the plaza being occupied by our artillery and the streets barricaded by piles of stones, but cramped as we were in our movements we determined with the Mexicans to make the most of the occasion. By 10 o'clock, the streets were filled with mounted Mexicans, whooping and charging upon each other. Gradually they all formed into one great party and rode by us in a bantering style. We were fewer in number but possessed an immense advantage over them in the size, weight, strength, and speed of our horses. Thinking that we did not accept or understand their first challenge, they formed to charge upon us. We were clustered in the mouth of one of the main streets that led to the plaza, and as we found them rushing down like a whirlwind upon our ranks, we suddenly opened to the right and left and allowed the whole body to pass to the rear. With a jeer of triumph they passed by when we wheeled like lightning on their rear and using freely our spurs charged the whole body at full speed. The weight of twenty large American horses is enough to overthrow all the ponies in Mexico, and as we had no arms to carry our whole attention was devoted to the management of our horses. We rode right full upon them, and at the first shock more than twenty men and horses were rolling in the dust, and our triumph was achieved for the rest of the party scattered in every direction, up alleys and into yards, in short, perfectly satisfied that *los cavallos Americanos son mucho buenos, y mucho grandes*. It was our turn now to ride in triumph up and down the streets, bowing to the senoras and kissing our hands to the senoritas who lined the streets and windows and who returned our salutations most graciously. The Mexican gallants followed after us but kept at a most respectful

distance. At length, one of them who spoke a little English rode up
and inquired if we would like to engage in a "chicken race." We
expressed our willingness to do so, and two or three of them dashed
off to procure a chicken. The conditions of the race were these: the
chicken was to be given to some man mounted on a good horse; the
rest of the party, both Mexicans and Americans, were to remain in
the plaza, while the man was to have about a hundred yards start;
at a given signal he was to run by a designated course which led
about two miles round town to our camp. If he reached camp in
safety, the chicken was his prize; but if he was intercepted or over-
taken by any of the Mexicans who were going to take short cuts
through the town for the purpose and the bird taken away from
him, why then he was to be laughed at and suffer the mortification
of defeat. A wild young Texian by the name of Clinton Dewit vol-
unteered to bear the chicken to camp, and seizing the bird by the
legs dashed off at a breakneck pace. After he had got a fair start,
about one-half of the Mexicans rushed after him, yelling like a legion
of devils; the remainder ran by a shorter route to intercept him at
different points of the road. We galloped out of town to see the
sport. They had purposely chosen a road for him to follow that was
covered with loose rocks and full of holes in hopes that his horse
would either stumble over the one or fall into the other. But Clint
Dewit was too good a horseman to suffer either of these mishaps
and picked his course over the uneven ground as coolly as if he
were gallanting a lady to church. The speed of his horse was so
much greater than that of his pursuers that he was soon able to
leave them far behind; but those who had run across and got before
him annoyed him exceedingly so that he was frequently obliged to
ride right over them (which he always did when he had a chance)
or task his horse's powers to the utmost to ride around and avoid
them. When he had nearly reached the camp, a big, stout fellow,
mounted on a strong horse, rushed out from behind a house which
he was obliged to pass and grasped the prize, and so eager was he
to secure the chicken that he momentarily released his hold of the

bridle while both horses were dashing along at full speed. Clint immediately perceived his advantage and grappling him by the throat suddenly reined his horse up. The consequence was that the greaser's horse passed from under him and left the rider in Clint's grasp. Dashing him to the ground, the young Texian clutched the prize and raising a yell of triumph bore it easily to the camp.

Another was brought out, and another chase succeeded, terminating like the first. Another, and another, and still with the same success. Until at last, we found ourselves pretty well supplied with stock in the poultry line, and the Mexicanos ruefully acknowledged that there were *no mas Gallenas in Reynoso*—no more chickens in Reynoso.

❊   ❊   ❊

The morning of the 4th of July found us busily employed in preparations to celebrate the day with suitable rejoicing. Every stray pig or chicken that ventured to show himself in our yard that day was unfortunately despatched—unfortunately, I say, since everybody said they came to their death by accident. As the boys said, "If the poor things would run in the way *just* as they were going to shoot off their guns in honour of the 4th, of course they could not help it if they *were killed.*" And then *just* to prevent them from spoiling, they were put on the fire.

Two large horse-buckets of whiskey was procured and a loaf of white sugar grated into it, with the due allowance of water. But to describe the scene of feasting, drinking, and revelry which ensued is beyond the power of our pen. Yet we would not have it for a moment supposed that we were unable to tell what happened after dinner, because—

Suffice it, that the dinner went off as all other dinners go off, with infinite satisfaction to everybody that enjoyed it. The wine—the whiskey we mean—was capital and circulated freely, and everybody was in such admirable spirits and such excellent good humour with everybody else, and the toasts that were given were received with such prolonged, vociferous and tumultuous applause that Col. Wilson, although nearly half a mile distant, was suddenly awakened from his *siesta* by the noise. He despatched a file of men to find out if the Rangers' camp had been unexpectedly attacked by a Mexican force or "what was the meaning of that disturbance, anyhow."

The men were furnished with several "horns" out of the "big bucket" and sent back to Col. Wilson, "with the compliments of the Rangers" and the polite request "that he would join us in a drink." The message was faithfully carried, and the colonel came up himself. But when he arrived and found no officer about (for McMullen was not present) and by looking over the fence saw the men were ripe for anything, he prudently concluded not to pay us a visit. He was perceived, however, and one of the most "far gone" of the party reeled to his feet and proposed as a toast, "the health of Col. Wilson," and three of the most vociferous cheers that ever rose upon the air burst from the group around. The old gentleman understood the joke and hurried off to his quarters so that we were allowed to enjoy ourselves for the remainder of the evening as we pleased.

*　*　*

Just before entering the town, we had to ford a beautiful stream which danced merrily along and rippled over its rocky bed, pure, cool, and as limpid as a mountain rivulet. As we rode up, still being concealed behind a high bank, a rare sight was presented to our view. Some fifty or sixty young Mexican girls were bathing in the lovely stream, making the air ring with their merry laughter and the water foam and splash with their sportive agile movements. Occasionally, their unveiled charms were exposed to our gaze as we peeped cautiously over the high bank at the lovely nymphs who continued their joyous sports, totally unconscious of our presence. Every form of maiden loveliness stood before us, from the girl of eighteen to the budding beauty of the laughing child. How long we might have gazed entranced upon this fair original scene, we cannot pretend to say; for, unfortunately for us, one of the young girls happened to glance above and descried a long line of strange, bearded-and-moustached faces peering earnestly over the bank at them. The sight we now witnessed afforded us the highest merriment. The alarm had been quickly given, and the girls, in confusion and dismay, paddling and splashing, quickly made for the shore with screams and shrieks. Scampering towards their garments, *rebosas*, mantillas, and gowns, picked up in all directions, were put on in a hurry, and then running—such a footrace for home, half-dressed as they were, made one of the most amusing and laughable scenes that we ever saw.

*   *   *

In the afternoon a heavy rain was seen coming up, and hurried preparations were made to preserve our arms from the wet. A young Ranger was seen taking off his clothes which he carefully rolled up in his blanket and placing them at the foot of a tree, covered the whole with his saddle when the rain commenced falling in torrents. He stood out in its midst with perfect indifference while the rest of his comrades were wrapped in their blankets and had sought the shelter of the trees from the storm.

"What are you doing out there, Harry?" said one of his messmates.

"Taking a shower bath," said Harry.

"Why, your clothes will get all wet, you fool."

"No they won't either, " said Harry, "for they are wrapped up in my blanket."

"And where is your blanket?"

"Why, under my saddle, snug enough!" said Harry, with a knowing look.

"Well, that *beats* me," said his messmate, bursting into a loud laugh, in which all heartily joined; "who ever would have thought of that way to keep dry!"

*   *   *

We had a funny scene in our company, this afternoon. Two or

three of the men while out on picket found a mule load of baggage belonging to a Mexican officer. The animal had probably stampeded during the retreat of the day before, and Torrejon's men were in too great a hurry to hunt up runaway mules. The letters found would show that the owner was Don Ignacio something or other, captain of the third company of Guanujuato cavalry, and to set forth that Don Ignacio was a man of some consequence he had a scarlet coat of the finest broadcloth, covered with pure silver buttons, ornamented with rich silver embroidery, and upon the breast of which was an order. His cap was of blue velvet, richly ornamented with silver band and tassels, while his cavalry pantaloons of blue broadcloth foxed with morocco had a wide stripe of red down their outer seams. Among the baggage was also a mattress, several pillows, the cases of which were elaborately worked, and other fine bed-furniture. In addition to all this, as if this were not enough, there were some half a dozen red, green, and figured petticoats, a dozen pair of beautiful little pink, blue, and white satin slippers, to say nothing of a dozen neatly wrought linen camisas—all the wardrobe of some pretty *poblana* girl who had doubtless followed Don Ignacio to the wars.

After all this large and elegant assortment had been opened, our orderly sergeant, the son of a member of Congress from Tennessee, rigged himself out in the showy uniform of the Mexican officer and strutted forth to detail a picket-guard, decidedly the best dressed man in the invading army, from Gen. Taylor down. In the meantime, there were others who girt the *poblano's* petticoats about them and then executed divers *cracoviennes* and *cachucas* to the great amusement of the bystanders and to the great danger of stampeding all our horses. Altogether, the scene was extremely diverting.

*   *   *

"Well," said the Ranger, as he resettled himself on his blanket, and knocking the ashes out of his pipe carefully put it away. "Well, I once knew a fellow who for many years was engaged in the smuggling trade with the Mexicans on the Pacific coast. He was said to have been born in the States. But it was hard to tell. He had black eyes and hair, and if he had ever been white the sun had shaded his complexion to a dark brown. He spoke the lingo perfectly well, and if he *was* born in the States his English somehow had a sort of a twist in it. There were many strange stories told about him, and it was said he once lived in Italy. No one ever knew his real name. The Mexicans called him *Capitan Bill*. He was about five feet six inches in stature and rather delicate than robust; his features were regular, and nothing about him very striking, except that one of his eyes had a notion never to leave the corner nearest his nose." Here the group smiled and turned a look on Tom.

"It was about fifteen years ago, at the time of the colonization of Texas, when I was that many years old," continued the Ranger, "that Capitan Bill first came down to our settlement, and there somehow he got the name of *Strabismus Bill*."

"Got the name of what?" said Tom.

"Strabismus Bill," repeated the Ranger.

"What did they call him that for?" said Tom.

"Why, I believe the way it came about," said the Ranger, "was that Bill fell in love with a lovely girl who at the same time was being courted by the doctor of our settlement. Kate Young was counted the most beautiful girl for miles around, and, as Bill played on the guitar and sang Italian songs, he *sorter took her* first. But the doctor told her one day that Bill had the *strabismus*, which so alarmed her that she would never see Bill again. It was known all about that Kate had *kicked* Bill on account of the *strabismus*, and so long as he remained about them parts they called him *Strabismus Bill*.

"Shortly after, Strabismus Bill disappeared from the settlement and was not heard of for some years. It was after the Texian war had closed that I met a friend who told me the sad end of poor Bill. It appeared, after he left us, he went back to his old trade. Well, it was while on his way from Mazatlan where he had been with some

Mexican smugglers, and were returning with a *cavallada* of some 500 mules, laden with teas and silks which had been clandestinely landed on the coast from the East Indies that he met with an incident that controlled his after life. They had so far eluded the vigilance of the excise officers as to gain the interior. So well did they know the geography of the country and every path and trail that, in case of an alarm, they would all scatter out in all directions so as to avoid pursuit, then strike for the trail on the course of their route, and thus all meet again after one or two days of separation. In those days the smugglers and the bandits made common cause of it, and afforded each other protection.

"One night as they were travelling along, they passed a rancho which had been attacked by the Indians and all the people massacred. On entering one of the huts, Bill thought he heard a sigh, and looking up into a little loft he discovered a young girl who upon perceiving him jumped down and, clasping him around the neck, to his surprise and amazement and amid a shower of kisses, greeted him as her brother! Notwithstanding Bill's protestations of the contrary, still clinging to his neck, she heeded him not and with sobs of grief told him how their parents had been murdered. Bill continued to disclaim the relationship, but all he could do would not convince her of the mistake; so he took her up on his horse and carried her to his home.

"A few days after their arrival, her true brother made his appearance, he having accidentally stopped at Bill's house on his way home. And, indeed, the resemblance between the two was so striking and remarkable that it was not strange that even a sister should have been deceived."

"Why, was he cross-eyed too?" said Clark.

"Of course he was," answered the Ranger, "or how could he *look* like Bill?"

"Well," continued he, "as the girl was very beautiful, Bill fell in love with her. Some months afterwards, it was ascertained that she was the niece of a wealthy Mexican Don, who having heard of her misfortune had written to her to come and live with his family at his *hacienda*. Bill accompanied her and asked her uncle's permission to marry her. He consented, but it was plain the girl married more out of gratitude than from love. She never seemed happy after the marriage. With others she appeared gay enough, but in the presence of Bill she was always sad. One day it was discovered that she had poisoned him."

"Poisoned him!" said Tom, with surprise; "poisoned him! what for?"

"Why, some said it was because she was in love with another, but it was generally attributed to the reason that he was so infernal ugly and always looked cross at her." A loud laugh burst from the crowd, while Tom rolled himself up in his blanket and was not heard of any more until next morning.

*   *   *

"Those who know anything about the emigration of Germans into Texas are well aware that thousands of them have made Indian Point near Port Lavaca a grand rendezvous before leaving for the interior settlement of New Braunfels, or the frontier station on the Pierdenales [Pedernales], the Llano, or the San Saba. Bill [Dean] said that he visited the Point last spring when some five thousand Germans were encamped there and was present at one of the most thrilling and heartrending scenes it had ever been his lot to witness. So far as his individual knowledge went, neither ancient nor modern history made mention of any case which might be considered as anywhere near parallel.

"Among the emigrants, remarked Dean, was a young, pretty, red-cheeked girl, the pride of the party, who strolled out alone one day to gather wild flowers in the chaparral. Her ramblings carried her farther than she intended, and when she turned to retrace her steps she found that she was lost, poor thing—bewildered and perplexed in a tangled maze. In vain she strove to recollect the position and bearings of the camp she had left, all so joyous, a short hour before—

reason had fled its throne. In an agony of doubt she ran to and fro in the chaparral, every step taking her farther from her friends, and darkness at length found her completely exhausted and crazed with thoughts of Indian peril and of starvation. Her sufferings during the night, continued Bill, you must fancy for yourselves—I shall not attempt to depict them.

"With the early morning light she was again on her feet. She gazed in every direction, she ran in every direction, but no sight of her friends gladdened her longing vision. While thus engaged she was discovered by a Mexican girl whose father had a small rancho some five miles from the Point, and now when succour was at hand the lost one fled at its approach. The Mexican girl called upon her in soothing terms, but she heeded her not. The former then went to her father hard by and told him that some poor straggler from the camp of the strangers was in the bushes and to all appearance was lost and bereft of reason. The old man mounted his horse, went out in search, and soon came up with her; but she fled at his approach as from one of the wild denizens of the prairie. The old man in the kindness of his heart with soft accents attempted to arrest her flight. She heeded him not. He knew that she must belong to the German camp, that she was lost, that she was crazed, and he determined to rescue her. Coiling in his hand, the lariat or leather rope which hung to his saddle, he set off full speed after the bewildered and frightened fugitive, threw it gently over her head, and thus checked her flight. To call his daughter, thinking that she might better assist in soothing the poor girl, was his first impulse; to proceed with her to the camp of her friends and deliver her safely to those who must be but too anxious for her, was his second.

"Great was the joy of her relatives, gladdened were the hearts of all who knew her as she was brought into camp; but soon these emotions were changed to bitter sorrow as one by one they discovered that the fairest flower among the emigrants was crazed. The sweet caresses of her mother and sisters she answered only with a vacant stare; the kind offices of those who crowded around were

uncared for, unregarded. Her half-frantic lover, as he uttered words
of comfort and endearment, was answered with a look that told
plainly she recognised him not, that he was forgotten. Restoratives
of every description were resorted to but without effect. A favorite
little dog wagged his tail in joy and endeavored to lick the hands of
his mistress in token of gladness at her return but was spurned as a
stranger. Songs that she had loved in childhood fell in soft cadence
upon her ear; yet she heeded them not. Presents from her lover—
gifts that she had treasured in her heart of hearts—were passed over
as idle toys. Her once-bright eye, so full of intelligence and life, was
now glazed, vacant and lusterless—her round, full face, once so
radiant with intellect, was now a meaningless blank—and as her
friends gazed upon her they wrung their hands in sorrow with sad
misgivings that the reason of the poor girl was lost forever.

"At length an elderly matron left the melancholy group and
started off as if intent on making one more effort at restoring the
crazed one to her senses. Presently she returned with a large plate
of hot, smoking sauerkraut in her hand. Elbowing her way in
among the sorrowing crowd, she presented the dish to the girl,
and"—

"And with what effect?" ejaculated a Ranger who had been listening all the while and who now dashed away a tear which had
gathered in his eye. "With what effect?"

"As-ton-ish-ing!" slowly ejaculated the wag. "It brought her right
to; and the way she skived into that kraut showed that twenty-four
hours' hard exercise in the chaparral is a great help to the appetite!"

❋ ❋ ❋

A Texas Ranger under Walker who had gone home after the fight
was relating the exploits of his commander and was describing the
battles, and so forth to a crowd of friends, when a young lad who
had been an attentive listener his face brightening up with enthusiasm at the glowing descriptions of the narrator, slapping his
hand upon his thigh, cried out, "D--n me if I don't go to the wars."

Attracted by this speech, the Texian turned round to see from whom it had emanated, and discovering the author of it to be a young delicate-looking lad, said to him with a significant look, "*You* go to the wars!—hum—you had better stay home!"

"Yes, *me*—why not *me?*" cried the lad, indignantly drawing himself up to his full height.

"Why, thar is a heap to do out thar, youngster," said the Texian, "which you mought not be able to do, that's all."

"And what have *you* done?" said the boy, making up to the Texian, who stood full six feet in stature.

The crowd now gathered around, anxiously leaning forward to catch the reply of the Texian, for the boy's question was thought a poser. "What have *I* done?" said the Texian, repeating the question several times and laying much stress upon the pronoun I, at the same time looking much confused for a reply. "What have I done? Why," said he, "I have done more than *you* will ever do, if *you* go."

"And what is *that?*" said the still indignant lad. "Why, *I've got back safe!*" said the Texian with a loud laugh of triumph, in which the crowd joined.

An Indian Story

"GREEN 'UN"

DURING A LATE SOJOURN through the Western part of the country, it fell to my lot to stop over night at the residence of an old friend, one with whom I have spent many a happy day. . . . It was a very cold evening in the month of January, a chilling north wind was blowing, and the sleet was falling fast around. I had rode upwards of thirty-five miles since breakfast and as a matter of course was quite tired and very cold. I did not make the usual salutation ("Halloo!") which is generally given when a person rides to a house in the country; but as soon as I had dismounted, I handed the reins of my bridle to a servant boy, who, upon seeing me ride up, had come out to take care of my horse. Just as I stepped upon the gallery, I heard a very familiar voice saying, "Well, I don't think so, for Sam Houston wasn't in that scrape—at least, I don't think he was." The conversation, whatever it was, was stopped upon my entering the room, where I found Major ————— and L————, both in fine *spirits* and so forth. The Major, after asking me about my health, the news, and so on at length said, "Well, my young friend, L. and myself were just talkin about the Ingin wars, and—and," continued he, (after turning over a huge quid of tobacco in his mouth), "about Sam Houston's fightin, and sich like."

He was just about to commence a tale when the little bell com-

---

From *Spirit*, XXI, 10 (April 26, 1851), 116. "Green 'Un" was probably a journalist; several journalists who also contributed sketches to *Spirit* used similar pen names: "The Old One" (Francis Durivage of New England), "The Little 'Un" (Coddington C. Jackson of Louisiana), and "The Middle Aged 'Un."

menced ringing, and we went in to supper; after partaking of which, we were soon again around the big log fire. The old Major sat down in the corner and commenced smoking his pipe; L. and myself also sat down. Nothing was said for some minutes when at last the Major broke the silence by saying, "Gentlemen, I was jist about to commence tellin you of one of my scrapes which I got into with some *Ingins*—and now if you'll listen I'll tell it."

We of course agreed to keep silence, and he commenced (as near as I can remember) as follows: "I suppose you know that jist about the time when I was Captain in that rigiment of men at Austin, the Ingins was monstrous bad—killin people and stealin horses, and cuttin up all sorts of capers. Well, I used to tell the boys that they must always sleep with one eye open, for them savages would come sometime when they wasn't thinkin and steal the blankets off of em, and them, too, if they didn't look out. Well, they was very careful, takin em in general, but once or twice the Ingins come and made out to get two or three horses. Well, that sorter made em more watchful-like.

"One time, some six or eight of my men went out to hunt and gather pecans, and thinkin that there was no Ingins about, they thought that they'd be safe; so they all went off without takin guns—all of em but a feller there that they called *Short*, jist for a nick-name though, I 'spose. Anyhow, Short took his rifle and a pair of five-shooters along, thinkin he *mout* see somethin to kill. Well, they hadn't been gone a bit over half an hour, when I seed em all comin back as hard as they could run, hollerin, 'Injuns! Injuns!'

" 'They've got Short, haven't they?' said I, for I seed he wan't with em.

" 'Yes,' said they, 'the Injuns has got Short.'

" 'No,' said I, 'they hain't, for I hear him shootin. Now he's fightin like all hundred, I know!'

"They then got their guns, and we started out to where we heard him shootin. But all at once we noticed that he didn't shoot any more, and so of course we was certain that he was dead. But anyhow, we kept on and presently we met him, walkin along as though nothin had happened. I was completely astonished.

" 'Why, upon my soul!' said I, 'what has been the matter?'

" 'Well,' said he, 'you jest sit down thar, and I'll tell you all 'bout it.'

"We all sat down on the grass, and he commenced: 'Now,' said he, 'them fellers (pointin to the other boys that had been with him) 'is the biggest cowards in this world! Don't you think that while we was out thar under an old pecan tree gittin pecans, they all broke and run without sayin anything. I thought they was jest runnin for fun, so I said nothin nether, nor, what was worse, I didn't care nothin. But, anyhow, I said to myself that I was goin to git as many pecans as I wanted before I left. While I was thinkin about it, I thought I heard somebody talkin. I looks up, and there cum about forty Injuns, as I thought, but when I cum to count em there wan't but seven! I begun to think my time was comin, but anyhow I concluded that if they got my life, they'd have to pay mighty dear for it. So I run to the tree whar my rifle was and picked her up. By this time the Injuns was within fifty steps of me. So I raised up and let one of em have it, rite in the knowledge box, and down he cum— the rest of em sorter held back then, (before I'd got my rifle loaded, now mind you). Well, I hauls out one of them pistols and lets another feller have it, and he fell—but they still kept cumin and shootin their arrows at me, but they didn't hit me nary time. I 'spose they thought that I couldn't shoot twice with a pistol. Anyhow, they kept comin and I kept shootin till I killed every darn one of em *but one,* and he run clear off, so I couldn't kill *him!*'

"And," (continued the Major), "after Short had done talkin, I told some of the boys to go back to camp and git some hoes or somethin, and we would bury the varmints. . . . Well, sir, we found six lyin dead. While we was lookin at em, the boys cum with the hoes, dug a big hole, throwed em all in, and covered em all up. Poor crectures! I thought I'd treat em with some kindness, even if they was Ingins."

A Drake-Pulling in a Frontier Camp

"VEVO VOMBO"

WE ARE NOW on Oak Creek about 200 miles out of creation and for the present living in tents; we hope, however, to be pushed far enough one of these days to get *in* again, if the present revolutionary system continues. Well, a young sub [subaltern] came on some few months since and having been stationed for some time in one of our gayest cities was pining away under the influence of the dull monotony of camp life, love, and all the *ennui* incident to that delightful situation, when looking around for some amusements that were suitable for Christmas, fell upon the idea that a gander pulling would be the most amusing and novel sport that could be engaged in. Naturally excitable and nervous in his disposition, the idea had hardly entered his mind before he ran from tent to tent canvassing it with his brother officers. Meeting with every encouragement, he took advantage of the leave of absence of a brother officer to send to the nearest village (only 200 miles distant) for a couple of ganders. After many strict injunctions from the sub, we started but could not procure ganders for love or money.

Returning much chagrined at our want of success, we were trying to find out the best means of breaking the sad intelligence to our friend, when who should we see coming to meet us about ten miles from camp but the same sub, and scarcely were the customary

---

From *Spirit*, XXII (February 5, 1853), 606. The author, who contributed his article from Camp Chadbourne, Texas, is unidentified. The popular backwoods sport of gander-pulling was first described in frontier humor in A. B. Longstreet's *Georgia Scenes* (1835).

words of greeting passed before the question was asked, "Have you got the gander?" Of course, we had to tell him of our want of success, and we were much relieved upon his saying, "It don't make much difference, for I have bought a couple of old drakes which will answer just as well."

Well, Christmas came and with it a sun as bright as ever shone in fairy land. The mounted company, the one to which our young sub was attached and which was to make itself glorious in the annals of drake pulling, was awakened long before the reveille sounded and the men were already busily prepared in saddling their steeds and in plucking the feathers from and greasing the heads and necks of the unfortunate victims. After all the preliminaries were gone through with, the sub on a snow-white charger, marshalled his men, and after giving them rules which were to be strictly observed, winded up in an excited and eloquent strain. Pointing to the assembled garrison, he said: "Men! today I wish each of you gallantly to do his *devoir* for the honor of his company, for recollect, the eyes of hundreds are upon you."

Off they charged to the field of action, and standing near we were wrapped in enthusiasm at the glorious sight, but while contemplating it, our feelings suddenly changed as one of the Emerald Isle—already at that early hour happy under the influence of several cheering glasses—exclaimed, pointing to the gallant quarry, "There go the ——— G's on their duck hunt."

At about a hundred paces from the scaffold, the company was halted, and one of the victims "run up." At first he did not seem to mind it much, but as he watched the stern glances of his bearded foes and then glanced at his ridiculous position, his heart misgave him, and he exhibited his unspeakable disgust by flapping wings and made strange contortions of his well-greased neck. The word was given, and from the battle array emerged an amateur sub who had been offered the first pull. Bounding under the exciting influence of the spur, his proud steed shot onward. An intense excitement was manifested, and each beholder in breathless anxiety

watched the strained eye of the rider as he approached the unsus-
pecting victim: his hand is raised, he is under the scaffold, itching
for blood, his hand seizes the dangling neck. Now he has it! now he
hasn't! or, "May-be-so! yes! may-be-so! no!" as an Indian spectator
observed. As the rider pursued his onward course, the disgusted
drake flapped his wings and shaking his greasy head prepared
for the next onset. And now on that snow-white charger comes
the youthful commander. Standing erect in his stirrups, with eyes
dilated, he makes a bold effort, but the wary drake is now equally
anxious, and simultaneous with the sub's effort, he skillfully places
his head under his wing. "He has it!" but the spectators rather think
not as they see the unsuccessful grasp at the air, and the drake
coolly unfolding himself. Peal on peal of laughter followed the unsuccessful effort, and on that bright morning many a merry laugh
and shout were answered by the echoing hills and borne away to
murmur among the rocks and trees. And now come the ――――― G's.
Many a gallant pull was made and many a gallant dodge, but still
the neck hung on and continued its eel-like efforts to elude the grasp
of its foes. And now a stout Irishman, rendered obstinate by repeated failures, vowed that either he and his steed must part company or that drake and his head. Off he started, but unfortunately
for Pat, at the critical moment, his stirrup leather broke, and Pat
hugged with convulsive grasp his horse's neck; unused to such
tokens of endearment, especially when accompanied with a simultaneous blow of the spur, his horse launched out both heels and
then reared high in the air. Pat dexterously changed sides, but his
steed scorned all his untimely caresses and finally landed him amid
peals of laughter upon his mother earth.

Finally the neck came off, and with it a great deal of our day's
sport. The young sub, who had not succeeded in catching the head,
challenged the field for a race, which was eagerly accepted by
another sub, equally ambitious of rendering himself immortal. Off
they started; their horses, already greatly excited, seemed to enter
upon the sport with the same feelings as their riders and strained

every muscle. On they came right gallantly neck and neck, and the hurrahs were equally divided. Before the goal was reached, that snow-white charger was seen gradually falling farther and farther in the rear, and it was no longer doubted his rider had bet on the bob-tail nag.

Everything passed off pleasantly, and probably the pleasantest part of the day's sport was in witnessing the good humor and stoicism which the young commander exhibited at each new failure. We observed, however, that he did not yet appear satisfied, and casting our eyes toward the circle in which he was standing, we noticed him in close conversation with another young sub about his own size. Without wishing to play the eavesdropper, we heard the following, "I know you beat me fairly in the race, but I'll bet you can't throw me down."

I won't say whether that wrestling match came off or not, but as it was Christmas and generous bowls of eggnog were brewed, I rather think it did, especially as a bump was exhibited on one of the sub's heads the next morning, a bump which has not yet been found in any of our books on phrenology.

The Smashing of the Mirrors

"JOHN OF OXFORD"

IMMEDIATELY AFTER the battle of Cerro Gordo and the unavailing pursuit by our dragoons of Ampudia on his white charger and Santa Anna on his mule, a detachment which I had the honor to command was ordered to take possession of his Excellency's hacienda, which lay some distance from the main route of the army and seize or destroy such military stores as might be found.

With fifty picked men, well mounted and armed, and Lieut. C. for my second in command, off I started. Gaily we cantered over hill and hollow, the chance of a brush with the guerillas only adding a "sauce piqante" of expectancy to the pleasure of the ride. The declining sun at length saw us throwing frightfully distorted shadows across the courtyard of the hacienda, the tall dragoon horses, with their riders, looming in the fading light like mammoth elephants with castles on their backs. The scene around was beautiful, but would require the hand of an artist to render it aught like justice in description. Suffice it to say that nature had offered every facility and wealth and art had been lavish in their efforts to improve and adorn it.

Having performed the first duty of a dragoon on service (seeing to the horses), we proceeded at once to search the premises and after a thorough rummagement from turret to foundation stone succeeded in collecting a sufficient quantity of munitions of different kinds to have equipped sundry regiments of guerillas. Such as could be of use to our own troops were set aside as *spoils,* the

From *Spirit,* XXVI, 24 (July 26, 1856), 278.

balance to be destroyed before we left. Upon entering the house we found that wealth had been as freely and luxuriously expended in embellishing the interior as in adorning the landscape without. Marbles, bronzes, and beautiful paintings, filled the niches and graced the walls; on every side magnificent mirrors multiplied to infinity the splendors around. In the banqueting hall, which was of princely proportions, mirrors covered one side of the wall from floor to ceiling; and when the glittering chandelier was lighted strange were the contrasts which their broad surfaces reflected. Here, a work of Grecian or Italian art, embodying the idea of some sculptor-poet's dream; there, a bronzed and weather-beaten dragoon, armed in all the panoply of war's rough trade. Here, a collection of ornamental furniture, flower vases, gilded and embroidered ottomans; there, a pile of war-saddles and holsters, carbines and sabres. It was like a scene of enchantment and produced a wild strange feeling of delight such as I never had experienced before and never can feel as vividly again.

> Now daylight dies, and over
> The valley reigns the night;

but if there were any lovers among us, as in the vale of Cashmere, they were not allowed to wander.

Videttes were thrown out and guards stationed, and a fire having been kindled in the hall to correct the chilliness of the air, we began to think of our creature comforts. A rude but plentiful meal soon smoked on his Excellency's mahogany, while from the rich and varied stores of *liquid* wealth in the crypts below, from ripe South-Side to sparkling Hock, we did not hesitate to appropriate a few dozen bottles with which to wash down our soldier fare. We ate and drank heartily, soldierly, and well; and then, the necessary orders having been given, C. and I retired to our private quarters, which for this night I had established in his Excellency's own apartments. 'Twas a cozy nest that, for a tired trooper, with its thousand

little lady-like elegancies scattered about, among which was a most
exquisite "bonnet du nuit" which I incontinently seized.

C. being a remarkably handsome young fellow, I insisted upon
his putting the captured article on and *looking the lady* on one side
of the bed, while I, with all due dignity surrendered myself to sleep
as his Excellency on the other. With the rich lace frilling drawn
under his chin concealing the incipient down of his whiskers, the
Lieutenant really looked very pretty indeed; I played Santa Anna
to the life, save and except the advantage in dignity of two legs
over one. C., who was my only audience, applauded to the skies and
flattered me much upon my chances of success as a *delineator of
dignitaries.*

The midnight hour had come and gone, the officer of the guard
had made his round and reported, and all save the sentries were
doing their best to sleep "twell mornin," when I was roused by a
roar and crash as though a tremendous battering train had dashed
the building to atoms about our ears and Old Totten were coming
Vera Cruz over the hacienda. For one moment, though roused, I
was bewildered; the next, I had seized my sabre and rushed to the
hall, where all the men who were not on *out* duty had been left
sleeping on their arms. As I burst into the room, a sulphurous
canopy of smoke was curling up toward the ceiling beneath which
the men were standing in line, weapon in hand, gazing toward the
wall where once there had been mirrors. Just then, and before a
question had been asked, a vidette was brought in, who reported
having fired upon a small party of guerillas, evidently reconnoitering
the hacienda, but on finding us, as they supposed, in force, dashed
off when challenged. The matter was now explained without a word
said! Hearing the report of the vidette's carbine, the half roused
fellows sprang to their feet, fancying themselves attacked, and mistaking by the uncertain firelight their own reflection in the mirrors
for the antagonist party had fired slap bang into them. *And that's
the way the mirrors were smashed.* The whole thing flashed across
me in an instant, and I screamed with laughter. The men looked

sheepish enough at first, but soon a general and expansive grin spread over every countenance, followed by perfect yells of merriment. The noise was deafening and prevented me from noticing what was occurring in my rear. All eyes being directed towards me, and not dreaming my uniform (drawers and sabre) so very ridiculous under the circumstances, I looked behind me. Oh! ye powers of fun! There stood C., who had just rushed into the hall, still rigged in the senora's night cap, flourishing his sword with one hand, and rubbing his half-opened eyes with the other, shouting *Charge!* through the frills of thread-lace, as though giving orders through the bars of a helmet. Had his Excellency himself been there, I think he would have forgiven both the breaking of the mirrors and the desecration of the "bonnet du nuit" in consideration of *that laugh.*

Knowing the Bull by the Horns

ANONYMOUS

AMONGST the various enterprises which followed the American flag into Mexico was that of furnishing American horses to the grandees of that country. Larger, better formed, and better adapted to harness than the native stock, American horses were in great demand, and although many were lost in crossing the Gulf and many fell victims to the diseases incident to acclimation, still the horse traders of the Mississippi valley pushed the business with spirit and success.

Certainly amongst the most energetic of those engaged in the business was John Howton. He was originally from an extreme Northern State but had gradually worked along the body politic as a needle point sometimes does through the physical system until he had successively presented himself in almost every State in the Union. Finding the States, however, rather a pent up sort of Utica, he had crossed the Gulf in the wake of our army and at the time of which we write enjoyed a current acquaintance from Maine to Mexico inclusive.

Howton's dress and address were such as might have been expected from extended social facilities operating upon a raw material originally very uncouth. His stature was short and square, his hair intensely crimson, and standing as it did in strands radiating from his head, presented a lively picture of an exploding rocket.

From *Spirit*, XXIII, 42 (December 3, 1853), 495-96. Titled "A 'Cute Yankee in Mexico—Knowing the Bull by the Horns" and signed "Two of Us," this is one of the few sketches devoted to civilians in the Mexican War; most newspaper sketches of the time concerned the humorous aspects of soldiering.

205

His mouth was wide and bad luck in a spirit of mischief had enlarged its apparent dimensions by the sear of a horseshoe. Where the natural soil of his countenance was visible through a beard that resembled a chestnut burr, it was ornamented with premium freckles about the size and color of brass farthings. His costume indicated the impressions of his erratic pursuits. He had a furred hat of a brown-red color which had undoubtedly been made in Missouri, since no manufacturers out of the very focus of the fur trade could have put so honest an excess of material into the fabric. His coat and overcoat were of New England, his leggings and whip of Ohio. In part pay for an American saddle, he had obtained a serape of many colors and a pair of Mexican leather breeches with an indefinite number of bell-buttons which he swore "took him as long to fasten as it would to curry two horses" and which he intended to have sewed up upon his return. Howton's language had become as varied as his clothing. He had picked up his phraseology according to the emergencies of his eventful life, and he "guessed" at the distances or "cara ho'd" the roads with equal facility.

We were upon the highway from Mexico to Vera Cruz. It was night with a very bright moonlight. Howton had made us familiar with every horse he had ever sold in Mexico, and we could, as commissioners, have assessed with sufficient accuracy everything he was worth in the world, since he had told us his losses with as much candor as his gains. His speculations on the last trip had varied somewhat from the usual operations of his profession. He had sold an Hidalgo a pair of horses bought out of an Ohio wagon, as having been begotten, bred, and broken, expressly for the use of "Ex. Sen. Pres. de los Unidos Estados," General Taylor, who unfortunately died, and therefore did not need them. During a stay of several days upon free quarters at the hacienda of the Hidalgo, where he recruited his steeds for a grand descent upon the city of Puebla, Howton had "possessed" his courteous host with the extreme value of the cattle of Ohio. He expatiated upon the effect which their introduction would have upon the rather diminutive stock of the

country, and putting them at a high figure to impress a proper esti-
mate of their value, he received an order to purchase a bull and
two cows on account of his host.

These splendid cattle, combining in their pedigree every possible
permutation of the Devon, Durham, and Norfolk were called "the
patent abbreviated short-horn." The cows with their calves were
purchased from a flatboat at New Orleans. The bull was procured
in the vicinity of that city from a sugar estate, partly in exchange
for a mule, partly in consideration of taking him out of the neighborhood. He had been in the habit of "roaming with the dew upon
his feet," pretty much wherever he was inclined, whereby one of
his eyes had been extinguished by a fowlingpiece and his dewlap
torn bodily off by the dogs. But the certificate of pedigree and performance represented him as the victor of numerous fights and even
set forth the American Don Joses and Jesuses that the ferocious
bull had slain. He was to become the progenitor of a line of bulls
destined to raise the renown of the hacienda to a lofty elevation.

Howton had met with another adventure which he had contrived
to turn to account. Coming down from Baton Rouge as a deck passenger, he had found an angry Captain preparing to land what
everyone proclaimed to be "a nigger" upon the testimony of a very
dark skin, an unintelligible tongue, and an inability to perform that
indispensable form of tribute known among navigators as "settling
with the Captain." Howton discovered the nondescript to be a
"Mexikin greaser." He joked the Captain about being taken in and
finally took charge of the greaser at a reduced fare, intending to
employ him in the capacity of vaquero, or cowdriver extraordinary,
near the court of Mexico.

The greaser, having escaped being marooned at a Mississippi
woodyard, was, like any other rescued captive, very grateful. He
prostrated himself at the feet of Howton, and to use the expressions
of the latter "the d----d thing carried on pitiful." He was promoted,
however, to be master of the cattle.

The veteran bull was provided with a large red hood and a blue

ephod, whereon was worked "GENL SANTY ANNY" in large letters. These ornamental garments were to be worn at the sale of the
bull and other state occasions, at the discretion of any subsequent
proprietor.

But when the stock of horses and cattle was disembarked upon
the Mexican shores, Howton saw that the majestic gravity with
which the hero of the arena proceeded would delay the progress of
his whole drove of horses, involve many unnecessary bills, and postpone his arrival in market. He, therefore, detached Fernando, who
was ordered to proceed with due care of the invaluable stock entrusted to him. He gave him no money but ordered the various
posaderos on the road to furnish whatever he might require. He
then hastened forward, heralding the merits and magnifying the
cost of the bull and his family at every place which he passed until
every *posada* was thronged with spectators to see "el toro Ameri-
cano grande." As Howton hastened to the metropolis, the passengers
in the stage were asked about the fine stock they had passed. At
first they reported them getting on very well, then rumors of their
illness were communicated by the same medium, and after a few
days the *bull*etins ceased altogether.

Howton was now returning with the most indignant reproaches
against the ungrateful Fernando, whom, besides having redeemed
from bondage, he had also accoutred with a pair of his own
breeches, the cost to be deducted from his salary as vaquero.

We were approaching the place where the Devons and Durhams
had been last heard from. It had been arranged that an American
who understood Spanish very well should inquire into the circumstances. Howton wisely determined to remain incognito for fear
bills might be presented against him. The passengers entered zeal-
ously into his grievances and sympathized with him, whereas they
should have extended their congratulations rather to the Hidalgo,
who escaped paying a very high price for bull beef. Such, however,
is nationality.

We all entered the *tienda* (a shop about the size of a dogkennel, or a No. 3 drygoods box, generally filled with a very stout yellow woman, a lot of fish, onions, bread, cotton cloth, cheap violins, wax dolls, chocolate, and *agua ardiente*). There were two men in the one we visited on this occasion, with the usual variety and with onions in festoons of triumph over the unlucky proprietor of the bull. The first enquiries were very general. They were based on a report that an American gentleman had lost some very valuable stock on the road. It was admitted that they had stopped at the *tienda*, and the proprietor hastened to exculpate himself from any responsibility in regard to them.

"Ask him," said Howton, "wha's Fernandy?"

The response was very unsatisfactory—a Mexican of the lower order being about as hard to distinguish or catch as one of the wild cattle of the pampas, or any particular one of the vermin upon his own person. He had stopped with the cattle but had abandoned them and gone off.

"Ask him what become of the cattle." The cattle had been taken sick, and "*a los pocos dies morio la vaccas*" (in a few days afterwards the cows died).

"Ask him what went with the bull."

"Ah, senor," said the shopkeeper, with an hypercritical whine, "*a los pocos dies desperes morio el toro*" (a few days afterwards the bull died also).

"Well," said Howton, very much exasperated, "ask him, G-- d----n him, what went with the calvcs."

"Ah, *el vacaros estaban muy malos*" (the calves were also very ill).

"D----n you," said Howton in great wrath, "I expect you give a big bull punchin (bull fight), and then butchered the whole business. Gentlemen," said he, turning to us, "I'll bet that bull's carcase has been strung out as long as a bed-cord and this d----d yaller thing has been a-retailing of his very chittlins by the yard."

The black eye of the Mexican glanced with mingled expression of delight and apprehension. His brother, apprehensive from our numbers, the manner of Howton, and his knowledge of the rascality which had been practiced, took the American side. He said, "Me American! Me go to New Orleans, quick."

"G---- d----n your yaller soul," exclaimed the indignant jockey, "you'd better stay whar you are. We've got niggers enough there a' ready."

The shopkeeper pursued his narration. He evidently played for a point. He thought to vindicate his innocence and strengthen the probabilities of his story by demanding payment for his services. He said in a musical voice, "*Acquester la quinter—que costeora per medicos y medicamentos que suma y quarante nueve pesos y siete reales.*" (The bill for the doctor's attention and medicine is forty-nine dollars and seventy-five cents). *Pero el efficacio del vacaro qui applicara varios medicinos, se allevio per lo cual ci gasto vente dos pesos y dos reallos en le cursceon de llos.*" (But for the curing of the calf, to which we applied various remedies, the bill had been increased two dollars and a quarter).

"Cured em be d----d! You eat em up and you want to get your pay twice. Ask him what become of the carcase." The shopkeeper could not say; they had been eaten up by *los perros* (the dogs).

"By G----;" said the desperate Howton, "ef the cows and the bull's been eat up, I don't reckon they eat up that bull's horns, and I'd know em amongst a thousand. Ask him whar's the horns. Whar's the bull's horns?"

"*Este, senor, pagara la cuenta?*" (Will that gentleman pay the account?) asked the cunning Mexican.

"No, by G--, I shan't; they're no cattle of mine. They belonged to a man near Puebly. But I hate to see such meanness." Then he added, turning to us, "I know em. Ef he had any hook upon me, he'd wring in one of thar d---d alkaldys, and I'd never git done payin as long as I had anything, and maybe nuvver see home itself agin. So I guess I'll let him slide. Tell him, mister," (to the interpreter) "that ef you see the man that owned the cattle, you'll let him know of the bill for doctorin em."

The call of the driver, and the impregnable position of the Posa-dero, who from a defendant had become an applicant for his bill, terminated the enquiry, and the committee rose. Howton swore as he climbed up on the coach that if he had time he could prove by the neighbors that the "yaller raskal had first showed old Santy Anny in a grand bull-fight, and then sold or made beef of the whole lot and that if he could be sure that he had included that d----d Fernandy in the slaughter and sale, he should be perfectly satis-fied. But," said he, as he showed his enormous mouth at the side of the coach, "did you notice how the thing looked when I asked him to show me the horns! I had him on the horns, didn't I?"

"But, Howton, how was it about the bill?"

"Why, by G--, gentlemen, the fact was, *thar* he had *me!*"

VI
Tales, Tall or True

VI. Tales, Tall or True

THE GOLDEN AGE *of tale-telling in newspapers, between 1835 and 1845, came almost too early for Texas. While William T. Porter was popularizing frontier and backwoods sketches in his New York weekly,* Spirit of the Times, *Texans were fighting a revolution, repelling invasion from Mexico, and getting ready for the Mexican War. As a result, there were fewer journalists and competent amateur writers in Texas to supply Porter with tales than there were in the older states of the Old Southwest—Louisiana and Mississippi, for instance. Military officers who had supplied sketches for the* Spirit *from other areas seemed to lose some of their sense of humor when confronted with frontier conditions in Texas.*

This is not to say that Texans did not tell tales—around campfires, in bars, on front porches. They did, but there were few aspiring authors around to copy down the tales and send them in to Porter. Those that did get into print, particularly the hunting yarns, are quite typical of the newspaper humor of the time. Two themes received more attention in Texas tales than in stories from other regions: the visiting foreigner who comes to Texas to hunt and is put through the initiation of the tenderfoot; and the border lawlessness which, whether real or fictionized, contributed to the bad reputation of Texas.

In these early tales may be seen the humor and violence that became important ingredients of the western tall tale as it emerged in Texas in a later period.

215

Panther Tales

CAPT. WILLIAM SEATON HENRY

A PARTY of officers left the camp for a three days' hunt on the Nueces. The second day we had all returned for some grub, except D., when we saw him coming on horseback with (as we supposed) a deer behind him. To our joy, instead of a deer, he threw down an enormous panther. "Well done, D!" was the involuntary expression. "Where did you kill him?—under what circumstances?"

"Easy, my boys—just hold your horses; I'll tell you; but just tip me some grog, for I am rather used up. Well, I shot a busting big buck and saw it fall about a hundred yards from me, in a mott. Knowing when 'Old King Death' (name of his Wesson rifle) sends a ball that it is all up with anything it hits, I gave myself no uneasiness about the buck and was crawling upon another when I heard the d----st fuss and growling where the buck fell and concluded the wolves must have got it. I ran up and got within six feet before I saw the cause of all this confusion. Simultaneously with my sight, with a sharp cat growl and desperate leap, a panther sprang at me. I had barely time to fall back a few feet, when he brushed past me in full leap, just missing my person, and alighting on the ground about twenty feet from me. He instantly turned towards me and prepared—with teeth shown, tail on his back, and death in his eye— to make another spring at me. I drew up 'King Death,' saying, 'It is

From *Spirit*, XVII, 40 (November 27, 1847). Captain William Seaton Henry, who wrote under the pen name "Guy de L***," contributed a series of sketches and dispatches to *Spirit*. Later he collected and edited them for his book *Campaign Sketches of the War with Mexico*.

you or I, old fellow,' cracked away, and shot him through the center of the forehead, a little lower than the eyes. He fell, and, with some desperate struggles, died, relieving me from rather an unpleasant predicament."

"Good! old fellow! Bring out that bottle of Cozzen's old brandy; none but the best drink for the panther-killer."

It certainly was a dangerous, most fearfully dangerous situation. D.'s coolness, daring, and ready command of nerve saved his life. The animal weighed one hundred and sixty pounds, was seven feet eight inches from tip to toe, and four feet high! The spotted tigers are terrible animals, and the fiercest hunting dogs cower at their approach. Col. C. of Texas told me that on the Bernard River while he was hunting coons with a friend, the dogs treed something in an immense live oak, over which they made an unusual commotion. Being the youngest, it was his fate to climb the tree and get, as they thought, the coon down. The tree was directly on the river bank, and its horizontal branches reached nearly across. (The trees are no saplings in that section of the country, the live oaks especially; for they do say that under the shade of some, five hundred persons could dine.) . . . He climbed the tree and crawled out on one of those horizontal limbs. Expecting every moment to see the coon, what should present itself, upon his rising up to look around but an immense spotted tiger with eyes "like balls of fire." What to do was the question. He could not back out; he dared not drop into the river, for it was full of alligators. He fell upon this plan: he swung himself below the limb and hung on by his hands! The tiger walked over him, descended the tree, and went through a crowd of nine dogs—as fierce ones as there were in Texas—which never even growled at him.

Panther Hunting

ANONYMOUS

ABOUT THE MIDDLE of November, a party of five or six persons under R. D. Kelly, of this city [San Antonio], were engaged in surveying land on the West Fork of the Rio Frio some seventy-five miles west of San Antonio, and their dogs suddenly gave chase to a bear. It being a very large one, the party followed; and after proceeding about half a mile, a huge panther crossed the track of the bear. The dogs, preferring the panther, followed him, and they had gone but a short distance when he sprang into a low tree, as the dogs were hard after him. The party soon came up, and their only weapons of defence were hatchets and bowie knives, they having carelessly left their guns and pistols at camp that morning, which was some three miles distant. They were within a few feet of the panther before they discovered him, and he was now making ready to jump upon them. There was no time for hesitation at this important crisis. While the dogs for the moment attracted his attention, one of the party, J. R. Davenport, drew his bowie knife, and walked fearlessly up to the tree, and stabbed him in a fatal spot. The panther, as soon as he felt the knife, sprang over thirty feet the first jump; he had not gone but a few yards before he was overcome by the effects of the wound and the dogs, came to a halt, and soon died, not, however, until he had severely wounded several of the dogs while even in the last agonies of death. He was between ten and eleven feet in length from the nose to the tip of the tail and two feet and a half in height when standing in his natural position. The next day Mr.

From *Spirit*, XXIV, 50 (January 27, 1855), 594.

Davenport killed another of the same size. He had raised his rifle to shoot a deer, when he saw the panther crouched a few yards before him, patting his huge paws, ready to jump. He drew his faithful rifle and shot him between the eyes. He died without scarcely a struggle.

Thereby Hangs a Tail

ANONYMOUS

IT HANGS to what the naturalists call a Puma, the Mexicans a Lion, the Texans a Mexican Lion. A splendid fellow he is, too, with great, sleepy, green eyes, a skin as soft as velvet and beautifully mottled, teeth a half inch long and sharp as razors, claws over an inch in length, paws four inches across, limbs as finely proportioned as a sculptor could desire, and as brawny as any ploughman's you ever saw, a chest broad as a young colt's, a body as flexible as a snake's. The fellow is playful, too; the only precaution to be taken is not to put your hand where he can get hold of it. To look at him, one would think him the gentlest of kittens, as weak and delicate as a mouse; but a look at his old cage, with the thick timber torn up as if struck by lightning, will change this opinion at once. Once or twice already he has got loose in the big warehouse where he is kept, and such a sudden disappearance of the human inhabitants thereof as then took place was never before witnessed. He did no harm, however, being mercifully inclined.

This specimen of what Texas can produce in the way of wild animals, was, when a cub, caught on the Rio Grande by an officer in the army, and was presented by him to a friend of his residing at Corpus Christi. He grew up under charge of a Mexican, who led him about without a chain and treated him as he would a favorite dog. The animal never attempted to harm his guardian and appeared to have a decided affection for him.

From *Spirit*, XXII, 44 (December 18, 1852), 520. Reprinted from the New Orleans *Picayune*.

Not long since an acquaintance of ours, a young man un-acquainted with the ways of the world and particularly the world of Texas, was out on horseback in the prairies, back of Corpus Christi, looking for what he could see. Presently, in moving along a road, he came across one of those low, odd, awkward-looking things called a Mexican cart. It occupied the middle of the high-way; the oxen harnessed to it were lying down, chewing the cud of animal reflection. The vehicle was apparently unoccupied.

Our adventurer rode nearer, and just as he was within a few feet of the cart, up rose suddenly a tall, black, oil-skin covered, steeple-shaped Mexican hat, and under it one of the strangest faces that ever astonished a stranger. It was no less an individual than our "lion," who had sprung up and sat there on his haunches, showing his teeth in a grim smile and staring out of his big, green, glistening eyes in no pleasant manner for a person unaccustomed to such ad-ventures. Our traveller felt "all overish" down to his boots; his horse, frightened out of his wits, snorted and reared and pranced around, getting as far out of the way of the cart as he could. The "lion" sat still, wagging his long tail and evidently enjoying the scene. His appearance, with the tall, queer hat, was ridiculous enough; still there was something about him that made it more natural to desire to get out of his neighborhood than to stay near and laugh at him.

Our traveller speedily regained his presence of mind and forced his horse up to the cart. A man's head now rose above the sides of the cart and asked in Spanish what the Senor wanted. The lion's companion was his guardian—a Mexican. He was going down to Corpus Christi to deliver him to his owner and at noon had stopped his cart and laid down to take a nap. The lion's haunch was an excellent pillow for the Mexican's head and the lion's head a superior deposit for the Mexican's hat. So both had gone lovingly to sleep together.

A Bear Story

"GREEN 'UN"

LET ME GIVE YOU a short yarn, as near word for word as I can remember, as it was related to me by an old hunter, a few days since. In the course of our conversation he remarked, "Jist two hours by sun one day, in the latter end of October last, I hearn my dogs barkin like sixty. I looks out'n the door and sees em arter one o' the biggest bars this side o' Fiddler's Green. The bar war runnin across the field, and while I was lookin on, I seen him attempt to jump over the picket fence at the corner. Jist as he was about to leave my premises, my dog Cuffy made a grab at his tail and cotcht it about two feet from the eend."

"Stop," said I, "a bear's tail is not longer than four *inches*, at most."

"That's a fac, that's a fac," he continued, "but I meant *two inches;* anyhow, Cuffy held him thar tight, for better un half an hour, leastways, till I could get my two five-shooters. I forgot to tell you, that my ole rifle got broke t'other day, while I was 'temptin to climb a tree with her in my hand. You see a gang of wild hogs were arter me, and—"

"But that's not the bear story," I remarked.

"Well, as I was sayin, he held the bar thar till I could git my two five-shooters to where the bar was, but the cursed dog begin to look around for me and let go his holt; the critter got loose and broke like a quarter hoss—me and t'other dogs arter him. Well, sir, we run that bar better 'an fifteen miles, durin which time, I *fired fifty-seven* shots at him with my pistols and at last brought him to the ground, and what do you think he weighed?"

"Don't know," I answered.

"Well, sir, I weighed him thar on the spot, and don't you think he weighed *two thousand three hundred pounds!*"

I tried to poke in an answer in the negative, but the old hunter continued, not waiting for an answer.

"So I jist shouldered him, and off I started for home. When I got thar, you had better be thinkin I was tired, and don't you believe that when I got home, my ole 'oman, thinkin as how I mout be some orful terrificatious animal, commenced on me with the fokes! That was orfullest bar I has seen since—since, oh, I don't know how long."

I doubted the truth of his story, considerably, and when I inquired more particularly concerning the weight, how he got it home, and so on the old hunter suddenly got into a notion to leave and suddenly *vanished* from my sight.

Uncle Pete's Bar Story

"ESPERANCE"

TRAVELING not long since high up on the Trinity, I remained one night with a worthy old gentleman whose humor was as celebrated in the neighborhood as his hospitality. As I rode up to the gate I heard such peals of laughter that, although I had never been in that part of the country before, I felt convinced that I could be no where else but at Uncle Pete's. Nor was I mistaken, for he soon met me at the gate, and after taking my horse and placing him in the stable, we proceeded to the house, where I was introduced to several young men who were collecting stock in the neighborhood and had camped for the night with Uncle Pete. They had evidently been enjoying themselves with rough jokes and tales, when my arrival interrupted them, but after supper was over one of them begged of Uncle Pete to give them a tale.

"Yes, yes," cried several, "let's have your fight with the bar, when you first came to these diggins."

"And let us know how many you *thought* you saw," said another.

"Well, boys," said Uncle Pete, "if you must have it, here goes, and I reckon if you had been in my place, some of you would have seen *more bars* than I did. Well, about two months after I had first squatted in this part of the country, I went over to Bill Davis's clearing one morning to grind my axe and get my gun lock mended. You know he lived about seven miles from my shanty, and I told my old woman before I started that I would be back again for supper. But Bill was putting up a corn crib and asked me to lend

From *Spirit*, XIX, 28 (September 1, 1849), 325.

him a hand until night, so I concluded to stay with him until after supper and then go home by moonlight.

"Well, boys, after we had got through working on the crib and finished supper, Bill Davis brought out some whiskey and some good tobacco and insisted that John Wills, Tom Barnes, and two or three others with myself should hold on for an hour or two and be sociable. We did so and I reckon it must have been nigh on to 12 o'clock, when I shook hands, mounted old Camanche, and started. The moon was shining mighty bright; whether the *red eye* had anything to do with it, I don't know, but it looked bigger to me than it ever did before—in fact it looked sometimes almost as if two moons had got together. . . . On I started, taking a small trail that John Wills told me to follow out of the swamp as it was a nigher cut to my house.

"Well, when I got to the edge of the prairie, I struck a bee line for home; but I hadn't gone more than half a mile from the timber, when I saw about one of the biggest bars that ever made a pig squeak, about fifty yards off, right ahead of me. Now, I have had some bar fights in my time, and some of them was not to be sneezed at, and although I reckoned on getting a few scratches from the critters, still, I never dodged a fight with any of them. But I do say that when I first saw *this* varmint—the biggest I had ever seen—my skin *had* a little touch of the goose flesh because I kinder thought it was the devil himself, he was so black and sassy. At first, I thought of taking the back track, seeing I had no gun, but then the idea of being laughed at kept me still, and I set my brains to work to find out some way to circumvent old shaggy. While I was planning against *him*, he was doing the same for me, for he kept edging and sideling along towards me, snapping his teeth and growling in a way that was anything but comfortable to my feelings. Thinks I, if I can only make some of the boys hear me in the neighborhood, old fellow, we'll make you smoke for this. With that I commenced yelling out, 'Bar! Bar! Ingins! Murder! Fire!' and everything else, for the critter was a-getting mighty close and me a-backing all the time.

It was getting too hot—it was either fight or run and that to be done in a hurry. Nobody heard me; if they did, they had no time to come, so I wheeled for a clear start somewhere. By this time the bar was not ten feet from me, champing and foaming at the mouth like a mad dog. As I turned, with a hop, skip, and jump, he had us. Grabbing old Camanche by the hind leg with one paw, he give me a rake in the back with the other, which slit my coat and shirt from my neck to my saddle tree. In a moment he had my bowie [knife] into him *some,* and old Camanche give him a somerset with his heels. Now, boys, I tell you that bar was mad when he gathered himself up, and no mistake, for he come agin full tilt at us with his teeth a-popping, making a noise like a parcel of hogs eating acorns. I didn't stop to see any more, for I thought it was time to be off, and the way Camanche made a blue streak along the edge of that timber was a caution; he didn't want any spurring *that time;* he was as bad scared as I was. Everytime I looked around I thought I could see one varmint close upon me—here he was—there he was— he seemed to start out of every hollow tree and briar patch I passed until at last I thought the woods was full of bar, and they were all after me.

"Well, I suppose I kept old Camanche at his best for at least an hour—going I didn't know where—and the old horse was pretty well done over, when I espied a house close by. So bad was I scared that I never thought of the fence before the door, but I bulged old Camanche through it—over his head I went, bang into the house, right in the middle of several fellows who were sleeping there. 'A bar! a bar! huzza! a bar's amongst you!' I shouted with all my might. And if ever you saw a scramble, there was one there that night. The way the shirt tails flew about was funny; such swearing, shouting, and kicking, some looking for one thing, some for another— some hollered 'Where's my gun?' 'Give me a knife!' screamed another. And one fellow I saw a-hiding under the bed, while another who looked out the door swore it was in the yard, big as a 'Brotti- mus,' snorting fire and brimstone.

"Old Camanche liked to have been killed for certain, for it took me some time to get a hearing and explain matters. However, after a while all was settled, and although some of the boys tried afterwards to raise a laugh on me for running from the bar, I had only to mention the 'Brottimus' with his fire and brimstone, and they would let me alone.

"And now, boys, you've got my story, and it's about time to go to bed. But let me advise you; when you leave a neighbor's house of a moonshiny night, be sure of two things—that you've *got* your rifle and that you haven't got no 'red eye' under your shirt."

Wolves on the Track

BIGFOOT WALLACE

ONE VERY COLD EVENING two or three hours perhaps before sundown, I concluded to take a little round in the woods by way of exercise and bring home some fresh venison for supper; so I picked up "Sweet Lips" [his rifle] and started for a rough, broken piece of country, where previously I had always found deer in abundance. But, somehow, the deer didn't seem to be stirring that evening, and I walked two or three miles without finding a single one. After going so far, I hated to return without meat, and I kept on, still hoping to find the deer before it got too dark to shoot; but at last I had to give it up and turned my course back toward home again.

By this time the sun was setting, and I hurried up as fast as possible to get out of the chaparral and into the prairie before night came on. All the evening I had heard the wolves howling around me in an unusual way, but I had no fear of them, as I had been told they seldom, if ever, attacked a man in Texas. When I had gone back perhaps a half mile or so, a large gray wolf trotted out into the path before me and commenced howling in the most mournful manner; and in an instant he was answered by a dozen other wolves in the hills around us. Thinks I, old fellow, if you are hatching a plot for my benefit, I'll make sure of you, anyhow; so I brought "Sweet Lips" to range on his shoulderblade, and at the crack of the gun he gave one spring into the air and dropped as dead as a hammer in his tracks.

From Duval, *Adventures of Bigfoot Wallace*, pp. 64-69.

But, somehow, although I can't say I felt any fear of them, my suspicions were aroused as to foul play on the part of the gentlemen who were answering him from the hills, and I loosened "Old Butch" in the sheath, rammed another bullet down "Sweet Lips," and as soon as I had done so, I put out for home again in double-quick time. But the faster I went, the faster the wolves followed me, and looking back after a little while, I saw twenty-five or thirty "lobos" (a large, fierce kind of wolf, found only in Mexico and Texas) trotting along after me at a rate I knew would soon bring them into close quarters; and in the bushes and chaparral that bordered the trail I was travelling I could see the gleaming eyes and pointed ears of at least a dozen others coming rapidly toward me.

I saw in a minute that they meant mischief, but I knew it was useless to try to beat a wolf in a footrace. However, I resolved to keep on as long as they would let me, and when they closed in I would give them the best ready-made fight I had "in the shop." So I stepped out as briskly as I could, and the wolves trotted after me, howling in a way that made my hair stand on end and my very blood run cold. A dozen times I wished myself back again safe in "old Virginny," where a man might travel for a hundred miles without meeting up with anything more dangerous than a possum; but wishing didn't stop the wolves, so I let out my "best licks," hoping that I could make home before they could muster up courage enough to attack me.

But, I reckoned without my host, for one big fellow, more daring or hungry than the rest, made a rush at me, and I barely had time to level my gun and fire, for he was touching the muzzle of it when I pulled the trigger. He fell dead at my feet, but, as if this had been the signal for a general attack, in an instant the whole pack were around me, snarling and snapping and showing their white teeth in a way that was anything but pleasant.

I fought them off with the breech of my gun, for they didn't give me any chance to load it, retreating all the while as rapidly as I could. Once so many of them rushed in upon me at the same time that in spite of all my efforts I failed to keep them at bay and they dragged me to the ground. I thought for an instant that it was all up with me, but despair gave me the strength of half a dozen men, and I used "Old Butch" to such a good purpose that I killed three outright and wounded several others, which appeared somewhat to daunt the balance, for they drew off a short distance and began to howl for reinforcements.

The reinforcements were on their way, for I could hear them howling in every direction, and I knew that I had no time to lose. So I put off at the top of my speed, and in those days it took a pretty fast Spanish pony to beat me a quarter when I "let out the kinks." I let em out this time with a will, I tell you, and fairly beat the wolves for half a mile or so, but my breath then began to fail me, and I could tell by their close angry yelps that the devils were again closing in upon me.

By this time I was so much exhausted that I knew I should make a poor fight of it, more especially as I could perceive, from the number of dark forms behind me and the gleaming eyes and shining teeth that glistened out of every bush on the wayside, that the wolves had had a considerable addition to their number. It may be thought strange that I didn't take to a tree, but there were no trees there to take to—nothing but stunted chaparral bushes not much higher than a man's head.

I thought my time had come at last, and I was almost ready to give up in despair, when all at once I remembered seeing as I came out a large lone oak tree, with a hollow in it about large enough for a man to crawl into, which grew on the banks of a small canyon not more than three or four hundred yards from where I then was. I resolved to make one more effort and if possible to reach this tree before the wolves came up with me again, and if ever there was good, honest running done, without any throw-off about it, I did it then. The fact is, I believe a man can't tell how fast he can run until he gets a pack of wolves after him in this way. A fellow will naturally do his best when he knows that if he doesn't in twenty minutes he will be parcelled out among as many ravenous wolves, a head to one, a leg to another, an arm to a third, and so on. At least that was the effect it had on me, and I split the air so fast with my nose that it took the skin off of it, and for a week afterwards it looked like a peeled onion.

However, I beat the wolves once more fairly and squarely, and not much time to spare either, for just as I crawled into the hollow of the tree (which was about as high as my head from the ground) the ravenous creatures were howling all around me. At the bottom of the hollow I found a "skunk" snugly stowed away, but I soon routed him out, and the wolves gobbled him up in an instant. He left a smell behind him though that was anything but agreeable in such close quarters. However, I was safe there at any rate from the attacks of the wolves, and all the smells in the city of New Orleans couldn't have driven me from my hole just at that time.

The wolves could only get at me one at a time, and with "Old Butch" in my hand I knew I could manage a hundred in that way. But such howling and yelling I never heard before or since but once, and that was when I was with the Keechies and a runner came in and told them that their great chief Buffalo Hump had been killed in a fight with the Lipans. The wolves bit, and gnawed, and scratched, but it wasn't any use, and every now and then a fellow would jump up and poke his nose into the hollow of the tree; but just as sure as he did it, he caught a wipe across it with "Old Butch" that generally satisfied his curiosity for a while. All night long they kept up their serenade, and as you may well suppose I didn't get much sleep. However, the noise didn't matter, for I had got several severe bites on my arms and legs and the pain I suffered from them would have kept me awake anyhow.

Just at daylight the next morning the wolves began to sneak off, and when the sun rose not one was to be seen, except three dead ones at the root of the tree, that had come in contact with "Old Butch." I waited a while longer to be certain they had all left, when I crawled out of my den, gave myself a shake, and found I was all right, except a pound or so of flesh taken out of one of my legs, and a few scratches on my arms. I hobbled back home, and for a long time afterwards when I heard the howling of wolves I always felt a little uneasy.

I found out the next day why the wolves had attacked me in the way they did. I had a bottle of assafoetida in my trunk, which somehow had got broken and run out among my clothes, and when the wolves pitched into me I had on a coat that had been wet with the confounded stuff and smelled worse than a polecat. I had often heard that assafoetida would attract wolves, but I always thought before this that it was a sort of old-woman's yarn; but it's a fact, and if you don't believe it, go some dark night into a thick chaparral where wolves are numerous and pour about a gill over your coat and then wait a little and see what will turn up; and if you don't hear howling, and snapping, and snarling, I'll agree to be stung to death by bumblebees.

Bill Dean, the Texan Ranger

GEORGE W. KENDALL

RARE WAGS may be found among the Texas Volunteers, yet the funniest fellow of all is a happy-go-lucky chap named Bill Dean, one of Chevallier's spy company and said to be one of the best "seven-up" players in all Texas. While at Corpus Christi, a lot of us were sitting out on the stoop of the Kenney House early one morning when along came Bill Dean. He did not know a single soul in the crowd, although he knew we were all bound for the Rio Grande; yet the fact that the regular formalities of an introduction had not been gone through with did not prevent his stopping short in his walk and accosting us. His speech, or harangue, or whatever it may be termed, will lose much in the telling, yet I will endeavor to put it upon paper in as good shape as possible.

"Oh, yes," said he, with a knowing leer of the eye: "oh, yes; all going down among the robbers on the Rio Grande, are you? Fine times you'll have, over the left. I've been there myself and done what a great many of you won't do—I come back, but if I didn't see nateral h—ll—in August at that—I *am* a teapot. Lived eight days on one poor hawk and three blackberries; couldn't kill a prairie rat on the whole route to save us from starvation. The ninth day come, and we struck a small streak of good luck: a horse give out and broke down, plumb out in the center of an open prairie; not a stick

From *A Quarter Race in Kentucky and Other Sketches*, ed. William T. Porter (Philadelphia, 1878). This sketch first appeared in the New Orleans *Picayune*, June 26, 1846, as a dispatch with the dateline Matamoros, June 13, 1846, sent by Kendall, founder and editor of the *Picayune*, who at the time was covering the Mexican War.

233

big enough to tickle a rattlesnake with, let alone killing him. Just
had time to save the critter by shootin him, and that was all, for in
three minutes longer he'd have died a nateral death. It didn't take
us long to butcher him, nor to cut off some chunks of meat and stick
em on our ramrods, but the cookin was another matter. I piled up
a heap of prairie grass, for it was high and dry, and sot it on fire;
but it flashed up like powder and went out as quick. But—"

"But," put in one of his hearers, "but how did you cook your
horsemeat after that?"

"How?"

"Yes, how?"

"Why, the fire caught the high grass close by, and the wind
carried the flames streakin across the prairie. I followed up the fire,
holding my chunk of meat directly over the blaze, and the way it
went was a caution to anything short of locomotive doins. Once in
a while a little flurry of wind would come along, and the fire would
get a few yards the start; but I'd brush upon her, lap her with my
chunk, and then we'd have it again, nip and chuck [tuck?]. You
never seed such a tight race—it was beautiful."

"Very, we've no doubt," ejaculated one of the listeners, interrupting the mad wag just in season to give him a little breath. "But
did you cook your meat in the end?"

"Not bad I didn't. I chased that d----d fire a mile and a half,
the almightiest hardest race you ever heer'd tell on, and never give
it up until I run her right plumb into a wet marsh. There, the fire
and chunk of horsemeat come out even—a dead heat, especially the
meat."

"But wasn't it cooked?" put in another one of the listeners.

"Cooked! No! just crusted over a little. You don't cook broken-
down horse flesh very easy, no how; but when it comes to chasing
up a prairie fire with a chunk of it, I don't know which is the
toughest, the meat or the job. You'd have laughed to split yourself
to have seen me in that race—to see the fire leave me at times and
then to see me brushin up on her agin, humpin and movin myself

as though I was runnin agin some of those big ten miles an hour Gildersleeves in the Old States.

"I'm goin over to Jack Haynes's to get a cocktail and some breakfast—I'll see you all down among the robbers on the Rio Grande."

A New Trial in Snowdon's Case

ANONYMOUS

NOT MANY YEARS AGO that capital good fellow, M----, was judge of a district in northwestern Texas. A chap of the name of Snowdon signed some kind of a bond or recognizance for $20,000 as surety and being required to "justify" was sworn in open court and asked if he was worth six thousand six hundred and sixty-six dollars and sixty-six and two-thirds cents, after payment of all his just debts and liabilities.

"Yes, sir," said he, "more than five times that sum."

He had hardly got out of the courthouse when the grand jury indicted him for perjury, and he, thinking the matter very serious, employed two small limbs of the law, went to trial, and before he knew what he was about, found himself *convicted*.

He then thought it high time to get a *good* lawyer, and so went to Gen. H----n and employed him to obtain a new trial, securing him a fee of a thousand dollars. The General made and argued the motion, and the Court took it under advisement and adjourned.

That night Judge M. and General H. occupied the same room. There was also another person in it who afterwards told what took place. M. tells the tale himself, accompanying it with that sort of denial which leads one to suspect there is a little truth in it. The other lodger in the room said that about two in the morning he waked and looking round saw the Judge and the General earnestly engaged in a game of poker. Just as he waked, he heard the Judge say, "Well, General, we have been playing all night without doing

From *Spirit*, XXVII (February 21, 1857), 7.

much. Now I have got a good hand, and I mean to make something of it. I go you a hundred and fifty dollars."

"I will see that and go you a hundred and fifty better," said the General, after looking at his hand.

M. examined his pocket, found he had just three hundred left in it, and deposited it on the table, saying, "By the Lord, General, I believe I can beat you, and we'll close the thing up this time. I go you that and a hundred and fifty better."

"You have a good hand, have you, Judge? I suppose *so*," said the General, "but I believe I have got a better. I go you that hundred and fifty, *and a new trial in Snowdon's case.*"

"Done," said M. "I call you."

The cards were turned over. M. was beat, broke up the game, and went to bed.

The court granted Snowdon a new trial the next morning, any-how.

"I Pass!"

"OLD NICK"

THREE GAMBLERS some short time since wandered into our church. They had strayed off from Orleans or some other place and landed on our island [Galveston], expecting to find green-horns here. They were mistaken as everybody else will be who expects to find such a class here, for let me tell you people here are as sharp as steel traps, and when you leave home to come here, all the fools are behind, not one before. After remaining here for several weeks and not getting even a nibble, the three gamblers concluded to turn virtuous and moral, to begin which they attended church and seated themselves on one of the back benches in the same pew. As the hat was going the rounds, it finally came to them; the first one saw the pile and went "four bits" better, the next went one dollar better, and passed the hat to the third one, who had fallen into a doze; by receiving a nudge in the ribs his eyes opened, and seeing the hat pretty well covered in the bottom with money, he threw his head back, yawned, and said in a loud voice, "I pass."

From *Spirit*, XXIII, 27 (August 20, 1853), 313. Excerpted from "Doings in Galveston." There is no information on the author. This anecdote was probably old when it appeared in *Spirit*.

How the Cockney Killed a Buffalo

"ESPERANCE"

THREE MONTHS AGO, I fell in with a party of young men, sixteen in number, some thirty miles from Austin, Texas, bound for the buffalo ranges. It was early in the morning when I rode up to their camp, and they were about breakfasting. To their friendly invitation to join them in their morning meal, I readily consented as my appetite was considerably sharpened by my early ride and the sight of the venison steaks, broiled prairie hens, and hot dodgers, which were spread out in tempting array on tin plates, flanked by pots of coffee. I need not say that our repast was enjoyed with a keen relish, for all who are familiar with prairie life, either as a hunter or traveller, know well the result produced by exercise . . . in the open air.

Among the party was an old hunter by the name of Stevens, who is well known as one of the best guides in the western country and whose services are in constant requisition by the various parties of young men, strangers, who are constantly arriving from the old countries looking for sport on our western prairies.

Many have been the parties that Stevens has guided safely to the haunts of the wild horse and buffalo. Many and rich are the tales he recounts of the disasters and mishaps which have befallen, both by flood and field, some of those adventurous youths, fresh from their mothers' apron strings and yclept "green," who, like many illustrious predecessors, have sought his aid in leading them to the spot where they could distinguish themselves by extinguishing a herd of buffalo.

From *Spirit*, XX, 23 (July 27, 1850), 271.

Whilst we were despatching our breakfast, I had endeavored, but in vain, to draw the old man out so that we might hear one of his adventures, but to my many questions he only replied in monosyllables. I had nearly given up in despair of finding the oil wherewith to grease his tongue, when a dispute between some of the party changed the state of things in my favor. Some three or four of the young men who were tying up their blankets and bundles and preparing their packs had got into an animated confab about their horses, guns, and their skill as marksmen. Most of them were on their first expedition of this kind and consequently had very imperfect impression as to the mode of hunting, as well as exaggerated ideas of their own prowess. In fact, it was not long before the talk waxed fast and furious and bets to a considerable amount were proposed and accepted as to which would kill the most deer or slaughter the most buffalo before their return.

Stevens, who was sitting at the foot of a tree smoking his pipe, listened for some time at the discussion going on and appeared highly amused at the excited disputants, but as one of them made a boast that he would kill a bull with every ball he fired, he broke in, "Well, my boys, you talk big, and some of you will do wonders no doubt with your fine horses and gimcrack guns, and not a few will make your everlasting fortunes from the hides carried home. But now, while we are talking about it, listen to an old man and take his advice—one who has grown old in the prairie and who has run mustangs and killed buffalo from the Sabine to the Rio Grande; therefore recollect what I tell you now. In the first place it is necessary when you are preparing to dash down upon a herd to keep cool—don't get too much excited, keep your horse under good control and a firm grip of your gun, and above all," said the old man, with a slight laugh, "don't fire unless you *are sure* it is a buffalo you're after, and not one of our horses—for I've seen such an accident before today."

"Tell us how it happened."

"I will. Two years ago this spring, as is my usual custom, I was

TALES, TALL OR TRUE

down on the Bernard with a few horses to sell—some of which I had caught on the prairies and others that I had traded for with the Indians. After I had got through with my business, sold all my horses, and was preparing to start back to my old occupation of running mustangs, I got a message from Major B----- on the San Antonio who wished to see me at his rancho. Well, I went over and found he wished to engage me as guide to two young Englishmen who had lately arrived in the country. They had letters of introduction to him and were very anxious, like yourselves, to hunt mustangs and shoot buffalo.

"They were just from college and were travelling about to see the world, but their governors, as they called their fathers, had better have kept them at home or sent some one along to take care of them, for they were the greenest chaps that ever I clapt sight on. As for hunting, why they hardly knew the difference between a rifle and a shot gun, and they sat on their horses like bags of meal. However, that was none of my business, and as soon as they had collected their traps we started. It was not long before I had them in the heart of the buffalo range."

"Were you not afraid of the Indians attacking you with so small a party?"

"Not at all. For myself, I trusted to my usual good luck in keeping out of their hands, and as for the two Englishmen, C----- and T-----, they were green enough to be afraid of nothing. Nevertheless, I advised them constantly how to act and gave them as well as I could an insight into the character of the bloody-minded heathens who were prowling about. The Englishmen seemed not to be much interested about them, however. 'Buffalo! buffalo! Show us the buffalo! Do let us kill a buffalo!' was their talk from morning till night. What their exact idea of a buffalo was (they never having seen one), it is hard to tell, and probably they themselves did not know. From their conversation, I inferred they supposed it to be the size of an elephant and having the fierceness of a lion. At all events, they were ready to see them in any shape, size, or form save the right one, as the conclusion of my tale will show. On the fourth night of our camping out, I was roused by C-----, who had been kept awake by his anxiety and who begged me to listen, as there was something infernally strange going on in the prairie. I did so, and it was not long before I told him and his companion to their great joy that the game we sought was close at hand.

"Although scarcely past midnight, they saddled up their horses and got ready for as early a start as possible. As day broke and the mist cleared away from the prairie, I found by the noise that the herd of buffalo were in a deep ravine about a mile off; consequently they could not be seen from the position we were then in. I directed C----- to take his stand near a high mound to the south and T---- about half a mile from him, whilst I would start the herd, and, if possible, run them in their direction, so they could get a shot. After seeing them off—not without many misgivings as to the result—I started myself, and zigzagging about, taking advantage of mounds, bushes, and briar patches, I managed to get to the very mouth of the valley unperceived. There, I had a good view of the whole herd which was quietly grazing and numbered about five hundred head. Although such a scene was familiar, still the excitement told on me, as it will on all at such a time let him be young or old, as you will find before you return. However, there were the buffalo, the nearest scarcely a hundred yards from me, and my old horse was getting as eager for the charge as myself. In a few moments my plan of action was formed; and mashing my old coonskin flat on my head, holding my gun ready, and putting the spurs into Gotch, with a yell amongst them I dashed. Whew! how they scampered! and how the ground shook! It was devil take the hindmost or equally as bad, for I was in his place. One young cow was knocked down and trampled on by the rest, and no sooner did she rise than down she tumbled again from my rifle bullet. There was such a punching of ribs, rattling of horns, such bellowing and snorting, and clattering of feet, that it was no wonder to me as we rose the hill where C---- was placed where he had a most excellent opportunity of taking his pick out of the number to see his horse pitch him over his head and then scamper away among the buffalo. T----, hearing the noise, seeing the dust and confusion, and burning with a praiseworthy ardor of doing he hardly knew what, came charging down full tilt, minus his hat, his mouth catching gnats and his eyes as big as dollars. 'Look out! there he comes! catch him!' I shouted, pointing to C-----'s horse, which, frightened nearly to death, had finally extricated himself from the herd. With mane flying and distended nostril, the horse came tearing down toward T----, his terror increased by the water gourd and bread wallet beating a tattoo on his hide at every jump. T----, hearing my shout and seeing something—he didn't know what—coming down upon him with a great racket, fired away with both barrels, and down came the horse, rolling over and over and smashing gourds, wallet, and saddle into a cocked hat."

" 'Huzza! I've really killed a buffalo at last! Huzza!' "

" 'So you have,' " I shouted, " 'but it happens to be the one your friend rode, and if this is your idea of a buffalo, that they go about saddled and bridled, why I'll take devilish good care of old Gotch and my own carcase so that we are well out of your way the next time you kill one.' Poor devil; how he hated it. He even offered me fifty dollars if I would never tell of it. I told him he had nothing to fear from me, at least as long as he was in the country but that we had better look for his friend, to which he readily assented. Poor C---- was indeed in a woful plight—though not much hurt. His face was begrimed with dust, nose skinned, pants torn at each knee, and gun stock broken. At a distance he had seen the fate of his horse, and to the words of explanation and consolation of his friend and the offer of making the loss of his horse good at the earliest opportunity, he merely remarked that he had come this far in the wilderness to see buffalo and was well repaid, for he had seen the elephant too."

"They were satisfied with buffalo hunting . . . and in a week more we were back where we started from. Such was the end of *their* hunt. May *yours* be more successful."

The Rio Grande

E. A. P.

The following lines were written by a young officer of the U.S. Army and fully set forth not only his own but the first impressions of all white men who have visited the delectable region of the Rio Grande:

> The Devil was granted permission one day
> To make him a land for his special sway;
> He hunted around for a month or more,
> And ripp'd, and snorted, and terribly swore.
> But at last was delighted a country to view,
> Where the prickly-pear and the muskeet-tree grew;
> After very brief survey, he took up his stand
> On the eastern bank of the Rio Grande.
>
> Some little improvement he wished to make,
> For his own reputation he felt was at stake.
> An idea struck him; he swore by his horns
> To make a complete vegetation of thorns.
> So he studded the land with the prickly-pear,
> And scatter'd muskeet trees every where;

From *Spirit,* XXIV, 7 (April 1, 1854), 80. The poem was submitted by an officer who signed his initials, N. L. C. In a note, dated August, 1852, he said: "I have seen the mercury in the shade at Ringgold Barracks at 108, and for a month in succession above 100 at 3 p.m."[1]

"Spanish bayonets," stiff, sharp-pointed, and tall,
Were spread around to outstick them all.
He imported Camanches direct from Hell,
The tide of his sweet-scented train to swell;
A legion of skunks, whose loud, *loud* smell,
Perfumed the region he loved so well.
And as, for his life, he couldn't see why
The river did not enough water supply;
So he swore, if he gave it another drop,
They might take his head and horns for a mop.
And he thought Rio Grande not crooked enough,
He twisted it up about "quantum stuff";
So the birds when they seek to fly over its tide,
Are surprised to alight on the starting side!
He fixed the least heat at one hundred and seven.
And banished forever the moisture of Heaven;
Though none must think (by his tail he swore)
But the heat *could* get up to five hundred or more.
He wish'd he'd be d----d if potatoes should grow,
Or anything else that was fodder, by Jo!
And when he had fix'd things, all thorny and well,
He said, "By the Lord! it's a joy to Hell!"

He was satisfied now; he'd done all that he knew;
And vanish'd from earth in a blaze of blue;
And no doubt, now, in a corner of Hell,
Gloats over the work he accomplish'd so well;
And vows that on earth is no *hellisher* land
Than the eastern bank of the Rio Grande.

The Wild Woman of the Navidad

H. T. HOUSTON

NEAR THE MIDDLE PART of this State, there is a stream called the Mustang Creek, so called, I suppose, from there being a great number of wild horses found on its banks and in the surrounding neighborhood. It is a very wild looking place and rendered more peculiarly lonely and desolate by a tradition which has long existed (and which in all probability is true) that the woods on the banks of the Mustang Creek and Navidad River are inhabited by a "wild woman," or some kind of animal in shape and form like a woman. This woman (or animal) is said to be covered with hair, always going destitute of clothes and peculiarly afraid of mankind. Often she has been seen, and oftener her camps have been found.

It is said that one night a man who lives on the Navidad River heard his dogs barking very fiercely, and it being a very clear and "moon-shiny" night, he looked out to see what was the cause of the noise. Just as he put his head out of the door, he saw the shadows of something as it leaped upon a dairy [milk house], around which the dogs were barking. He started out to see what it was, but he had hardly got off the doorstep, when he was struck on the head and knocked down by a big club. He asserts that just as he touched the ground out in the yard, he saw the "wild woman" jump off the dairy and run, the dogs after her.

From *Spirit*, XXI (April 5, 1851), 81, presented as an excerpt from the book, *Adventures in Texas*. No information on the author is available. This is the most widely known of several wild man or wild woman folk tales in Texas.[2]

246

At another time, a man was riding across the prairie, when he saw what he supposed to be either a traveller or a runaway Negro, walking along at a distance before him. He started his Spanish pony into a gallop and soon saw that it was the "wild woman" whom he was pursuing. She ran as soon as she discovered him, and, although he urged his horse on with whip and spur, he found that he could gain very little on her. However, he gained his half a mile and over-took her before she got to the timber, which, when they started, was about three miles off. Our hero agreed that the best way to do was to rope her; this he attempted, but she, having a large club in her hand, took advantage of the first opportunity and struck his horse quite a fair lick in the forehead with it, which, of course, made the animal very much afraid of her. However, the adventurer kept on trying to throw the rope over her head and accidentally again got too near her, when she struck his horse again but evidently with more force than before, and down came the horse, rider and all. The "wild woman" then made her escape.

It has been reported throughout the country, during the past few weeks, that the "wild woman of the Navidad" has been taken prisoner. The report runs thus: Some four or five hunters were pur-suing a bear along the banks of that beautiful little river (the Navidad), when suddenly they came upon this strange being, as she was sleeping by a fire, it being a very cold day. They had no difficulty in catching her; and what was their surprise to find that this mysterious creature, either of the human or brute creation, was nothing more nor less than an African woman, supposed to have run away some fifteen or twenty years since, or about the time of the massacre of the brave Fannin and his noble band of Texian volunteers. It is also stated that this woman talks with other Africans on the plantations in that country.

Now, this latter report seems to me to be, as the saying is, "a made-up thing." It seems very unlikely that an African would live for years in the neighborhood of his or her countrymen and yet be entirely destitute of all kinds of clothing, both summer and winter and, notwithstanding all this, be on very good terms with other Africans.

And as to those "scrapes" of adventurers getting knocked down, etc., by the "wild woman," you must "let them go for what they'll fetch," for I have told them just as I heard them.

The Shot in the Eye

C. WILKINS KIMI

SHELBY COUNTY, lying in Western Texas[3] on the border of "Red Lands," was rather thinly settled in the latter part of 1839. What population it had was generally the very worst caste of border life. The bad and desperate men who had been driven over our frontier formed a rallying ground and headquarters here—seemingly with the determination to hold the county good against the intrusion of all honest persons and as a sort of "Alsaua" of the West for the protection of outlaws and villains of every grade. And indeed to such an extent had this proscription been carried that it had become notoriously as much as a man's life or conscience was worth who settled among them with any worthy purpose in view; for he must either fall into their confederacy—leave—or die. This was perfectly understood; and the objects of this confederacy may be readily appreciated, when it is known that every now and then a party of men would sally out from this settlement, painted and equipped like Comanches, with the view of carrying off the horses, plundering, or murdering some marked man of a neighbouring county; then returning with great speed, they would re-brand their plunder, resume their accustomed appearance, and defy pursuit or investigation. Not only did they band together for their operations in this way, but a single man would carry off a fine horse or commit a murder with the most open audacity and if he only succeeded in escaping here was publicly protected. I do not mean to have it

Reprinted from the *Democratic Review* in *Spirit*, XIV, 51 (February 15, 1845), 604-5, as "A Story of Texas Border Life."[4]

understood that the whole population at this time were men of such stamp avowedly.

There were some few whose wealth to a degree protected them in the observancies of a more seemly life—though they were compelled to at least wink at the doings of their ruffianly and more numerous neighbours. There was yet another but not large class of sturdy straightforward emigrants who, attracted solely by the beauty of the country, had come into it, settled themselves down wherever they took a fancy with characteristic recklessness neither caring nor inquiring who were their neighbours, but trusting in their own stout arms and hearts to keep a footing. Of course all such were very soon engaged in desperate feuds with the horse thieves and plunderers around them, and as they were not yet strong enough to make head efficiently were one after another finally ousted or shot. It was to exterminate this honest class that the more lawless and brutal of the other associated themselves and assumed the name of "Regulators." They numbered from eight to twelve, and under the organization of rangers, commanded by a beastly wretch named Hinch, they professed to undertake the task of *purifying* the county limits of all bad and suspicious characters or in other words of all men who dared refuse to be as vile as they were or if they were, who chose to act independently of them and their schemes. The precious brotherhood soon became the scourge of all that region. Whenever an individual was unfortunate enough to make himself obnoxious to them, whether by a successful villainy, the proceeds of which he refused to share with them or by the hateful contrast of the propriety of his course, he was forthwith surrounded, threatened, had his stock driven off or killed wantonly. If these annoyances and hints were not sufficient to drive him away, they would publicly warn him to leave the county in a certain number of days under the penalty of being scourged or shot. The common pretext for this was the accusation of having committed some crime which they themselves had perpetrated with the view of furnishing a charge to bring against him. Their hate was entirely ruthless and never stopped short of accomplishing its purposes . . . until at last there were few left to dispute with them. . . .

Among these few was Jack Long, as he was called, who neither recognized nor denied their power, and indeed never troubled himself about them one way or the other. He kept himself to himself, hunted incessantly, and nobody knew much about him. Jack had come of a "wild-turkey breed," as the western term is for a roving family. Though still a young man, he had pushed on ahead of the settlement of two territories and had at last followed the game towards the south; finding it abundant in Shelby County he had stopped here, just as he would have stopped at the foot of the Rocky Mountains had it been necessary to pursue it so far. He had never been in the habit of asking leave of any power where he should settle and of course scarcely thought of the necessity of doing so now, but quietly set to work and built himself a nice log cabin as far off from everybody as he could get. And the first thing that was known of him, he had his pretty young wife and two little ones snugly stowed away in it and was slaying the deer and the bears right and left.

The honest brotherhood had made several attempts at feeling Jack's pulse and ascertaining his availability, but he had always seemed so impassively good natured and put them off so pleasantly that they could find no ground for either disturbing or quarreling with him. What was more, he was physically neither an ugly-looking "customer" with his six feet four inches of brawn and bone . . . with a broad, full, good-humored face. . . . Jack Long might have been left for many a day in quiet, even in this formidable neighbourhood, to cultivate his passion for marksmanship at the expense of the dumb, wild things around him but for an unfortunate display he was accidentally induced to make of it.

Happening to fall short of ammunition, he went one day to the store for a fresh supply. This cabin, together with the blacksmith's shop and one or two other huts, constituted the county town, and as powder and liquor were only to be obtained there it was the central resort of the Regulators. Jack found them all collected for a great shooting match, in preparation for which they were getting drunk as fast as possible to steady their nerves. Hinch, the Regulator captain, had always been the hero of such occasions; for in addition to being a first-rate shot, it was known that it would be a dangerous exertion of skill for any man to beat him; he was a furious and vindictive bully and would not fail to make a personal affair of it with any one who should ruffle his vanity by carrying off the prize from him. In addition, the band of scoundrels he commanded was entirely at his service in any extreme so that they made fearful odds for a single man to contend with.

Everybody else in the county was aware of the state of things but Jack Long, and he either didn't know or didn't care. After they had fired several rounds, he went lounging listlessly into the crowd which had gathered around the target, exclaiming in admiration over the last brilliant shot of Hinch which was triumphantly the best. The bully was as usual blustering vehemently, taunting every one around him, and when he saw Jack looking very coolly at the famous shot with no grain of that deferential admiration in his expression which was demanded, he snatched up the board, and thrusting it insultingly close to his face, roared out:—

"Here! You Jack Long-Shanks—look at that!—Take a good look! Can you beat it?" Jack drew back with a quiet laugh and said good-humoredly, "Pshaw! You don't brag on such shootin as that, do you?"

"Brag on it! I'd like to see such a moon-eyed chap as you beat it?"

"I'd not know as I'd be very proud to beat such bunglin work as that."

"You don't! don't you!" yelled the fellow, now fairly in a rage at Jack's coolness. "You'll try it, won't you! You must try it! You shall try it, by G--d. We'll see what sort of a swell you are."

"Oh, well!" said Jack, interrupting him. . . . "Just set up your board, if you want to see me put a ball through every hole you can make!"

Perfectly astounded at this rash bearding of the lion—for it was difficult to tell whether contempt or simplicity dictated Jack's manner—the men got up the board, while he walked back to the stand and carelessly swinging his heavy rifle from his shoulder, fired seemingly as quick as thought. "It's a trick of mine," said he, moving towards the mark, as he lowered his gun; "I caught it from shootin varmints in the eyes;—always takes em there. It's a notion I've got—it's my fun." They all ran eagerly to the target, and sure enough his ball, which was larger than Hinch's, had passed through the same hole, widening it!

"He's a humbug! It's all accident! He can't do that again!" shouted the ruffian, turning pale, till his lips looked blue, as the board was held up. "I'd bet the ears of a buffalo calf against his, that he can't do it again!"

"If you mean by that to bet your own ears against mine, I'll take you up!" said Jack, laughing, while the men could not resist joining him. Hinch glared around him with a fierce chafed look, before which those who knew him best quailed, and with compressed lips silently loaded his gun. A new target was put up, at which after long and careful aim he fired. The shot was a fine one. The edge of the ball had just broke the center. Jack, after looking at it, quietly remarked, "Plumbing out the center is my fashion. I'll show you a kink or two, Captain Hinch, about the clear thing in shootin. Give us another board there, boys!"

Another was set up, and after throwing out his gun on the level in the same rapid careless style as before, he fired. When the eager crowd around the target announced that he had driven the center cross clear out, he turned upon his heel and with a pleasant nod to Hinch started to walk off. The ruffian shouted hoarsely after him:

"I thought you were a d----d coward! You've made two good shots by accident and now you sneak off to brag that you've beat me. Come back, sir! You can't shoot before a muzzle half as true!"

Jack walked on without noticing this mortal insult and challenge. Hinch laughed tauntingly long and loud, jeered him with exulting bitterness as long as he could make himself heard, as "a flash in the pan," "a dung-hill cock, who had spread his white feather." The men who had been surprised into a profound respect for Long were now still more astonished at what they considered his "backing out" and joined clamorously in hooting his retreat.

The fools! They made a fatal mistake, in supposing he left the insult unresented from any fear for himself. Jack Long had a young and pretty wife at home, and his love for her was stronger than his resentment for his own indignity. . . .

This was an ill-starred day for Jack, though; from this time troubles began to thicken about him. The even tenor of his simple happy life was destroyed, and indignity and outrage followed each other fast. Hinch never forgave the unlucky skill which had robbed him of his proudest boast, that of being the best marksman on the frontier, and he swore in base vindictive hate to dog him to the death or make him leave the country. Soon after this, a valuable horse belonging to a rich and powerful planter disappeared. He was one of those men who had compromised with the Regulators, paying as much blackmail for exemption from their depredations and protection against others of the same stripe. He now applied to Hinch for the recovery of his horse and the punishment of the thief. This, Hinch under their contract was bound to do and promised to accomplish forthwith. He and some of his men went off on the trail of the missing horse and returning next day announced that they had followed it with all their skill through a great many windings, evidently intended to throw off pursuit, and had at last traced it to Jack Long's picket fence. There could be no doubt but he was the thief. The planter knew nothing of Jack but that he was a newcomer and demanded that he should be forced to give up the horse and punished to the extremity of the frontier code. But this was not Hinch's policy yet awhile. He knew the proofs were not strong enough to make the charge plausible, even before a Lynch Court, of which he himself was both the prosecutor, judge, and executioner. His object was to first get up a hue and cry against Long and under

cover of a general excitement accomplish his devilish purposes. . . .
He proclaimed far and wide that he had found the horse at last, hid
in a timber bottom near Long's. This, of course seemed strong confirmation of his guilt, and though the mob were most of them horse
thieves to all intents, yet it was an unpardonable crime for anyone
to practice professionally among themselves. Long was loudly de-
nounced, threatened on every side, and ordered to leave the country
forthwith.

These proceedings Jack by no means comprehended or felt disposed to be moved by. He gave them one and all to understand
that he meant to remain where he was until it entirely suited his
convenience to go and that if his time and theirs did not happen
to agree, they might make the most of it. And Jack was such an
unpromising snaggish-looking somebody, and his reputation, which
had now spread everywhere—of possessing such consummate skill
with the rifle that he thought it a condescension to shoot game anywhere else but in the eyes—was so formidable that no individual
felt disposed to push the matter to a personal conclusion. He
might still, therefore, have been left in quiet, but Hinch had unfortunately taken up the impression from Jack's conduct in the
shooting match affair that he must be a coward, and if this were true
then all his skill amounted to but little. . . . Besides, Jack had given
fresh and weighter matter of offence in that he had refused to obey
and defied his authority as Regulator. . . . Several horses now disappeared, and robberies of other kinds perpetrated with singular
dexterity followed in quick succession. All these things he managed
through the clamors of his scoundrelly troops to have laid directly
or indirectly to Jack's door. . . .

About this time not only Hinch himself but every other person
who had made himself conspicuous by insisting upon Jack's guilt
and the necessity of punishing him summarily began to lose every
day or two valuable stock which was wantonly shot down sometimes in sight of their houses; it soon began to be remarked that
every animal lost in this way *had been shot in the eye*. This was

instantly associated, of course, with Jack's well known and curious predilection for that mark in hunting. A perfect storm of indignation followed. A meeting was at once convened at the store, of which the plotter was the chairman; and by a unanimous vote a resolution was passed condemning Jack Long to be whipped and driven out of the country—and Hinch with his Regulators appointed to carry it into effect. Hinch could hardly contain himself for joy. . . .

It was the third day after this meeting. . . . Jack had just returned from hunting and laying aside his accoutrements partook of the simple meal his wife had prepared for him; then stretching himself upon the buffalo robe on the floor, romped with his two rosy-cheeked boys . . . ; but mother wanted some water from the branch. . . . So jumping up, he left the little folk pouting wilfully as they looked after him from the door and started. The stream was only about a hundred yards from the house, and the path leading to it was through a dense high thicket. It was against Jack's religion ever to leave his house without his gun, but the wife, whom he loved above all the universe of sentiment and everything else, was in a hurry for the water, and the distance was so short—so he sprang gaily out with the vessel in his hand, leaving the rifle behind. The water had been dipped up, and he was returning along the narrow path closely bordered by brush when he felt a light tap on each shoulder and his career strangely impeded. He had just time to perceive that a lasso had been thrown over him which would confine his arms, when he saw himself suddenly surrounded and was rushed upon by a number of men. He instantly recognized the voice of Hinch, shouting, "Down with him! Drag him down!"

The men who had hold of the lasso about his body jerked at it violently in the effort to throw him. All his tremendous strength was put forth in one convulsive effort which would have freed him, but the infernal noose had fallen true and bound his arms. As it was, he dragged the six stout men who held it after his frantic bounds nearly to his own door before he was prostrated, and then it was by a heavy blow dealt him over the head with the butt of a gun. The last objects which met his eye as he sank down were the horrified faces of his two children and wife looking out upon him.

The blow deprived him of his senses for some time, and when he recovered he found himself half stripped and lashed to a tree a short distance from his house—Hinch in front of him with a knotted rope in his hand, his wife on the ground, wailing and clinging with piteous entreaty around the monster's knees, his children weeping by her, and outside this group a circle of men with guns in their hands. That fearful awakening was a new birth to Jack Long. His eye took in everything at one glance. . . . When the blows . . . fell upon his white flesh . . . he felt them no more than the dead lintel of his door would have done. . . . His wide-open eyes were glancing calmly and scrutinizingly into the faces of the men who stood around—those features are never to be forgotten. . . . The man's air was awful—so concentrated—so still—so enduring. He never spoke, or groaned, or writhed—but those intense eyes of his!—the wretches couldn't stand them and began to shuffle and get behind each other. But it was too late; he had them all—ten men. *They were registered.*

. . . . After lashing him until he fainted, the Regulators left him, telling his wife that if they were not out of the country in ten days, he should be shot. He did go within the specified time and it was said returned with his family to Arkansas, where his wife's father lived. The incident was soon forgotten in Shelby County amidst the constant recurrence of similar cases.

About four months after this affair, in company with an adventurous friend, I was traversing Western Texas. Our objects were to see the country and amuse ourselves in hunting. . . . My friend happening to remember a man of some wealth who had removed from his native county and settled, as he had understood, in Shelby County, we inquired for him and very readily found him. . . . We were frankly and kindly received, and horses, servants, guns, dogs, and whatever else was necessary to insure our enjoyment of the sports of the country, as well as the time of our host himself, were forthwith at our disposal. . . . One day we had all turned out for a deer drive. . . . We divided in the morning and skirted up opposite sides of a wide belt of bottom timber, while the drivers and dogs penetrated it to rouse the deer which ran out on either side by the stands, which were known to the hunters. We were unusually successful and returned to a late dinner at our host's, the planter's house. By dusk all had come in except my friend, whose name was Henry and a man named Stoner, one of the neighbors, who had joined our hunt. Dinner was ready, and we sat down to it, supposing they would be in in a few moments. The meal was nearly over, when Henry, who was a gay, voluble fellow, came bustling into the room and with a slightly flurried manner addressed our host, "Squire, this is a strange country of yours! Do you let crazy people range it with guns in their hands?"

"Not when we know it. Why? What about crazy people? You look excited."

"Well, I think I've had enough to make me feel a little curious."

"What is it? What is it?" exclaimed everybody, eagerly.

"Why, I have met with either the Old Harry himself—a ghost—or a madman—which it is, I am confoundedly puzzled to tell!"

"Where? How?"

He threw himself into a chair, wiped the perspiration from his forehead, and continued, "You know, Stoner and myself, when we parted from you all this morning, took up the right hand side of the bottom timber. Well Stoner accompanied me to my stand where we parted, he to go on to his, and I have seen nothing of him since. Soon after he left me, a deer passed out—I shot it—wounded it—and jumped on my horse to pursue it. The deer had staggered at my fire but was not so badly wounded as I supposed and led me off until it suddenly occurred to me that I might get lost, and I reined up. I soon found that this sober second thought had come too late and that I was already out of my latitude. I wandered about nearly all day, though taking care not to go very far in any one direction, before I came across anything which promised to set me right again. I at last came upon a wagon trail and felt relieved, for I knew it

must take me to some point where I could get information. The
trail was narrow, leading through scrubby thickets, and I was
riding along slowly, looking down, in the hope of detecting the
tracks of some of your horses, when the violent shying of my horse
caused me to raise my eyes. And, by George! it was enough to have
stampeded a regiment of horses! On the left of the trail stood a very
tall skeleton-like figure, dressed in skins; one foot advanced, as if he
had stopped in the act of stepping across it, and a long heavy gun,
just swinging down to the level, bearing on me. Of course, my heart
leaped into my throat and my flesh shrank and crept. Before I could
think of raising my gun, my eyes met those of this strange figure.
Such eyes! Surprise at their cold, unnatural expression suspended
my action. Burning with a chill singular brillancy in deep-sunken
sockets, they looked as if they never had winked. Dwelling steadily
upon my face for a moment, they seemed to be satisfied and the
gun was slowly thrown back upon his shoulder; plucking at a long
grisly beard, with an impatient gesture of his bony hands, the figure
made a stride across the trail and without speaking a word plunged
into the thicket. I was so confounded by this curious dumb show
that he was nearly concealed in the brush before I found my tongue
to shout to him to stop, but he kept on not even turning his head.
I was provoked and spurred my horse in after him as far as I could
penetrate, but he kept on, and I lost sight of him in a moment and
whether he can talk at all or not is more than I can tell!"

"Did you look at his feet, Henry?" interrupted one of the party.
"I expect it was old ----"

"Never mind what you expect. Bear me out," he continued. "I
followed the trail, which wound about it seemed to me towards all
the points of the compass, for an hour or more. At last it led me out
into a prairie, which I thought I recognized. I stopped and was
looking around to make out the landmarks when a horse with a
saddle on burst from the woods behind me and tore off across the
prairie, as if he too had seen the devil."

"What color was he?" exclaimed half a dozen voices in a breath.

"He was too far off for me to distinguish more than that he was a dark horse—ay about as much so as mine. I could distinguish the pummel of the saddle and the stirrups flying!"

"Stoner's horse was a dark bay," was buzzed around the table in low tones everyone looking seriously in his neighbor's face.

"Yes!" said the Squire, rising and stepping uneasily to the window, "Stoner's horse was a good deal like yours; he must have got away from him, and that is what detains him. But then the nag was a very kind creature and well trained. I wonder it should have behaved so."

"Don't believe Bay would have done it, Squire," said one of the men. "Something's gone wrong, I think! Was the bridle down, Mr. Henry?"

"It was too far off for me to tell. I followed in the direction the horse took and soon found myself here, and expected to find it here too."

"No. Stoner is beyond here," said the Squire. "That wagon trail you were turning and twisting about in is a road I had opened to a number of board-trees we cut and rived out there; you might have followed it for hours and not been more than a mile or so from the place you started from. That ghost of yours, by the way, may be some crazy fellow who has wandered off into these parts with mischief in him! Did you hear no gun!"

"I thought I did—about an hour after parting with that man, or devil, or whatever he was—but the sound was so faint and distant that, for fear I might be mistaken, I did not go to it; and the road had turned so frequently I could not tell whether it was in the direction he went off or not."

Here the driver interposed, saying that he had heard a rifle about that time on the right, but supposing it to be Henry or Stoner, he thought nothing of it. A half laughing discussion followed as to the probable character of the wood ghost Henry had reported of—some asserting that he was quizzing us—for these men were too much accustomed to the exigencies of a hunter's life to be for more than a moment seriously affected by the circumstance of Stoner's nonarrival. In the midst of this, a horse's feet were heard galloping up to the door, and a loud "Hulloa!" followed. The Squire rose hastily and went out. In a moment after he entered, looking pale and excited.

"Tom Dix (one of Stoner's neighbors) says that his horse has come home without a rider, the reins upon its neck, and a clot of blood upon the pummel of the saddle! Boys, he's been shot! Just as I suspected from the very first."

Everybody rose at this announcement—looking in the face of him opposite with a blank pallid stare.

"The crazy man!" ejaculated several. "Strange! Very mysterious business," said others.

"I tell you what," said the Squire after a pause, "has struck me from the first. It is that this strange-looking fellow Henry saw, mistook him for Stoner, until he looked into his face, for Henry's horse and general appearance are not unlike his, and when he found that he was wrong got out of the way and went on till he meet Stoner himself and has shot him."

"No doubt of it," said several.

"But it's a very mysterious affair," continued he. "I know of no such-looking man in this region as Henry describes, but at any rate he will be hunted down tomorrow, for Stoner was one of the Regulators, and Hinch's a perfect bloodhound. He can hardly escape, crazy or not crazy."

This seemed to be the most satisfactory explanation of the difficulty, and as it was too dark for us to do anything that night we resumed our seats to discuss over and over again these details. The Squire sent off a messenger summoning Hinch and the Regulators to be on the ground early in the morning.

Before sunrise in the morning, Hinch arrived with six men. I was waked by his loud blustering and swearing. He was raving, as I afterwards understood, about Henry, calling his story about the meeting with the remarkable personage all humbug and asserting his belief that if a murder had been committed, Henry was its author. Our host quieted him in some way, and when we came out to join them he greeted us with a snarling sort of civility. He was a thick-set, broad-shouldered, burly-looking wretch with blood shot eyes and a face bearing all the marks of riotous debauchery. Our search was for several hours entirely unsuccessful until Henry by accident found the place where he had encountered the Bearded Ghost as some one christened him. Here one of the keen-eyed hunters found the traces of a large moccasined foot. These were pursued for several miles and lost, but on spreading our line and continuing the same general course for some distance farther, we at last found dead the body of Stoner. It had been so much mutilated by the wolves and ravens that little examination was made of the bones. We gathered them together to carry them home to his family, and in doing this I noticed the fracture of a bullet through the back of the skull. It had been stripped bare of flesh; both eyes had been plucked out by the birds, and it was too shocking an object for close examination. But what puzzled all parties most was the discovery, a short distance off, of the trail of a shod horse. Now, there was perhaps not a horse in Shelby County that wore shoes and certainly not one in our party. Shoeing is never thought of, being unnecessary where there are no stones. This was as perfect a pozer as even Henry's story and threw yet a greater air of inexplicability around the affair. It was thought that this track might be easily traced to any distance, but after worrying about it for several days it was given up in despair, and the Regulators, fatigued and disheartened, scattered for their respective homes.

But one of their number never reached his. Being missed for two days, there was a general turnout to look for him and as had been the case with Stoner his body was found torn to pieces by the wolves. The report was that he too had been shot through the back of the head.

These murders and the singular circumstances accompanying them created great sensation. Hinch and his troops scoured the country in every direction, arresting and lynching suspicious persons, as they called them. One poor inoffensive fellow they hung and cut down four or five times to make him confess, but nothing was elicited, and they left him with barely a spark of life. That evening as they were returning to their headquarters at the store one of them named Winter missed a portion of his horse furniture which had become accidentally detached. He said he had observed it in its place a mile back, that he would return to get it and rejoin them at the store by the time they should be ready to commence the spree they had determined on going into that night. He left them and never returned. They soon got drunk and did not particularly notice his absence until some time the next day, when his family, alarmed by the return of his horse with an empty saddle, sent to inquire after him. This sort of inquiry had come to be so significant of late that they were instantly sobered and mounting rode back on their trail. Very soon a swarm of buzzards and wolves near a line of thicket ahead designated the whereabouts of the object of their search, and there they found his fleshless bones scattered on every side. They were appalled. The reddest-bloated cheek among them blanched. It was terrible! They seemed to be doomed! Three of their number dead and torn to pieces within ten days; and yet not the slightest clue to the relentless and invisible for but that ghostly story of Henry's and the tracks which only served to tantalize them. They shivered while the great drops started from their foreheads, and without thinking of looking for any trail or even gathering up the bones they started back at full speed, spreading the alarm everywhere. The excitement now became universal and tremendous. Nearly the whole country turned out for the purpose of unravelling this alarming mystery, and the superstitious frenzy was in no small degree heightened by the report that this man had been shot in the same way as the others—in the back of the head.

These incidents were all so unaccountable that I own I felt no little sympathy with the popular association of a supernatural agency in their perpetration. Henry laughed at all this but insisted that it was a maniac; and to account for the peculiar dexterity of his escapes and whole management related many anecdotes of the proverbial cunning of madmen. The wildest, most absurd, and incredible stories were now afloat among the people concerning this deadly and subtle foe of the Regulators, for it was now universally believed and remarked that it was against them alone that his enmity was directed. Henry's story was greatly improved upon and added to: as some reports had it, the Madman—as others the Bearded Ghost—was seen in half a dozen places at the same time; now on foot, stalking with enormous strides across some open glade from thicket to thicket—passing out of sight again before the observer could recover from his surprise; then mounted, he was seen flying like the shadow of a summer cloud over the prairies or beneath the gloom of the forest, always haggard and lean, dressed in skins with the hair on, and that long, heavy, terrible rifle on his shoulder. I noticed that there was only one class of men who ventured to assert that they had actually seen with their own eyes these wonderful sights and that was constituted of those who either had suffered, or from their characters and pursuits were most likely to suffer persecution from the Regulators—the class of hunter emigrants. These men were most industrious in embellishing all the circumstances of character, feats, and relentless hatred to the Regulators, as highly as the excited credulity of the public would bear. They never saw him except in the vicinity of the homes of some one of these hated tyrants. In their version this being was forever hovering around them, waiting the moment to strike while they were alone and far from any help.

They carried this thing so far as to attract attention to it and arouse in the cunning mind of Hinch the same suspicion which had occurred to Henry and myself, namely, that all this was the result of a profoundly acute and thoroughly organized scheme of this class, headed by some man of peculiar personality and consummate skill with the object of exterminating or driving off the Regulators. It seemed impossible that without collusion with many others the murderer should have been able to so baffle all pursuit. Hinch and his band had been thoroughly cowed and awed, but the moment this idea occurred to them the reaction of their base fears was savage exultation. Here was something tangible; their open and united force could easily exterminate an enemy who had acknowledged their weakness in resorting to secret combination and assassination from "the bush." They forthwith proclaimed war to the knife with the whole class, and during the next week several outrages so revolting that I will not detail them were perpetrated upon these men in different parts of the county; and the fact that during this general tumult nothing more was seen or heard of the mysterious Rifleman encouraged them with the belief that they had succeeded in getting rid of him through the intimidation of his confederates.

They had now been for nearly a fortnight in the saddle—had glutted themselves with vengeance and, as they conceived, broken down this dangerous conspiracy against their power, and if they had not succeeded in detecting and punishing had at least frightened off their singular foe. They now concluded that they might safely disband. That day, after they separated, one of their number, a man named Rees—almost as bad and savage a man as Hinch himself—was riding past a thicket in sight of his own house when he was shot. His Negroes heard the gun, and seeing his horse galloping up to the house riderless and snorting wildly, they ran down and found him stretched in the road dead. He was *shot in the eye* and the ball passed out the back of his head.

When Hinch heard this, he turned perfectly livid, his knees smote together, and with a horrible oath he exclaimed, "It's Jack Long, or his ghost, by G----! come back for vengeance!" It was now perceived for the first time that all the men had been shot through the eye instead of in the back of the head, where the ball had only passed out after entering at the socket. The other heads had been too unpleasantly mutilated for examination, and this fact had not been before observed. Of course, everybody was satisfied now that this terrible

being was in one way or another identified with Jack Long; the
notoriety of his favorite mark and his matchless skill instantly occurred to all as accounting for much that was unaccountable in
these occurrences. This produced a great change in public feeling.
The better sort began to conceive that they understood the whole
matter. The lynching Jack had received was fresh in their memories,
and they supposed that its severity had shaken his mental balance
and made him a monomaniac and that the disease had endowed
him with the marvelous cunning—the staunch, murderous hate—and
the unnatural appearance which had created such sensation. They
could not understand how a being so simple-hearted and sluggish
as he was reputed to have been could have been roused or stung
to such deeds by the mere depth and power of his natural passions.
But monomaniac or not, such a vengeance and the daring conduct of the whole affair were very imposing to their associations
and prepossessions, and they sympathized heartily with him. It
was only while the general uncertainty left every man in doubt
whether his own person might not be next the object of this murderous aim that the public were disposed to back the Regulators in
whatever violent measure they might choose to resort to to drag
the secret to light and the actor to punishment. Now that it was
apparent his whole hate was levelled against the Regulators and all
the uncertainty was confined to them, be he devil, ghost, madman,
or Jack Long, the public had no intention of interfering again. It
was a personal issue between him and them—they might settle it
between themselves. Indeed, men felt in their inmost hearts that
every man of the ten engaged in the lynching of Jack Long deserved
a dozen times over to be shot, and now they looked on coolly, rather
enjoying the thing, and earnestly hoping that Jack might have the
best of it.

And of this there seemed to be a strong probability. The Regulators made only one more attempt to get together, but another of
their number being killed on his way to the rendezvous—his body
bearing that well known and fearful signature of skill—the remain-

ing five, perfectly unnerved and overwhelmed with terror, retreated to their houses and scarcely dared for several weeks to put their heads outside their own doors.

The class to which Jack had belonged, at least those of them who had managed to keep a footing during the relentless proscription of the Regulators, now began to look up. They hinted that they had known of Jack's return from the time of Stoner's murder and had aided and abetted his purposes in every way in their power: furnishing him with fresh horses when the noble animal he rode back from the States became fatigued, assisting his flights and concealments, and furnishing him with information as well as spreading the exaggerated stories about him. . . .

Jack was now frequently seen, but it was known that his work was only half done and that he meant to finish it. He was regarded with great curiosity and awe. The five wretched men were entirely unstrung and panic-stricken. They made no attempt at retaliation, but all their hopes seemed to lie in the effort to get out of his reach. That long, heavy rifle haunted them day and night. They saw its dark muzzle bearing on them from every bush and through the chinks of their own cabins.

One of them, named White, who was an inveterate toper, with all his terror could not resist his inclination for liquor and after a confinement in his house of nearly three weeks determined to risk all and go to the store and buy him a barrel. He went in a covered wagon, driven by a Negro, while he lay stretched on the bottom in the straw. The barrel of liquor was obtained; he got into the wagon, lay down beside it, and started for home. All the way he never raised his head until, near the mouth of his lane, a log had been placed on the side of the road which tilted up the wagon in passing over it so as to roll the barrel on him. He forgot his caution and sprang up with his head out of the cover to curse the boy for his carelessness, and at that moment a rifle was discharged. He fell back dead—*shot through the eye.* The boy said that his master suddenly cut short his oaths and exclaimed, "There he is!" at the moment the gun fired. He saw a tall man with a beard hanging down on his breast and dressed in skins walking off through the brush with his rifle on his shoulder.

The next man, named Garnet, about two weeks after this, got up one morning about sunrise and in his shirt sleeves stepped to his door and threw it open to breathe the fresh air. He was rubbing his eyes, being about half asleep; when he got them fairly open, there stood the gaunt avenger beside a tree in the yard—the fatal rifle levelled, waiting till his victim should see him distinctly. He did see him—but it was with his last look. The bullet went crashing through his brain too! Long is said to have told one of his friends that he never in a single instance shot one of these men till he was certain the man saw and recognized him fully.

All were gone now but Hinch and the two youngest men of the party, Williams and Davis. The two latter were permitted to escape. . . . They made a forced and secret sale of their property and cleared out during the night. But it was for Hinch that Long had with passionless calculation reserved the most inconceivable torture. He had passed him by all this time, while one after the other he struck down the tools and companions of his crimes. He doomed him to see them falling around him with the certain knowledge that the avenging hate which slew them burned with tenfold intensity for his life. . . .

From the time of Rees's death Hinch looked a changed and stricken man. In a few weeks he had lost a great deal of flesh and became piteously haggard; his eyes and gait and voice were all humble. His turbulent and fierce animality faded before the harrowing suspense of this fear. The bully and murderous ruffian trembled at the rustling of a leaf. His own imagination became his hell and hungry remorse grew stronger and stronger with feasting at his heart. He never left his house for weeks, until the escape of Williams and Davis inspired him with some hope. He procured a fine horse and set off one dark night for the Red River. Everybody regretted his escape. Men had looked in quiet expectation upon the progress of this affair and in strong faith that the sense of wild border justice would be gratified in seeing this stern, righteous, and unparalleled vengeance consummated by the fall of Hinch, the monster instigator and chief actor in all the grievous outrages which had roused the simple-hearted Long into a demon-executioner of doom.

Hinch reached the bank of the Red River, sprang from his foaming and exhausted horse after looking cautiously around, and threw himself upon the grass to wait for a steamboat. In two hours he heard one puffing down the stream and saw the white wreaths of steam curling up behind the trees. How his heart bounded! Freedom, hope, and life—once more sprang through his shrivelled veins and to his lips. He signalled the vessel; she rounded to and lowered her yawl. His pulse bounded high, and he gazed with absorbing eagerness at the crew as they pulled lustily towards the shore. A click—behind him! He turned with a shudder, and *there he was!* That long rifle was bearing straight out from the top of the bank. And so the vengeance was consummated. . . .

Long did not remain in Shelby County, but in what direction he had intended to go after returning to Arkansas for his wife and children, I could never hear. He is probably living now his old quiet and good-natured life in the heart of the green wilderness. It is as likely as not that of those two chubby boys who rolled with him about the floor of his logcabin . . . will some of these days come to Washington from congressional districts beyond the Rocky Mountains.

NOTES TO SECTION VI

1. There are many parallels between this poem and one which was widely circulated a few decades later called "Hell in Texas." Mody C. Boatright's "More about 'Hell in Texas'" (*From Hell to Breakfast,* Texas Folklore Society Publication XIX, 1944, pp. 134-38) supplements an earlier article in the same series (*Southwestern Lore,* 1931) in which the poem was attributed to E. U. Cook, a lawyer who came to Texas from Iowa in the 1880's. Cook's poem appeared in his book, *The First Mortgage.* Copies of the poem were distributed by the Buckhorn Saloon, San Antonio, and it was printed on the back of a business card distributed by a livestock commission company.

2. "The Wild Woman of the Navidad" is treated at length by J. Frank Dobie in *Tales of Old-Time Texas* (Boston, 1955), pp. 14-33. A version of the story in the "Creed Taylor Manuscript," Texas Archives, furnished by James M. Day, Director, follows:

"I think it was sometime during the year 1830 that parties who owned a large body of land on the Brazos below Richmond brought over a lot of Africans to work on their new plantations. Several of these Negroes ran away; some went to the Cronk Indians, others made their way into Mexico and one in particular took up his abode in the wilds of the Navidad bottoms. He was a giant in strength and was almost as fleet on foot as an ordinary cow pony. In appearance he had all the repulsive facial features of the African savage and would have passed in Barnum's show as a human gorilla. His voice was gutteral and sonorous and his yell would have shamed any Comanche on earth. He never molested anyone, other than by his occasional nocturnal raids on the settlers' smoke houses and hen-roosts, and in these foraging expeditions he was always successful. If an ax was left at the wood pile overnight, it was sure to disappear with him. If there was beef hanging out on the line to dry, the meat was taken and also the line. Clothing left on the line shared the same fate, but to what uses he appropriated it was never known since he was never seen to wear anything but some kind of a skin about his loins, reaching half way to his knees. The territory to which he confined his operations was of vast extent along the Navidad, and his visitations were so irregular and uncertain that the settlers never could forecast his coming, hence, his immunity from capture. He was often seen in the jungles of the Navidad and could have been shot on diverse occasions, but as he had never shown violence towards any-one, nobody wanted to kill him, preferring to capture him when opportunity offered and sell him to some of the slave holders on the Brazos. He was a terror to the women in all the settlements and mothers quieted their children by threatening them with the 'Wild Black Man.'

"I have never seen any account of this savage in any of the Texas Sketch-books, although his existence was well known to all the first settlers. For this reason I enter this brief record of him, but I want it clearly understood that he was not one of my old comrades. He disappeared sometime in the early 40's and it was supposed that he got with the Cronks and went to Mexico."

3. Only a small part of the area that now comprises the state of Texas was settled by the 1840's; hence, the western Texas referred to here was generally east of a line running roughly from northeast to southwest through Bonham, Dallas, Waco, San Antonio, and Laredo.

4. In 1846 Charles Wilkins Webber published, without his name, *Jack Long; or Shot in the Eye: A True Story of Texas Border Life* (New York, 1846), from which was adapted the play, *Shot in the Eye, or, the Regulators of Texas*. This play "gave New Yorkers their first glimpse on the stage of the notorious society in the piney-woods section of Texas. Opening on September 3, 1849, it shared the billing at the Bowery with *Macbeth* for more than a week. This play, which was published as *Jack Long; or, the Shot in the Eye* by John Beer Johnstone, was only one of several stage adaptations [of the book]. It received more press notice than any previous Texan play. The *New*

York Sun hailed its first performance with a warning to the public that it should secure its seats early, for the Bowery was sure to be crowded for many nights to come." (Joseph Leach, *The Typical Texan: Biography of an American Myth* [Dallas, 1952], p. 90)

VII
Jokes and Jokers

VII. Jokes and Jokers

MANY *of the Anglo-Americans who came to Texas from the southern states brought with them the lively story-telling tradition of Old Southwest humor. In that tradition, much of the amusement turned on the practical joke, that excessively masculine form of nineteenth-century humor which found favor with American frontiersmen everywhere. The practical joke worked best among members of a congenial group, since its success depended upon a shared situation and common knowledge of an individual's peculiarities. The practical joke emphasized physical discomfort, and the raw humor of it barely obscured its inherent violence.*

Another form of Old Southwest humor that blossomed in Texas was the deception of the newcomer, or "breaking in the tenderfoot," as it was called. The amusement stemmed from the newcomer's ignorance of the environment, local customs, and wild animals of the area; thus, the tenderfoot was subjected to physical discomfort or other embarrassment merely by withholding information from him and letting him make a fool of himself.

The violence characteristic of the practical joke and the deception of the newcomer was in many instances amplified in Texas, partly in response perhaps to the violence of the environment itself. Though it may be difficult for twentieth-century readers to appreciate the humor of scaring people with rattlesnakes and fake Indian raids, early Texans evidently enjoyed this form of amusement which, figuratively, teeters on the precipice of catastrophe. This laughing in the face of danger thus became a part of the Texas myth.

Ingins About

ANONYMOUS

ABOUT THE YEAR 1832-33, there lived a family of some note on the Guadaloupe River in western Texas. Among them were several young ladies of the upper-tendom of those days—sensible, handsome looking creatures—happy as larks and always fond of fun. It happened that among the fifteen or twenty young men residing in that section, there was one, by name C., a surly faced, grizzly-haired, chuffy, and moon-eyed chap who became wofully smitten with the most charming of the aforesaid young ladies, and who, of all the buckskins in the wilds of Texas, was most unlikely to be a successful diplomatist in matters wherein the gentler sex were to be consulted, won, and wed.

C.'s visits became less and less like angels'—first once a month, and then doubling to twice a month, once a week, and soon, said the old man, "the ambier-spitting,[1] deer-killing fellow, was almost every day forcing his company on Miss Betty." Many jokes at her expense followed, of course, and she resolved, after suffering under them for some time, to get clear of her admirer or quit the ranch herself. An opportunity offered on the Sabbath following. It being the watermelon season and Betty's father having a fine supply, all the youngsters for miles around assembled there on the holy day to feast on melons. C. was prominent in the circle till in the afternoon; Betty held private interviews with the other young men and arranged that C. should be decoyed from the house and frightened

From *Spirit*, XX, 48 (January 18, 1851), 567.

by the cry of Indians from some of his comrades, which it was thought would wound his pride and drive him away. Five young men, with C., walked out. A bath in the river three hundred yards distant was proposed by one and seconded by several. Of course, poor C. "was in." They went down to the ford near the melon patch and began undressing. In the meantime eight or ten others with guns had gone down under cover of the bank and secreted themselves along the path from the bathing place to the house. The company with C. were in fine glee and in going down spoke of the recent outrages of the Indians, of their increased boldness, and so on, thus exciting the anti-combative bumps of C. to the highest pitch. "Now boys," said one, "who shall be the first to dive in that 'er pool, eh?"

"I will," said C. "Be-gosh, ain't I first with the gals? In course, I'm first here."

Off went coats, shoes, pants, and so on. Just as C. had doffed everything barring a short, red flannel shirt—bang! bang! bang! "Who-wo-yeh!" Bang! went two, three, four guns—loud and shrill rose the Indian yell in the dense brush and under the bank.

"Oh, Lord! I am a dead man, boys!" said James Simpson.

"My leg is broken. Oh, save me!" cried George Williams.

"Run for life, men! Run, for mercy's sake, run!" cried Jack Parsons. "One of my eyes is out and both arms broken!" All was said in an instant, when—do you see that red blaze along the path? Look a moment—what velocity! That jagged hair all straight out behind! That's C. a-streaking it for the house, shirt and all—see him about the corner of the field, by the thicket—bang! bang! went half a dozen pieces—louder than ever rose the hideous warcry.

"Oh, Lord!" grunted C., redoubling his speed—the red blaze getting larger, bunches of his bushy hair dropping out as he "spread himself"—see him leap the yard fence, high in the air, red shirt and all!

The porch was full of ladies—off went two or three more pieces— C. glanced at the ladies, then at his short red shirt. "Run for your life, C.," screamed Betty. "The house is full of Indians! Father's dead and brother Sam wounded! Run, speed!"

In the twinkling of an eye C. was out of the yard. Supposing premises surrounded, off he shot, the red blaze more brilliant than ever, and striking directly into a thick, thorny bottom, he reached and swam the river. Although it was near sunset, C. got into a settlement fifty miles distant by breakfast next morning, still retaining the sleeves and collar of his red shirt, and reported all the family and visitors, among the slain. As for himself, he said he fought as long as fighting would do any good.

Betty was never troubled with C. after that snap.

Mr. Keen's First Cow Drive

"GREEN 'UN"

THE RAISING of cattle is followed by a great many persons in Texas, some individuals owning several thousand head which run at large upon the prairies and are generally gathered twice during the year, once in the spring and once in the fall, and the calves marked. It is often the case that the cattle stray off to a distance of twenty miles, when a parcel of cow-drivers go in pursuit of them and drive them back. These cow-drivers are by no means noted for their tender feelings toward a green 'un, as the sequel will show.

In the latter part of September, 1850, while some of the stockbreeders of one of the interior counties were taking their fall drive, a verdant youth from one of the old states expressed a wish to join them. As the boys thought a little fun would not be amiss, they acquiesced. About one o'clock p.m. the company started, accompanied by Keen, the freshman, intending to go to a point of timber on the San Bernard, known as Buffalo Point, where they expected to camp for the night and commence driving early on the following morning. Their route lay across a prairie some twenty miles wide, and as there was no business for the evening but to make their point, they of course spent their time in fun and frolic.

Two of the crowd (Bill and John) appeared to notice Mr. Keen more than the rest. They rode a short distance from the rest of the company in close conversation and finally joined the stranger who, in reply to their queries, informed them that he had never seen a

From *Spirit*, XXI, 28 (August 30, 1851), 326.

bear and was unacquainted with their habits, but ventured to assert that bears never attacked a party so numerous as that one.

"Don't they?" said Bill. "I knowed one once to tear the scalp off a fellow's head while he was asleep and then get clean off; there's a heap of the varmint about here."

The three rode on together in silence for some distance, the stranger evidently ill at ease on the subject of bears and scalps, and Bill and John concocting "divilthry." At last Bill opened his head and spake in the following terms: "*Mister* Keen, bein as you is not used to sleepin out, I guess it would be best for you to sleep close to the fire, 'cause you mought catch cold—and then again if a bar happens to come into camp, you can consider yourself safe, 'cause they don't often come near fire; but they'll be sartain to be arter you, bein as you're a stranger, and a bar can tell when strangers is about same as a *pusson* could."

This helped Keen some and did not set Bill and John back any, but no further business was transacted until they reached Buffalo Point, at about dark. A fire was soon kindled and supper consisting of cornbread, bacon, and coffee prepared. All sat down to enjoy the repast in good humor, except Keen, who was thinking only of what would be the best way to manage in case a bear should happen to come. After supper, Bill and John strolled out of camp and held converse with each other for a short time, when John returned to camp, Bill taking an opposite direction. Before many minutes, however, he came running towards camp shouting at the top of his voice, "Bar! bar! Boys, there's a bar out there a little piece—the most terrificatious one you ever seed!"

This announcement produced a deep sensation in camp, which of course had a powerful effect upon the mind of Mr. Keen—indeed it rendered him almost speechless—but his glaring eyes and trembling limbs spoke volumes.

All apprehensions of an attack from *that* bear having been dissipated, it was proposed that they should consign themselves to the embrace of Murphy [Morpheus] instead of Bruin; Bill "looked" to the fire, secured Mr. Keen a good place near it, enjoined all to preserve strict silence, and flung himself on his blanket. Half an hour passed, and Mr. Keen betrayed evident signs of uneasiness from his close proximity to the fire. Another half hour and he betokened symptoms of being done brown—indeed, he was about to remove his body to a more genial situation when—hark! a cracking of bushes near by! Yes, and every man in the camp jumped to his feet, as if to be ready to fly should the alarming prognostication be repeated. Soon a low growl was heard and a noise like the snapping of teeth. The darkness was almost impenetrable, and every one ran a few steps toward the prairie, except Bill, who dropped to the ground to ascertain the cause of alarm. In a few moments Bill called them back, declaring that all was right; but in a moment after, and before Keen had recovered himself sufficiently to know what he was about, Bill cried out, "Yes! yes! it *is* a bar! Run for your lives!"

"Run, run!" was heard from each, and every one scampered off. Poor Keen was frightened nearly to death, and the way he made his stampers move was a caution. He leaped upon the first horse he came to, but the animal being tired would not run with him. After trying in vain to get the horse to travel, Keen jumped off and took leg bail once more, when the drivers raised another outcry. Keen was convinced that the bear was at his heels; he outran the party, stumbled against his own horse, took the rope from his neck, mounted him, and was off in a jiffy without bridle or halter to guide his animal—*bear*-backed and his master *bear*-headed, *bear*-footed, and what was worse, a *bear* chasing them.

Away he went, flying across the prairie, not knowing in which direction he was going. John, who had kept close to Keen from the first, as soon as he saw him mount his horse, cried out, "Boys, boys! it aint a bar! it's somebody stealin horses. Come on! come on! We'll catch him!" Keen urged his horse to his utmost speed, but alas! he reached a gully containing soft mud to the depth of about eighteen inches, into which he fell. He soon scrambled out, covered with mud, and looking as black as a nigger. Bill and John soon came up, swearing vengeance against horse thieves in general, and the one they had just caught in particular, who in vain protested his innocence. The drivers plunged him into a part of the gully containing some water, which served to whiten his face some, and enabled Keen to prove his identity to the surprise (!) of all. After an interchange of explanations, they returned to camp, where our verdant friend kept watch till daylight and then cut for the settlement, swearing that he never again would be found on a cow drive in Texas.

The Grapevine "Rattlesnake"

BIGFOOT WALLACE

THE NEXT DAY I rode along with our author, knowing if there was a rattlesnake on the road he would be sure to find it; and in fact he soon stirred up one, and I got down and killed it and pulled off its rattles which I slipped into my pocket, unnoticed by our author. "Captain," said he, as I remounted, "how in the world have you managed to live so long and camp out so much at night in this wilderness without ever having been bitten by a rattlesnake?"

"Why, you see," I answered, "if you don't lose your presence of mind, there's very little danger of a rattlesnake's biting you, even when he crawls to bed with you at night. When you discover one crawling under your blankets, all you've got to do is to lie still and let him fix himself to his notion (and they always pick out the warmest places) and as soon as he is fast asleep, you can jump up without the least danger of being bitten; but if you should move a peg before he has settled himself, he'll nip you to a certainty."

"Yes," replied our author, "but who could lie still under such circumstances?"

"I have," said I, "a hundred times. One dark night about a year ago when I was camping near the edge of a thick chaparral, I felt a fellow crawling under my blanket. I lay perfectly still and let him select his own locality, and nothing would do him but a place right along side of my face. I tell you it was pretty hard work to keep quiet when I felt his scaly sides rubbing up against my neck and face as he slowly wound himself in his coil. After he had fixed him-

---

From Duval, *The Adventures of Bigfoot Wallace*, pp. 137-42.

self to his notion, I lay perfectly still a few moments longer to make sure he was asleep and then sprang up suddenly, and striking a light soon had the gentleman's head mashed as flat as a pancake. Remember, Mr. Author," I continued, "there's no danger at all of a rattlesnake's biting you at night if you only lie still and keep quiet until he settles himself."

"Yes," said our author, "but who could lie still and keep quiet unless he was made out of castiron while a rattlesnake was slowly coiling itself up in his bosom? Ugh! the bare idea makes me shudder from head to foot."

I saw that my "snake story" had produced the desired effect upon him, and for the time I dropped the subject. The next night we encamped in a very snaky-looking locality, and I cut off a piece of grapevine about as thick as an ordinary rattlesnake, which I slyly slipped under the edge of our blanket just before we turned in. About half an hour after we had lain down, I drew out the slip of grapevine and ran it slowly along the author's back, at the same time gently shaking my rattles which I held in the other hand. He was just on the eve of dropping off to sleep, but the crawling motion and the "rattling" aroused him in an instant.

"Oh! murder, Captain," said he, "there's a rattlesnake crawling along my back! What in the world am I to do?"

"I know it," I answered, "I hear him rattling now (and I gently shook the rattles I held in my hand). Lie still and don't move a muscle until he coils up."

"Oh, yes," said the poor fellow (and his teeth fairly chattered from fright), "it's easy enough for you to say lie still when I am between you and the snake, but it isn't so easy for me, for I can feel him squirming along my back now."

"I know that," said I, "but you must lie still, for the first motion you make he will have his fangs into you, sure."

"Oh!" said the poor fellow, as I gave the vine another serpentine twist along his back, "this is more than human nature can bear— ugh! ugh! Captain, can't you do anything for me?"

"There's no danger at all," I said, "if you will only keep still; he will soon settle himself, and then you can jump up without the least risk of being bitten. When he quits rattling altogether," said I, shaking the rattles in my hand, "you will know that he's asleep."

"Captain," he replied in a faint and husky voice, as I gave the vine another twist and shook the rattles, "this is past endurance. I *must* get out of this at all hazards."

"Unless you want to die," said I, "don't do it, but lie as still as a mouse when puss is about. By the way, Mr. Author," said I, "can you tell me whether the rattlesnake is confined to the American continent, or if he is to be found also in other countries? I have heard a great many opposite opinions on the subject, and some pretend to think," I continued, giving the vine another twist, "that they are a species of the Cobra di Capello, the most poisonous serpent in the world."

"Captain," said our author, getting the better of his fright for the moment, in his indignation at being asked such an untimely question, "I like an inquiring mind, but I must say that you select the strangest occasions imaginable for obtaining information upon such subjects. Why, man," he continued in a rage and totally unsuspicious that I was playing upon him, "do you suppose a man is in a condition to answer any question rationally with a rattlesnake spooning up to his back?"

"There is no doubt," said I, pretending not to notice what he had said and giving the vine another rake along his back, "that if they are not a species of the Cobra, they are just as poisonous, for I have seen a man die in twenty minutes after he had been bitten by one of them. There was Jake Thompson, who was bit on the foot by one when we were scouting a year or two ago on the Nueces, and he didn't live long enough to say 'Jack Robinson, Junior'; and yet in that little time he turned as black in the face as a Negro, and his body swelled up till he was as big as a skinned horse."

"Captain," said he, "will you do me the favor to postpone the balance of that interesting story for another occasion? I'll back you against the world for picking out the most unsuitable times for telling your yarns."

"Oh, I beg your pardon," said I, "I forgot you wasn't broke into the ways of the wilderness yet. When you have bunked with a hundred rattlesnakes as I have done, you won't mind it a bit. I recollect about six years ago, when Bill Hankins and me were out hunting on the headwaters of the Leon, we camped one night—"

"Oh! good gracious," said our author, "Bill Hankins again and the headwaters of the Leon! Captain, I want you to distinctly understand that I've heard just as much as I desire of Bill Hankins and the headwaters of Leon, and—"

"Oh! very well," I said, interrupting him in turn, and shaking my rattle, and screwing the vine into the small of his back, "I've no wish at all to force my stories upon you."

"Ugh!" said the poor fellow, "this is past all endurance. Captain, remember me to all inquiring friends, and don't forget that the manuscript of the 'Wayworn Wanderer' is in my saddlebags. Give it to the world with all its imperfections!"[2]

"Hold on just one minute longer," I said, giving the rattles a vicious shake, "and you will be all right."

"Not another second," he cried, "it's no use talking, I may just as well die one way as another," and he made a desperate bound from under the blanket and pitched head foremost on the ground ten or twelve paces off.

I seized a bottle of chili peppersauce and ran to where he was lying. "Here, Mr. Author," I said, "drink this quick!" He took it and in the hurry and excitement of the moment hastily swallowed about a pint of the content.

"Gracious," said I, "you have made another wonderful escape."

"I don't know so well about that," said he, sputtering and gasping for breath. "I'm afraid I'm bit."

"Do you feel," I asked, "as if you were up to your waist in a kettle of melted lead?"

"Not exactly," he replied, drawing his breath sharply through his teeth, "but I feel as though I had swallowed a quart or so of it."

"Then," said I, "you are all safe, and you have made the most wonderful escape on record. No one before has ever missed being bit, who sprang off as you did, before the snake had coiled himself up. A most extraordinary escape, truly," I continued.

"What in the world," said he, "was that stuff you gave me just now?"

"That," replied I, "is an antidote I always keep for the bite of snakes. I got it from 'Puppy's Foot,' the Tonkawa chief, and if taken in time it will kill the poison of the most venomous snake."

"I have no doubt of it," said our author; "it would kill old Satan himself. It is hot enough to scald the throat out of a brass monkey. For mercy's sake, give me some water to cool my coppers."

I handed over the gourd to him, and he took a long swig at it, then seating himself on a log by the fire, in spite of my remonstrances, he persisted in sitting up the balance of the night.

More Snake than Bear

"AN EX-TEXAN"

JOE, on the bear hunt, as a matter of course, took the lead; next came the redoubtable Poke, armed with a double-barrel, which excited both the sneers and the laughter of his compatriots; Dave, Baze, and Sam composed the main body, while old Africa and young New York, in the persons of Caesar and myself, brought up the rear. Caesar was evidently in an especial bad humor, so bad, indeed, that the forced absence of his favorite "Bose" would hardly account for it. He stumped along behind me with a fire-pan[3] on his shoulder and an axe in his hand. Every time that he made a misstep or hurt his toe or when his shin—the seat of African honor—came in rude contact with unexpected substances, so brimful was he of ire and bitterness that no small quantity—spilled as it were by the jolt— would overflow in the form of a round dozen of African oaths, succeeded by a continued rumble of mutterings, for all the world like distant Dutch thunder.

"Doggone, de fool! who ax him for come, hey? Antee gwain coach dis child wid the pups, no how. Mass Joe's sense mus be done gone any how, das a fac."

"Why, Caesar," said I, at length, "what can be the matter; what has disturbed your equanimity?"

"Stub'd my ekalimity? Massa Phil, dah's nuff to stub enny white folks' ekalimity, let lone poor nigga, sah. Dar's Mass Dave's gone leff Bose home—knows more'n him, any day—an dat no count Mass Poke, he got dern fool scatter gun, wid cussed (*Caesar*, for percus-

From *Spirit*, XXII, 9 (April 17, 1852), 105. Reprinted from the *Democratic Review*.

sion) looks and bofe of de hammers down. Whose gwain to hunt de dogs ahead ob him, I like to know; t'aint dis nigga. F'e's gwain to shoot somebody, best send in white folks; dey don't cost nuffin; nigga's worth de money; can't ford it."

Caesar was quite right in the matter of Poke and his gun. The gentleman was a sportsman and horseman of the Winkle school, never of any benefit in expeditions of this kind and generally the cause of mischief. . . . By the time we had reached the timber, the short-lived twilight had waned and night had fairly set in; the moon was quite low down in the horizon, but a thousand pretty inquisitive stars were peeping down upon us through the foliage of the old oaks.

We were pushing lustily forward in Indian file, the canine portion of the party, at least, in fine spirits, when a loud shout from the rear brought us to a halt and to the right about; and in a few moments a newcomer was received with a hearty greeting from all hands. He was the pioneer of a race that is destined ere long to overrun this region—a shrewd, thorough going Yankee peddler who had brought with him into the wilderness a large stock of clocks and other notions, now mostly converted into cows and calves. He disposed of his wares at exhorbitant prices, receiving in pay the above-named bovine currency of the country as the customary trade price—ten dollars per pair—and bid fair to become one of the largest stock owners in the prairie. Good natured, ever-ready for trade, quick at rude repartee, seemingly liberal, and by no means deficient in either tact or courage, he was a great favorite with all.[4]

Caesar, despite all remonstrances, was now ordered ahead with the dogs and went off very sullenly, having previously entrusted our Yankee friend Biggs with the fire-pan. For some time both Joe and the Negro had their hands full with the curs which were running and yelping in every direction and at all kinds of game, but before long a shout from the men and a prolonged and general chorus from the dogs told us that something of consequence was up. Off we dashed, hurry-scurry, in hot pursuit of the clamor, but little heeding briars and brambles, rents or tears, in the excitement of the moment. Joe and Caesar were soon in sight, then disappeared for a moment as they rushed down a steep gully. Joe's "yip" had just announced that he had reached the opposite bank, when our evil genius Poke, so full of the chase that he had not noticed the dry bayou before him, pitched headlong down the precipitate bank. Off went he and off went his gun, and in an instant a yell that no white man's throat could have uttered announced that the shot had told.

"O, ki'! bress de Lor', Mass Poke, d--m you, sar, got dis nigga to pay for; tank de Lor' for dat, massy, anyway. Whafor you no shoot yuself and do somethin good? Who axed you hit dis chile? Pray de gorry mity ye broke yer dern fool no-count neck"—came up from the hollow in broken sentences as the poor fellow rolled down the opposite side and finally landed right on top of Poke, who lay on his back shouting for help and insisting upon it that, at least, every other bone in his body had been broken.

In spite of the certainty that some mischief had been done and the uncertainty of its extent, we were fairly convulsed with laughter; and when, after an evident tussle between the two, a crash was heard and Caesar's voice proclaimed in triumphant tones: "Dar, dat gun's fixed for slow shootin; won't kill no mor niggas; smash him to pipe stems, dat's some comfit." We had perforce to roar. In a moment after, both made their appearance and anger had evidently obtained the mastery of pain and fear. No serious damage had been done to either, and the return of killed and wounded exhibited no greater disasters than a barked nose upon Poke, a slight graze of two shots upon a very pinguid and prominent portion of Caesar's person, and a double barrel—the parent of all this mischief—put entirely *hors de combat*.

Having repaired damages and patched up a temporary truce between the contending parties, we dashed off at the best speed we might after the dogs, whose yelping sounded more dim in the distance. Joe declared that he had started a bear and have him he would. To all appearance the bear had either taken a tree or else relieved from the fear of his great enemy—man—turned upon his tormenting pursuers.

The latter proved to be the case, and having squeezed through a thick piece of cane we came suddenly upon as pretty a scene of confusion as ever a somewhat dull moon—one half the beams being tangled with, and intercepted by, the over hanging branches— partly illumined. An ungainly object in black, dimly visible near a huge tree, was surrounded by a dozen or more dogs of all colors, breeds, and sizes, barking to the manifest danger of their lungs. They dashed at him whenever his back was turned and he for a moment quiet, but retreated in a most undignified manner in all directions when he launched at them, which operation he performed sometimes upon four feet and sometimes upon two, accompanying his demonstrations with particularly edifying growls.

The crackling of the cane and the shouts of his pursuers, partly audible amid the general din, at length aroused Bruin to a lively sense of the true danger of his situation. Abandoning in haste his inglorious conflict, he did, in his hurry, the very worst of all things possible—take a tree. Now all of this, although occupying some time in recital, was in transaction but the work of a moment, and the bear had mounted some twenty feet before a gun was leveled at him.

"Hold on—don't fire," cried Dave—the shot on all great occasions— to Moore, who was raising his old musket, as I thought, with an insane intention of shooting the moon. "Hold on, let him get quiet." Too late. Moore blazed away and very luckily, considering who it was, did no particular mischief. Another gun was fired, and then Joe's voice was heard in tones of warning. "Look out, boys! He's a-coming; stand back."

Bruin had discovered his error and although more frightened than hurt was evidently meditating a retreat. An instant after, and any doubts that might have been entertained on the subject were dissipated; for, being somewhat pressed for time and under the circumstances preferring the shortest way, Bruin suddenly let go all and down he came with a tremendous thud, plump in the midst of the dogs and very narrowly escaped making a general average among them.

Every gun yet undischarged was immediately fired at him and evidently with some effect, for although the gentleman in black made off again upon three legs, there was anything but "grace in his steps," and his pace could scarcely be termed tiptop.

Moore snatched the axe from old Caesar's hands, and was after the quarry on the instant. Away went Bruin and away went Moore. The rest of us followed closely and in too much haste to think of a reload.

It was becoming tight times with Bruin. Moore neared him, aimed a blow with his axe, missed, and went down stem foremost with all sail set; up again, [he] ran fairly alongside with the intention of boarding the enemy; and the axe was again poised for an effective blow, when Bruin turned and made a claw at him, tearing his nether garments, carrying off one of the over-grown brogans as a trophy and making his mark pretty legibly upon the foot and ankle of the unfortunate Milesian, who, jumping back, went down this time stern foremost, impinging on Joe and involving him in the general decline and fall. While we gathered around the prostrate pair, Bruin plunged down the banks of a bayou near at hand, and the crash of the dense cane told that he now was upon pretty safe ground.

Moore's wounds were neither deep nor dangerous. If he was somewhat deficient in coolness, he certainly was not in courage but seemed ready to come up to the scratch upon all occasions, as the late affair had proved. After rubbing his leg a minute, he declared his readiness to go on as soon as the missing shoe could be discovered.

"Shoe," said Joe, "whar's yer boots?"

"At home," answered Dave, "a-waitin for him. Lucky he didn't hev one of em on, or the bar would hev put his foot in it!"

"Which shoe have you lost?" demanded Poke.

"The off one, to be sure," said Biggs.

"Hurroo, murther, the curse av Cromwell on ye! it's myself 'tis got it now," yelled poor Moore, in anguish.

Poor fellow, he *had* got it. Stumping along, he had absolutely stuck his unprotected toe into the open jaws of a large rattlesnake and received a very dangerous wound. Joe and Dave commenced masticating tobacco furiously, and Biggs produced a gourd of whiskey, of which at least a tumbler full was poured down the sufferer's throat without any decided effort at resistance upon his part; then a great poultice of the tobacco was bound upon the wound and more of the whiskey poured upon that. The internal application operated admirably, and the patient recovering his courage, now increased by no slight addition of the Dutch article, insisted that he was perfectly able to get home with no other help than that of Biggs—and the gourd of whiskey.

As he limped off, Poke edged up to old Caesar and asked in a low and tremulous voice, if he thought there might be many more snakes about here. "Ki, yes, Massa," replied the Negro, delighted to witness his fear, "dar's more'n a cart load to de acre, just whar we stand."

"I—I rather reckon I'd best go after em," said Poke aloud. "Moore 'll want to be carried afore he gets far, and Caesar and Sam had best come along too."

"No, No," answered Dave, "they'll do well enough; if you want to go, go. I'm not a-goin to give this up yet."

All the remainder of the party coincided with Dave, except Joe, whose faith in the adverse omen of the morning was marvellously strengthened and now insisted that all chance for overtaking the bear was at an end for the present, that he could be found in the morning with the aid of old Bose and the hounds, and that then he would not be far off. The stiffness from his wounds and weakness from loss of blood would render him an easy prey.

Poke endorsed all of Joe's arguments and called our attention to the threatening appearance of the sky, which was fast becoming over-clouded. Dave, Sam, Baze, and old Caesar were for having the bear at any rate, and how the affair would have terminated I know not if the Negro had not cut the Gordian knot.

I noticed his stealing slyly behind Poke, who was too much engaged in the discussion to notice him. In a moment after, the long-legged Alabamian gave one terrific yell and flopped over upon the ground.

"Snake! sna-a-a-ke!! sna-a-a-ke!!! Oh Lord, I'm a dead man. Help, murder! I'm done for. Carry me home. Send for a doctor. I'm as good as dead now. I feel it a-comin. My hands cold already. Can't somebody pray?

> "Now I lay me down to sleep—"

> "Your little hands were never made
> to tear each other's eyes."

These rather heterogeneous lines were probably the only remnants of early piety in the storehouse of his memory. We tried to comfort him and to ascertain the situation of his wound, but all in vain; he would die. Nothing could help him. We must carry him home and let him die in his bed. His limbs were stiffening now; he yelled and roared again like a mad bull.

There was no help for it. So shouldering him bodily, we started for home at a slow pace. The Negro would not go near him. Snake-bit people bit others he had heard, and he wouldn't risk it. After a while, Caesar approached Joe and whispered something in his ear which caused him to give an emphatic whistle. Joe announced that he was quite tired and must deposit his precious burden for a moment on mother earth. In spite of all Poke's remonstrances and groans this was done. Then Joe whispered the secret to me and the rest, and leaving the wounded gentleman reclining upon a bed of leaves, we quietly walked off.

"Hollo, don't leave me; I ain't dead yet—don't, oh don't," shouted Poke.

"Keep cool," said I. "We are only going to make a litter for you and will be back in a moment."

We pushed on, regardless of his cries, and very soon our laughter, no longer to be controlled, broke forth. The would-be dying man heard it, and, recovering the use of his limbs in a miraculous manner, came up in a run—swearing at us for our inhumanity, appealing to our compassion, and insisting that he would not live to reach home—all in a breath.

"Shut up," said Joe, "the niggar only spurred you a little with a piece of cane, that's all the harm you've had—don't be a fool."

Instead of a fool, there seemed to be more danger now of his becoming a madman, and it was as much as we could do to keep him from laying violent hands upon the sable joker.[5]

A Practical Joker

ISAAC MC GEARY was among the early settlers. He was a genial fellow with a passion for practical jokes in which he sometimes found a boomerang. While I was working down at Colonel Bell's, McGeary and a stranger one day rode up, their feet encased in moccasins and their heads covered with rude caps made of a green deerskin. The caps and moccasins so at variance with the balance of their attire, especially that of the stranger, whose name was Dickerson, at once suggested a misadventure. Inquiry elicited the remarkable story that they had camped out on the prairie the night before and the coyotes had stolen their hats and shoes. I saw by the twinkle in Mc's eye that there was a sequel to the story and as soon as he got a chance he unbosomed it to me. Dickerson was as verdant as a meadow in May, and on their ride down from San Felipe Mc amused himself by imposing on his credulity—telling him among other things of the penchant of coyotes for hats and shoes, cautioning him on retiring to put those parts of his apparel under his head, himself setting the example. After Dickerson fell asleep, Mc softly arose and stealing the hat and shoes from under his companion's head he carried them, together with his own, a little way aside and hid them in the high grass. Great was Dickerson's consternation when he awoke in the morning and felt for his hat and shoes. Mc felt for his and they too were gone. He commenced looking around, and when he had carried the joke far enough, he sauntered out to the place where he had deposited them intending to explain

From *The Evolution of a State,* pp. 73-74.

their disappearance, but behold they were not there; the coyotes had gotten them. The hats they found torn to fragments, but the shoes were gone. McGeary dared not cheep then, so they went across to Captain Martin's on the river where they were fitted out in the manner above described. Dickerson often told that story as he understood it to illustrate the stealth of the coyote.

McGeary played a worse joke on me, and [one] that I should have liked to lick him for had I been physically able. Old Martin Varner had a lot of wild hogs running in the bottom and when he wanted pork went out and shot one. Having occasion to replenish his larder, Varner invited McGeary and myself to go out with him. We all went out on foot accompanied by several dogs. The first game we flushed was a boar with tusks three or four inches long. The dogs caught him and Varner seeing that he was not marked took the opportunity of establishing his claim, an operation that somewhat riled his porcine lordship's feelings. McGeary and I held the struggling beast while his ears were being mutilated,[6] and when I released my hold McGeary, who had him by the hind feet, deftly slued him around with his head toward me and shouting, "Look out, here he comes," turned him loose. With gnashing teeth and bristling hair, the enraged beast sprang to his feet and made for me. I was considered fast on foot, and there seeming to be no alternative I took to my heels, the boar after me and the dogs after him. For about sixty yards I led them till, catching my foot on a stub, I fell flat. My pursuer was being too hotly pursued by the dogs to assault me. When the chase passed I rose to my feet; there was McGeary fairly rolling with merriment. I was mad for a few moments and as before stated would have licked him had I been able. McGeary swore it was the fastest foot race he ever saw and would want nothing better than to travel with me if I could run like that on a bet.

Duck Hunt Extraordinary

"GUILLERMO"

IN A COUNTRY filling up as Texas is and has been for some years past, it is but natural that we find a large number of persons who well merit the title of "green 'uns." Of this class was John McL-----e, a native of old Virginia, who became a citizen of Texas soon after it was admitted into the Union. Now friend John was passionately fond of hunting, and scarcely did his foot press Texan soil before he was running in all directions in search of game. Unfortunately he wound up his first exploit by slaying three *tame turkies,* the property of an old lady living in A[ustin]. This threw such a damper on his feelings that it caused him to forego this amusement for some time until one day, when I wished to go hunting and having no company, I called by for John and after some persuasion prevailed upon him to accompany me. Now be it known that north of the city of A[usti]n about a mile, there lives a wealthy butcher, who, at the time I speak of, possessed a large flock of sheep and goats, and among the latter a tremendous "William goat," which was famous for his implacable hostility to "seats of honor" in general, and those of the genus "boy" in particular. Many a lad he had given a "lift in the world" and had caused as many more to discover that their legs were not made merely to stretch cloth over, but to protect their bodies when prudence advised a retreat.

Well, on the evening in question, as John and I were moving noiselessly along the banks of a small creek that wanders through

From *Spirit,* XXV, 40 (November 17, 1855), 471. The author is unidentified.

the butcher's pasture grounds, I noticed that friend "Billy" of the horns was eyeing us rather closely to bespeak much comfort in the prospective, and being myself a very prudent personage and possessing a great relish for a joke, I soon decided upon what course to pursue. "John," said I, "you see that tree at the bend of the creek about forty yards from here? Well, you sneak along here by this underbrush on the bank until you are about twenty yards from the tree; then you must get on your hands and knees and crawl to the foot of it. When you get there don't put more than your head through the underbrush and see if any ducks are in the pond."

"Very well," he answered, "I'll do it exactly right, but what are you going to do in the meantime? Take my flask, I may lose it."

"I am going down here and cross over the creek so as to get a shot as they rise. Now do be careful, John, and don't show more than your head, and don't fire till I am ready—I'll give the signal."

So saying I bounded off towards a little mound just behind where we were and out of the reach of his goatship, who had now left the flock and was approaching John with his head, ears, and tail erect. In the meantime, eager for a shot at the ducks, my friend followed my instructions to the letter, and having arrived at the point designated he dropped down on all fours and crawled carefully and quietly along. Friend "Billy" followed with the most inquisitive motions, being entirely at a loss to account for the sudden metamorphosis of his intended victim.

John finally reached the tree and pulling his head slowly through the bushes to his great delight perceived five or six plump paddlers on the water, all unconscious of the cruel death impending over them.

"Billy," during this survey on the part of John, had approached within two or three feet and was scanning him very carefully, as if to pick the most vulnerable part of his body. Having at length apparently decided, he took two or three steps backward, and rearing upon his hinder legs, he sprang forward and planted his horns and forehead in that part of friend John where honor is generally supposed to be located with such good will and effect that he vanished with most unbecoming haste, and a second afterwards the ominous sound of a heavy body falling into the water told but too plainly the fate of the duck hunter. I ran down and crossed the creek opposite to where John was and found him just getting out of the water and heaping curses upon *me for pushing* him in, while "Billy" was standing upon the other bank complacently viewing the scene as though he was innocent of all participation in it.

John not having perceived his goatship, made the very comforting assertion that he intended "to give me a d---d good licking for it," and was *coolly* preparing to put his words into effect, when I pointed to the real perpetrator of the mischief and burst into a laugh. He gazed at "Billy" for a moment, then taking up his gun and starting off, he quietly remarked—

"Well, W., d----n me if you mayn't use my head for a football if I ever again come *ducking* and go home *ducked*."

An "Upper Crutch" Fishing Party

L. M. H.

BUT DID YOU EVER hear how to catch "Upper Crutches?" Perhaps not.

A few years ago, when El Paso (opposite this point) had a large proportion of Americans amongst its population, a lively party of them assembled at _____'s one night, who had for some hours been engaged in a brisk game of "pull." L. was some hundreds out in a "bad streak" and thought of quitting soon, as he had just come in from the mines for a little county visit and didn't "sabe" the game much. To relieve the monotony, it was proposed to go and catch some "Upper Crutches." Says L., "Agreed. What kind o' things are they?"

"Oh," said D., who is very crafty and always plays it very low down, "they are a sort of thing something like a duck, but jest sort o' live along the banks of the 'cacias, you know, and catch fish and things." (Acacias are artificial streams for irrigation.)[7]

"Well, how do you catch um?"

"Why you jest hold bags for em, you know, and keep sort o' quiet, and drive em in," replied D. slowly.

L., eager for a meat breakfast, hurried everybody off, fretting like a little pot boiling because the party stopped at old C.'s on their way to the acacias to get a big grass bag and lantern. Old C. said that he would hold the bag, as he understood it. D. thought that he

From *Spirit*, XXVIII, 14 (May 15, 1858), 164. The author is not identified. A version of this same gag was still being played on uninitiated boys in the 1920's and 1930's in the Texas Panhandle, where it was called a "snipe hunt."

301

had better. But L. believed that by doing this they wanted to get his share and swore that he would hold it himself, "d---d if he wouldn't."

"But," replied old C., "you don't know how to act. Suppose they should come this way, what would you do?"

"Why," says L., "I should jist easily slip the bag around to um."

"But they might come up around you."

"If they should I'd lay mighty low and spread the bag, and I'm small and could fix um."

Finally, it was decided that as L. was a "little feller," he might hold the bag, while the rest of the party were to go up the acacia and drive the "Upper Crutches" along down to him, and into the bag, by low whistling. He was duly instructed how to hold—getting on his knees on the bank and spreading the bag open with his hands and teeth with the lantern by the side of its mouth. The party then started off, and the occasional laugh greeting his ears only made him open the sack wider with a chuckle to himself how he had out-witted them and got to hold it. He was left to himself and his game for a time, until he attracted the attention of a big strolling Mis-sourian who sneaked up to him on tiptoe to get a look at the bag. "Keep back," says L., "you scare um." The fellow, only the more anxious, whenever the wind rustled the leaves would draw himself up to get a look. "Stand back," L. would hiss, "I tell you, sir, keep back—I can't catch nothing." L. now told him in a whisper that he was after "Upper Crutches" and to keep still and he should have some. But "big ugly" was now crazy to get to hold the bag. Finally L., a little tired and slightly suspicious, gave him a chance, trans-mitting his instructions in case emergencies should arise and saying that he would go and drive them in, followed his friends back to _____'s.

They all laughed some, and he *a very little*, but to relieve him-self invited them down to take a little look at his friend. On getting near, there he was, like a spread eagle, reaching nearly across the stream with the bag, but looking somewhat discouraged. L. approached *very* respectfully, and said in a low voice, "How do you come on?"

"D---n um, I've heard um two or three times but can't get um in."

"Well, stranger," says L., "I don't believe it's a very good night for 'Upper Crutches,' but you just come tomorrow night and bring a bag and lantern, then I'll take one side of the 'cacias and you the other, and we'll catch plenty of um."

A Texas Joker

ANONYMOUS

DURING THE HARDEST of the storm the day before yesterday [in Houston], we took a lounge down to the steamboat landing. While standing on the brink of a deep gulley that emptied its torrent of water into the bayou, our attention was attracted to the bottom of the gulley, where a drunken loafer was stemming the torrent holding on to a root fast anchored in the bank. The poor fellow, not knowing anyone was near him, was combating his fate manfully and in calculating his chances of escape gave utterance to the following:

"Haynt this a orful sitivation to be placed in nohow? If I was a steamboat, a rail, or a wood pile, I'd be worth fifty cents on the dollar [more] than I'll ever be agin. Unless I'm a gone case now, there haynt no truth in frenology. I've weighed all the chances now like a gineral and find only two that bears in my favor: the first is a skunk hole to crawl into, and the second a special interposition of Providence; and the best chance of the two is so slim, if I only had the change, I'd give a premium for the skunk hole—them's my sentiments. If I could be a mink, a muskrat, or a water snake for about two months, prehaps I wouldn't mount the first stump t'other side

From *Spirit*, XXV, 39 (November 10, 1855), 461. Editor Porter introduced this sketch as follows: "Some three years ago we copied the following startling bit of fun from the 'Texas Morning Star' published in Houston. It lately fell our way again, and we were so tickled upon reading it once more that we determined to start it for a second heat. We will take small odds that in three months' time it will have been re-published in half the newspapers in the country." The *Morning Star*, printed in the office of the *Telegraph and Texas Register*, was issued from 1839 until the 1850's.

of the Bio [bayou] and flap my wings and crow over everlastin
life, skientifically preservated. But what's the use holdin on this
root! There haynt no skunk hole in these ere diggins; the water is
getting taller about a feet, and if my nose was as long as kingdom
come, it wouldn't stick out much *longer*. Oh, Jerry! Jerry! you're a
gone sucker, and I guess your marm don't know you're out; poor
woman! won't she cry the glasses out of her spectacles when she
hears her darlin Jerry has got the whole of Buffalo Bio for his coffin?
What a pity 'tis some philanthropis or member of the human society
never had foresight enough to build a house over this gutter with
a steam engine to keep out the water! If they'd done it in time,
they might have had the honor and gratification of saving the life
of a feller being; but it's all day with you, Jerry, and a big harbor to
cast anchor in. It's too bad to go off in this orful manner when they
knows I ollers hated water ever since I was big enough to know
'twant whiskey. I feel the root givin way, and since I don't know a
prayer, here's a bit of Watt's Doxologer to prove I died a Christian:

> On the bank where droop'd the willer,
> Long time ago."

Before Jerry got to the conclusion, he was washed into the bayou
within a few feet of a large flat that had just started for the steamboat; his eye caught the prospect of deliverance, and he changed
the burden of his dirge into a thrilling cry of, "Heave to! Passenger
overboard and sinking, with a belt full of specie! The man that
saves me makes his fortune!" Jerry was fished ashore by a darkey
and to show his gratitude invited Quasbey "to go up to the doggery
and liquor."

NOTES TO SECTION VII

1. Ambeer or ambier, that is, tobacco juice. The practice of chewing
tobacco was widespread in the nineteenth century.

2. Earlier in the book Duval introduces the Author as a determined writer
who had come to San Antonio to gather factual information for his proposed
novel, "Wayworn Wanderer of the Western Wilds." The Author meets Wallace

and obtains permission to accompany him and his Rangers on an expedition to punish the Lipan Indians for stealing horses. The Author turns up in a costume entirely unsuited to the brush country, carrying an umbrella, a portable ink-stand, and a memorandum book. While breaking in this greenhorn, the Rangers have fun with his umbrella, his "pepperbox" gun, his stovepipe hat, and his misadventures with various wild animals. But the Author persists and is eventually accepted by the men.

All the while, the Author holds several discourses with Wallace about James Fenimore Cooper's delineation of Indians. After some experiences with Indians, the Author concludes that Cooper's picture of Indians and camp life is false; "Mr. Cooper is a humbug, sir!" he exclaims. In the light of this revelation, he plans to rewrite his own novel completely when he returns to civilization.

Duval rather skilfully combines this satire on the romantic novel with an excellent example of the western version of the breaking in of the tenderfoot, which occupies over fifty-six pages of the book.

3. A fire-pan was a metal container in which live coals were carried for fire hunting, a night hunt in which such game as deer and woodcock was located by the reflection of torchlight in the eyes of the animals or birds. A popular hunting practice in the South and Southwest in the early nineteenth century, the technique is explained in Thomas Bangs Thorpe's "Woodcock Fire Hunting" (*Spirit*, XI [May 1, 1841], 103) and "A Defense of Woodcock Fire Hunting" (*Spirit*, XII [October 15, 1842], 386). A humorous treatment of the subject is "The Fire-Hunt," in *Traits of American Humor by Native Authors*, ed. T. C. Haliburton (London, 1852), III, 169-87, in which a hunter shoots his own mule that he had left tied to a tree while he was hunting deer at night.

4. The Yankee peddler in nineteenth-century popular humor was a blending of the characteristics of real people and the stage Yankee, a figure firmly established as early as 1800. He was not usually so favorably presented as he is in this sketch. For a discussion of this and other character types in popular humor, see Jennette Tandy, *Crackerbox Philosophers in American Humor and Satire* (1925); Constance Rourke, *American Humor* (1931); Arthur P. Hudson, *Humor of the Old Deep South* (1936); and Walter Blair, *Native American Humor* (1937).

5. In a note the unidentified author says: "This is no coinage of the writer's brain, nor is it the only instance within his knowledge of the fanciful effect of fear upon a cowardly mind. One Dave H-----s, well known to every old settler in the Bay Country of Texas, soon after his arrival, set forth upon a land-hunting expedition and like all newcomers prepared himself for his journey in the extreme of old Mexican style. A pair of spurs with rowels at least four inches in diameter formed part of his equipment. The first night the party camped near Clear Creek and had just gathered around the fire when Dave jumped up and shrieked out that he was snake bitten. Upon examining his person, no marks of the bite could be found, and a careful scrutiny of the ground about them was had without effecting the discovery of a snake. At length Dave was pacified and sat down again *upon his knees* by the fire. In an instant he was up again, again having been bitten by his secret but remorseless enemy

which proved after all to be nothing more dangerous than the long sharp rowels of his spurs." This situation led to a traveling anecdote, told over and over again in Texas.

6. The allusion here is to the widespread southern-southwestern custom of showing ownership of range hogs by slitting their ears with distinctive marks, two of which were called "swallow fork" and "under bit."

7. An acacia is, of course, a tree. The word with which it is being confused here is *acequia*, Spanish for irrigation ditch.

Index